The Political Dynamics of Japan

The Political Dynamics
of Japan

Jun-ichi Kyogoku

Translated by
Nobutaka Ike

UNIVERSITY OF TOKYO PRESS

Publication assisted by a grant from The Japan Foundation and the Suntory
Foundation

Translation based on the Japanese original NIHON NO SEIJI
(University of Tokyo Press, 1983)
English translation © 1987 UNIVERSITY OF TOKYO PRESS

ISBN 4-13-037015-4
ISBN 0-86008-409-4

Printed in Japan

Contents

Foreword

The number of general works in English on Japanese politics that has been published since 1945 is sufficiently large so that if they were to be placed side by side they would occupy several feet of shelf space. With a few exceptions, these books have been written by American scholars. Works by Japanese academics on their own politics are conspicuous by their absence. The most important reason for this lacuna is probably the fact that few Japanese professors have sufficient confidence in their ability in English to write in that medium. I have long felt that it was a pity that we did not have a view of Japanese politics as seen by someone who is a participant. This is because I am inclined to believe that outsiders and insiders are likely to see things from a somewhat different perspective.

Thus, when I was asked by the University of Tokyo Press as to whether I would be interested in producing an English edition of Professor Jun-ichi Kyogoku's new book, *Nihon no Seiji* (Japanese Politics), I responded affirmatively. Professor Kyogoku, whom I had the pleasure of working with many decades ago, is one of the relatively few Japanese scholars who has specialized in the study of Japanese politics. His new book represented a summation of a long career of teaching in the Faculty of Law at the University of Tokyo, and of research and writing in his specialty.

This may help explain why *Nihon no Seiji* struck a responsive chord among the Japanese book-buying public. Following its publication in the fall of 1983, it enjoyed brisk sales so that during the following nine months it was reprinted eleven times. In writing this book, the author has obviously cast his net wide. Thus, the work has an encyclopedic quality, and instead of dealing with personalities and events that have occupied center stage in recent years, it seeks to probe the more basic problems, currents, and processes at work in the political arena. Because of this, the book has an enduring quality.

The original edition ran almost 400 pages, and contained some material that would be of less interest to foreign readers. In any case, the publisher desired a shorter English edition. Accordingly, the reader should be warned that the present work is not a line-by-line translation of the original book, but rather is a revised, abridged edition. Parts One and Two of the original book were rewritten by the author and are now presented in Chapters One through Three. Chapters Four through Nine, except for some shifting of material, are based closely on the material in Part Three of the original book.

It was my good fortune that I was able to consult the author in preparing the translation. Professor Kyogoku spent some time at Stanford in the summer of 1985, so I was able to turn to him for assistance in clarifying passages that puzzled me, and in deciding appropriate English renderings of certain Japanese expressions and concepts. Needless to say, I am solely responsible for any errors in translation.

Finally, it may be appropriate to make some brief comments about the material in *Nihon no Seiji*. Because of its encyclopedic quality, each reader will find gems that will strike his or her fancy. What I found particularly interesting may be summarized as follows:

First, most Western scholars have not referred to any great extent to the religious aspects of belief systems in Japan as they relate to politics. By contrast, the author devoted considerable space to religion. This is because, I believe, an important feature of Japanese religious life is that it involves not only the individual, but fellow human beings, and the cosmos, of which individuals are a part. According to Shintō, the cosmos contains many kinds of deities, including the spirits of the deceased ancestors. These spirits can affect the welfare of the living, so appeasement of the soul is a sacred duty.

Second, whereas the judiciary is scarcely mentioned, there are many references to the mass media, especially the press. In fact, the press appears to represent a fourth branch of government.

Third, the battlefield paradigm in which individuals are depicted as leaving their families and villages to go out into the world in order to carry on a struggle for existence may come as something of a surprise to many readers. This is because Western works on Japan tend to stress the prevalence of harmony, unity, and social peace in that country.

Fourth, the discussion of ideological politics in terms of *seiron* and *zokuron* is something new. To the best of my knowledge, no Western writer has treated the subject in this way.

Nobutaka Ike

Stanford, California
May 1986

Acknowledgment

In Tokyo in June 1986, I participated in a series of editorial conferences with the author and Ms. Nina Raj, of the editorial staff of the University of Tokyo Press, who is responsible for seeing this book through the press. I feel that the revisions that resulted from those meetings helped produce a better product. Accordingly, I wish to thank my colleagues for their cooperation.

The Political Dynamics of Japan

Chapter One

Political Structure and Policies

The Parliamentary System

Political Reorientation

Following Commodore Matthew Perry's visit in 1853, Japan concluded treaties of friendship and commerce with the Western powers, thereby ending a period of national isolation that had lasted more than 200 years. This change, however, led to political instability, and a power struggle that resulted in a brief civil war. The new government that came into being following the Meiji Restoration made the transfer of Western technology to Japan one of its basic policies. In 1889, a written constitution was promulgated, and in the following year, the Imperial Diet began its deliberations.

The twentieth century saw the emergence of party government and parliamentary cabinets. After World War I, and during the 1920s, party governments became the rule. But, the military, especially the army, used the doctrine of sovereignty residing in the Emperor to thwart control of the government by the civilian cabinet. This led to a kind of dual structure. During the 1920s and 1930s, the army, ignoring the cabinet, invaded the Chinese mainland, especially on a large scale after 1937. Moreover, the army, assuming an active role in politics, replaced the party government with one dominated by the military, as can be seen in the emergence of the Tōjō cabinet in 1941.

Faced with a demand by the United States during the 1941 negotiations in Washington, D.C., that all troops be withdrawn

3

from China, Japan attacked at Pearl Harbor, leading to war with America and Great Britain. When Nazi Germany under Hitler also declared war on the United States, World War II spread from East Asia to Southeast Asia and the entire Pacific area. It ended in 1945, after more than three and a half years of fighting, with Japan's defeat. As a result of the defeat, both Japan's army and navy were demobilized.

The present structure of international society was more or less set at the end of World War II. The United Nations was established. The United States and the Soviet Union, after the Yalta Conference, entered into a situation of conflict and coexistence. The former colonies in Asia and Africa, including Japanese colonies, obtained their independence. Today there are more than 160 countries that are members of the UN.

Constitutional Revision
It was also true that political changes were instituted in other countries. Examples would be Germany, Italy, Japan, and the nations of Central and Eastern Europe. Japan's present political system is a product of reforms instituted by the Allied Forces that occupied Japan following its defeat in World War II.

The idea that occupied countries would be compelled to undertake political reforms in the interim period between surrender and the signing of a peace treaty was different from, and did not coincide with, what the Japanese government had in mind when it accepted the terms of the Potsdam Declaration. A new precedent was set in international law. But an occupied and disarmed Japanese government could not resist.

With respect to the attitude of the Allied Powers, a Japanese textbook on constitutional law contains the following interpretation: "The Allied Powers believed that World War II was more than a war as understood in traditional international law, that is, an armed struggle among sovereign nations involving disputes about right and wrong. They saw it as civilization vs. barbarism, humanity vs. inhumanity, and justice vs. injustice. Accordingly, they planned for a series of postwar reforms, something fundamentally different from what had happened in previous wars, when after victory on the battlefield, the victors would seek to annex territory and collect war reparations. The Allied Powers felt that they were given a free hand, as a result of unconditional surrender, to reform the domestic politics of the defeated countries. Hence they tried to make basic changes in the political system and even in the mental outlook of the people."[1]

The General Headquarters of the Allied Command (GHQ) took up constitutional revision as the central measure of political reform. But the Japanese government, although under Occupation, was not anxious for such reform. So on February 13, 1946, GHQ presented its draft of a new constitution to the Japanese government and sought its adoption. After successfully negotiating such modifications as changing the original unicameral legislature to a bicameral one, the government, making it appear that it had taken the initiative, announced it as a draft of a revised constitution on March 6. GHQ then took steps to oversee the adoption of the document by the Imperial Diet. Thus, the new Constitution was adopted in November, 1946, and became effective on May 3, 1947. But any public reference to the fact that this Constitution was the work of the Occupation authorities was subject to censorship and was forbidden during the period that Japan was occupied. This was to maintain the facade that the Constitution had been revised by "the freely expressed will of the Japanese people," as enunciated in the Potsdam Declaration.

The new Constitution came into being (1) by amending the Meiji Constitution, thus preserving legal continuity, and (2) through "the freely expressed will of the Japanese people," as assured by the 22nd General Election of 1947, thus carrying out the instructions of the Far Eastern Commission of the Allied Powers. However, there was another side to the story. First, in occupied Japan sovereignty rested in the Supreme Commander for the Allied Powers (SCAP), and neither the Emperor nor the people legally had sovereignty. Second, the original draft and the subsequent revisions were undertaken by GHQ with the power that was inherent in the Occupation. Third, the Occupation established the Constitution, giving sovereignty to the people by amending the Meiji Constitution, which had placed sovereignty in the Emperor, thereby shifting its locus. These points became the subject of the "constitutional debate" after Japan regained its independence in 1952.

Of course, it should be added that although Japan's sovereignty

1. Tsutsui Wakamizu et al., ed., *Hōritsugaku Kyōzai, Nihon Kempō-shi*, (Tokyo: Tokyo Daigaku Shuppan-kai, 1976), pp. 23–24.

was restored by the San Francisco Peace Treaty of April 28, 1952, the Japanese people have not repudiated the new Constitution. Furthermore, to this very day, the members of the Diet, and all of the government officials, beginning with the prime minister, hold their positions and carry out their duties on the basis of the Constitution.

The chief goal of the Allied Powers in reforming Japan's political system was to prevent Japan from becoming a militarist nation again and threatening the peace of the world. For this purpose, Article 9, which prohibits Japan from bearing arms, was expressly put into the Constitution. On the theory that democratic states will not become militaristic, provisions for a parliamentary cabinet system were included to guarantee the existence of parliamentary government in Japan. In this way the principle that the House of Representatives, which takes precedent over the House of Councillors, would elect the prime minister was established. The prime minister, in turn, would choose his cabinet ministers, thereby assuring the collective responsibility of the cabinet. Under the system of a tripartite division of powers, the National Diet was designated as the highest organ of state power.

The Emperor System

These reforms completely changed the old system, wherein sovereignty resided in the Emperor, who ruled with the consent of the Imperial Diet, and which enabled an autocratic bureaucracy to hold sway, using the Imperial prerogative as its shield. The Emperor was not merely a head of state as stated in Western-style constitutions, but also a religious head.

The Emperor's prerogative as head of state included the right to exercise legislative, judicial, and administrative power. But he exercised these powers in accordance with the provisions of the constitution, which was a "self-imposed limitation," according to Professor Minobe.[2] In terms of Western constitutional law, this made the Emperor a constitutional monarch, which was the official interpretation in Japan until about the middle 1930s.

2. Minobe Tatsukichi (1873–1948), an authority on constitutional law, tried to reconcile parliamentary government and the Emperor system with his theory of the Emperor as an "organ" of the state. In 1936 he was attacked by the rightists and forced to resign his professorship at Tokyo Imperial University, and his writings on the subject were banned.

On the other hand, the Preamble of the Meiji Constitution proclaimed: "The rights of sovereignty of the State, We have inherited from Our Ancestors, and We shall bequeath them to Our descendants." Thus, Imperial sovereignty rested on theocratic, patriarchal principles. In this way, the legitimacy of the Emperor system did not rest on Western-style constitutional theory. Instead it rested on a government-supported religion, State Shintō, with its numerous shrines, and on political education in the lower schools. In short, its legitimacy rested on the principle that the Emperor was a living god and the chief priest of State Shintō. After the esoteric rite that took place when a new emperor assumed the throne, in a religious sense, he was reborn as a god.

Thus, the Emperor system had two faces and two sources of legitimacy. The school of thought which stressed the constitutional monarchy aspect of the Emperor and put him above politics argued that by freeing him from political responsibility, it was possible to preserve the throne "inherited from Our Ancestors." As far as the actual operation of government went, by and large, it was consistent with this view, even in the case of the independence of the supreme command. By contrast, the military, which rested on the idea of the independence of the supreme command, utilized the view of the Emperor as an actual ruler. They used the image of the Emperor as commander-in-chief dressed in military uniform to indoctrinate a sense of loyalty among the troops. In order to instill among soldiers a willingness to die for the Emperor, they stated, as in the Imperial Rescript to Soldiers and Sailors (1882), that the armed forces in all ages were "under the command of the Emperor." Later, in the 1930s, when the military came to dominate the domestic political scene, they stressed the view of the Emperor as a living god, pressed for the clarification of the basis of the Japanese state, and rejected Minobe's interpretation of the Emperor as an "organ" of the state.

Now the control of the military was a prerogative of the Emperor. After the surrender of Japan, the Japanese people and the armed forces followed the orders given by the Emperor, and so the Occupation proceeded smoothly, without the armed resistance that had been anticipated. The military was quickly disarmed, and the soldiers, whose duty it had been to defend the islands against invasion, were demobilized. For the Americans, who dominated the Allied forces, this contributed greatly to their security.

The American forces, while assuring their own safety in the U.S.-Soviet bipolar world, sought to continue the Occupation. They proceeded with the political reforms and encouraged the emergence of democracy. They came to look positively on the role that the Emperor system could perform in the pursuit of these goals. Moreover, the retention of the Emperor system fulfilled the desires of the old political elite (prior to the rise of the military) and the great majority of the people. This made for a peaceful Occupation. However, now that neither Hitler nor Mussolini was alive, some of the Allied Powers wished to charge the Emperor with war crimes. There were also groups in Japan that wanted to either abolish the system or force the Emperor's abdication. In order to retain the Emperor system in the face of these pressures, it was necessary to purify the system of its "unjustness, inhumanity, and barbarism," or to change its character.

The first step in this change was to take Shintō out of the control of the state, and to renounce the divinity of the Emperor by means of an Imperial rescript to that effect. This removed the element that had previously given the system its legitimacy. The second was to establish another way to legitimize the system. This was to transfer sovereignty from the Emperor to the people (Article 1), with the Emperor serving as the "symbol" of national unity. The third was to abolish his position as commander-in-chief of the armed forces, and to sever any connections with nationalism by means of Article 9 in the Constitution, which forbids the possession of armed forces. This changed the nature of the system. The fourth was that these changes were made by the new Constitution, representing the "freely expressed will of the Japanese people," and that was clearly apparent to those inside and outside of Japan. The revision of the Constitution thus had a decisive impact on the preservation of the Emperor system.

The Diet in Power

The Prewar Diet

Parliamentary government in Japan is almost one hundred years old, when one considers that the Meiji Constitution was promulgated in 1889 and the first parliament was convened in 1890.

However, those who won the civil war and attained leadership positions in the new Meiji government, that is, the so-called clan oligarchy, now sought to monopolize its power by manipulating the political system.

In the newly established Western-style parliamentary regime, sovereignty was legally in the hands of the Emperor, and so diplomacy, military affairs, criminal justice, and governmental organization came under the Imperial prerogative. The regime also took measures to restrict party politics, based on the control of the popularly elected legislature by the majority party, as well as the establishment of a parliamentary cabinet.

The Meiji oligarchy, in order to remove administrative power as much as possible from the control of the Diet, instituted a number of political measures. For instance, they restricted the number of voters by a system of limited suffrage, and established a bicameral legislature with a popularly elected House of Representatives paired with a House of Peers, whose members were not elected. They also set up a Privy Council, which would "deliberate on important state matters." Also in administration, instead of having a cabinet with collective responsibility, each cabinet member was made directly responsible to the Emperor. As for the military, they adopted the system of the independence of the supreme command, and in military administration, the army and navy ministers in the cabinet had to be officers on active duty with at least the rank of lieutenant general or vice admiral. While they could interfere in politics, civilians could not intrude in military matters.

The political struggles between the Meiji oligarchs and the party politicians taught the former that supraparty governments were not possible, and so the two groups reached an accommodation. After Itō Hirobumi formed the Rikken Seiyūkai in 1900, the struggle for power largely involved parties led by high-ranking bureaucrats (most of whom were lined up with the oligarchy), leading eventually in the 1920s to party politics and cabinets based on parliamentary majorities. But later, the parties used the doctrine of "clarification of the basis of the Japanese state" that was advocated by the military as a weapon in the political struggle. This brought about their own downfall. Party governments were then replaced by those led by the so-called senior statesmen.

The Postwar Diet

In 1947, the postwar Constitution became effective, paving the way for parliamentary politics. The opportunity of the people to participate in politics was greatly expanded, and their freedom was assured. The right to vote is guaranteed to all by the Constitution. At present, the official lists of eligible voters for all elections at the national and local levels are maintained by election commissions in villages, towns, and cities. Also the number of elective positions has been increased. The House of Peers has been replaced by the popularly elected House of Councillors. The executives of prefectural and local governments are also elected. Moreover, people can now vote on the retention of Supreme Court justices, on referenda and initiatives, on the recall of elected officials, and dissolution of local legislatures.

The right to participate in politics has also been guaranteed. The old Peace Preservation Act[3] was repealed, and free speech and assembly as well as the right to form political associations have been guaranteed. Unlike the situation before the war, the Communist Party can exist as a legal party.

The coverage of election campaigns has become an important matter for the press. The election turnout is reported by and commented on by the press.

The allocation of seats in the House of Representatives to the various electoral districts that was made in 1947 has remained in place, although some efforts have been made to alter it. As a result of industrialization extending over a forty-year period, imbalances in representation have appeared. If one takes the number of voters per representative as a measure, there are a number of districts that are severely overrepresented and others that are underrepresented. The difference reached as much as three to five times. During the forty-year period, some adjustments have been made, but the imbalance has become even worse. In response to voters who have sued to try to correct the problem, the Supreme Court, on a number of occasions, has declared that the situation violates the Constitution. But there is no law nor constitutional provision that can force the Diet to act. It is up to the legislature to reallocate the seats.

An early reallocation is unlikely because it would affect the

3. This law was enacted in 1925 to suppress leftist political thinking and activities.

fortunes of the incumbent legislators and also the balance of power among political parties. Thus, reallocation necessitated by industrialization and urbanization will certainly be delayed, and for voters, this imbalance may be considered something like a chronic disease.

The Political World

Because the Constitution expressly provided for a cabinet system based on parliamentary majority, the means and ends of political struggles became clear. Those political forces seeking a place in the legislature had to try to attain a majority in the House of Representatives. However, because of institutional factors, the political struggle came to be centered on factional contests within certain political parties.

In this connection, it is useful to look at the electoral system. Following the 1946 election with large electoral districts, the 22nd General Election in 1947 adopted medium-sized districts with three, four, and five members. This system is still in effect today. It was originally adopted in 1925 by the first Katō Takaaki cabinet, which was a three-way coalition of the Seiyūkai, Kenseikai, and Kakushin Club. The system was revived in 1947 when there were three parties, the Liberal, the Progressive, and the Socialist. Thus, both the political world and the electoral districts reflected the tradition of the Seiyūkai, Minseitō, and the proletarian parties that prevailed in the 1930s.

The conservative merger in 1955 led to a system where the Liberal-Democratic Party (LDP) obtained a long-term monopoly of power. This led to the LDP and the conservative independents competing for seats in the electoral districts. Such intraparty competition made it handy to have a party system that would cut across districts and provide mutual help: that is, party factions. Also the political contests came to be focused on the selection of the president of the LDP, a process that made it useful to have more or less permanent factions that could be put together for coalition-building purposes. In this way, party politics came to be concentrated in factional politics. As factional politics intensified, a weeding-out process took place. The number of factions was reduced to one-half over a 30-year period. Power came to be wielded by large factions, the so-called corps.

Compared with the system of small districts, the medium-sized one tends to be more favorable to the growth of multiple parties. It has resulted in multiple opposition parties, and within the ruling party to coalitions of factions. Political journalists have taken a great interest in factional politics and have widely featured this phenomenon in the press.

As more people gained the right to vote, the number of eligible voters has increased. The present population of Japan is 120 million, with 80 million eligible to vote. With the land reform in the rural areas and continued economic growth, the old order dominated by local notables has disintegrated. Voters are no longer mobilized indirectly through local notables for the purpose of winning elections. It has become necessary to approach voters and their families directly and organize them on a continuing basis. The organization of support groups in electoral districts throughout the entire country in the 1960s was a response to this development. Today, the support organizations serve as the link between voters and the political parties.

In the big cities, however, there are many people who are not members of any organization, including political support groups. Young people in their early twenties who fall outside the networks that mobilize voters and who thus have low voting rates have also become the subject of newspaper comment.

Participation in politics is, however, not limited to voting alone. The freedom to participate has led, on the radical side, to mass demonstrations and marches, and, on the conservative side, to lobbying and pressure-group tactics. One form of lobbying is that used by local government officials. In order to secure more funds from the central government, mayors and governors, and members of city councils and prefectural assemblies go to the capital for lobbying purposes. There are also many other forms of lobbying and pressure-group activities. For example, after the end of the war, farmers formed their own organizations to promote the interests of tenant farmers, but after becoming land-owners as a result of land reform, they formed agricultural co-operatives, which apply pressure for favorable farm policies, such as keeping rice support prices high.

Workers also are guaranteed the right to form unions and participate in labor movements, but labor organizations are highly fragmented. Unions have become the source of manpower for mass demonstrations and marches put on by progressive politics. In addition, they engage in spring offensives every year in order to get wage increases.

Other organizations, such as women's, consumers' and citizens' organizations have made political demands and achieved good results. In many instances, there are governmental agencies that can deal with the disparate demands that emerge from a pluralist society. Moreover, in the LDP, there are sections in its Political Affairs Research Committee, and in organizations composed of Diet members, that can deal with political demands.

Professional politicians serve as temporary or permanent advisers to these pressure groups in order to seek their electoral support. They manage to obtain the benefits these pressure groups seek, either through the government agencies or the LDP. Specifically, these benefits are acquired either through legislation or budgetary allocations from the government. This is the way constituency service is provided. These activities are important not only to maintain support organizations but also to secure votes to get elected to office. Accordingly, in elections, incumbents who are able to show how much they have done for their constituents tend to enjoy tremendous advantages.

Policy Orientations

Pacifism and Defense

Self-Defense Policy

The Allied Powers occupied Japan, revised the Constitution, instituted land reform, legalized the labor movement, reformed the educational system, and put into effect other changes. While all this was going on, there emerged a bipolar world. The increasing military confrontation between the United States and the Soviet Union finally led to the Cold War. There was in Western Europe the Berlin airlift between June, 1948, and May, 1949, followed by the signing of the North Atlantic Treaty, and in East Asia, the establishment of the People's Republic of China in October, 1949. Then in 1950 the Korean War broke out. In the midst of all this, there was a reexamination of what part an occupied Japan should play in America's overall strategy in world affairs. There were three considerations. First, there was Japan's geopolitical position, second, its potential industrial power, and, third, its potential military power. The question of what would happen if Japan were to remain in the American sphere or were to join the Soviet sphere was considered, and this resulted in the recognition of Japan's value, militarily speaking.

Japan's position thus changed from that of a former enemy to a future ally. This also produced a shift in Occupation policy. The first policy change was to encourage Japan to become economically independent. Occupation policy that called for an agricultural economy to assure that Japan would not become militaristic was altered, after the abandonment of any attempt to collect reparations from Japan, to one of an industrialized, foreign-trade oriented economy. The second was the increasing use of American military bases in Japan. In order to assure long-term use of such bases, there was a shift in the system from one where the United States unilaterally secured them to one where they were provided by an allied country. As a result, when the San Francisco Peace Treaty was signed with Japan, a former enemy, the latter was now able to rejoin the world community. After Japan became a member of the UN in December, 1956, except for mainland China, Japan's status as an enemy came to an end. Also in Article 5 in the San Francisco Treaty it was affirmed that Japan, as a sovereign nation, "possesses the inherent right of individual or collective self-defense." On this basis of the right to arrange for collective security, Japan signed the Treaty of Mutual Cooperation and Security and the Mutual Defense Assistance Agreement with the United States immediately after the signing of the San Francisco Treaty. The Japanese government, which "desired that the United States maintain armed forces in and near Japan for the purpose of providing for its defense" offered, under the terms of the treaty, military bases to the United States. In this way, Article 9 became linked to both the San Francisco Treaty and the Security Treaty with the United States when Japan regained sovereignty.

Two weeks after the outbreak of war in Korea in June, 1950, SCAP ordered the Japanese government to organize a National Police Reserve of 75,000 men. This was four and a half years after the Constitution drafted by the Occupation provided for an unarmed Japan. In this way, Japan began to acquire de facto military forces. Two years later, in 1952, the Yoshida Shigeru government changed the Police Reserve to National Safety Forces and added a small navy. A National Safety Agency was also created. Then two years later in 1954, a law was enacted creating the Self-Defense Forces (SDF), with three branches—army, navy, and air force—and the National Safety Agency became the Defense Agency. The "chief mission of the Self-Defense Forces will be to maintain peace and security, and to defend our country against direct and indirect aggression." Thus, this law came to take its place side by side with Article 9. As a result, the question of the compatibility of the Constitution and the Self-Defense Law has sparked both legal and political debates to this day.

Those who see no conflict between the two defend the constitutionality of the SDF. Those who see a conflict argue the opposite. Also with respect to the national security policy, there are those who, from a political point of view, use the argument that the SDF should be maintained or even strengthened, while others wish to see it abolished. There are also views that combine legal interpretations and political opinion. For instance, the conservative school that wants to revise the Constitution would like to see Article 9 amended in order to remove any doubt about the constitutionality of the SDF so that the forces can be strengthened. Another group argues that the SDF are constitutional so they can be strengthened without a constitutional amendment. The government has been taking this position for 30 years. The third school are the leftists who say the SDF are unconstitutional and should be abolished.

Actually, on January 1, 1950, six months prior to the establishment of the National Police Reserve, General MacArthur issued a statement that Article 9 did not negate the right of self-defense, thereby signaling a change in Occupation policy. Moreover, the Preamble of the Security Treaty indicated the American expectation that "Japan will itself increasingly assume responsibility for its own defense against direct and indirect aggression." In the 1960 revised Security Treaty, it was stipulated that "the parties . . . will maintain and develop, subject to their constitutional provisions, their capacities to resist armed attack." Finally, for 30 years, or one generation, the great majority of the Japanese people have been caught between an antiwar and unarmed neutrality position that rests on Article 9 of the Constitution, on the one hand, and acceptance of the Security Treaty with the United States and a gradual build up of the SDF, on the other. In this way, Japan's defense system has changed from total reliance on the United States under the Occupation to a system that is based on "the inherent right of individual or collective self-defense."

Now, even if Japan were to gradually build up its defense forces, there are conditions that would assure that Japan would not become militaristic again. Japan's security vis-à-vis the Soviet Union is preserved by the American nuclear umbrella. Moreover, Japan is a signatory to the Nuclear Non-Proliferation Treaty, and it is likely that the United States does not envision Japan becoming a superpower armed with nuclear weapons. What America expects at most is that Japan would aid in the defense of the western Pacific region. What the United States wants in the way of Japanese military build-up is more in the area of weapons systems. Discussions have been going on in this area and progress is being made. Actually, Japan's defense capability is subject to the advice of the United States.

The strong pacifistic sentiment among the people also remains a deterrent to a return to militarism. They are very reluctant to see a rapid, large-scale build-up of the armed forces. Among the wars that Japan has participated in during the modern period, World War II was the first to bring the horrors of war to the Japanese islands. Through the wars that were fought since the Meiji Restoration, the invasions of the Korean peninsula and the Chinese mainland, the people indirectly experienced the effects of war: soldiers were killed and maimed; some were missing in action, others taken prisoner; and the families of the soldiers suffered too.

World War II brought requisitioning by the military, mobilization, and forced delivery of goods to the state. From the latter half of 1944, civilian deaths and casualties mounted from enemy air raids and gunfire from warships on major cities, and the travail of the populace reached a climax with the atomic bombings on Hiroshima and Nagasaki. There were other burdens: mass evacuations to the countryside, food shortages, repatriation of civilians from overseas areas, lack of consumer goods, and inflation—all of which made the people feel despondent. Some were able to make fortunes creating the black market, but most people ended up literally sick of war. These costs were not repaid by victory in war; defeat meant they had been paid in vain. That the people should harbor antiwar feelings was to be expected.

From the point of view of the people, legally the Emperor was sovereign when the country was defeated, and politically they were under the thumb of the military. They took part in the war that was started by the army and navy, and it is true they fought hard in it and got some benefits from it. Still, it was not the case that they collectively on their own initiative decided to go to war. As a result, even when the victorious Allied Powers pressed on the people the issue of their responsibility, they took the view that "the military were responsible, they were the ones who brought it on." Their response was that "the Japanese people were innocent victims in World War II." In this way there was no facing up to ethical questions, such as repentance for having been aggressors. Nor did they make any effort to come to grips with basic philosophical issues about human existence, such as "might and right," "good and evil," and "life and death." The war experiences that formed the basis of antiwar sentiments remained just that, and with the passage of time they became tales of wartime suffering that were recounted from time to time.

Article 9 of the Constitution
Article 9 of the Constitution gave a legal basis to and made legitimate antiwar sentiments derived from the war experiences. It also institutionalized such sentiments and provided for their renewal via political education. A political objective of this article that was included in the GHQ draft was to change the nature of the Emperor system, as we have already noted. Another objective was to make sure that Japan would never again become a military threat to the United States. This was done by inserting a clause against Japan's rearmament in the Constitution so that it might also be unnecessary to include it in a future peace treaty with the United States. The memory of the failure of the Versailles Treaty after World War I was still strong. In the final analysis, SCAP said that Japan should become an unarmed "Switzerland in Asia" in light of the fact that the Occupation forces were going to propose a security treaty wherein America would make a unilateral commitment to defend Japan. As can be seen from the Draft Treaty on the Disarmanent and

Demilitarization of Japan, the United States might have had the idea that the Allied Powers would oversee and guarantee the neutrality of an unarmed Japan.

In any case, there is a widespread feeling that the Japanese people made an original contract with the United States that Japan would accept Article 9 and unarmed neutrality in exchange for an unilateral commitment on the part of the United States to provide comprehensive security for Japan. In this way, unilateral dependence on Japan's part, and unilateral protection on America's part became almost self-evident. The Japanese accepted renunciation and rejection of war. This was institutionalized, and since then it has strongly influenced Japan's relations with the United States, Japanese foreign policy, and defense policies, as well as domestic politics.

In keeping with the strong pacifist sentiments of the people and the image of unarmed neutrality, the government has responded grudgingly to the American demand that Japan increase its defense efforts, and has kept increases to a minimum. One reason has been to limit the financial burden. This policy has been praised as one that has contributed to economic growth. But it has also led to accusations by the United States that Japan is getting a "free ride."

The Japanese policy has been to avoid entanglements in international politics. This has been in response to the feeling of the people that they "don't want to get involved," a kind of isolationist inclination. Despite its stated desire for peace, Japan has rarely been actively involved in efforts in various parts of the globe to promote peace. For example, it has never contributed to UN peace-keeping forces. Even in the case of defectors and refugees, Japan has only provided temporary shelter for those bound for other destinations, but has not granted permanent settlement. Again, this is to avoid entanglement. This system, which openly displays isolationist feelings, has changed somewhat in recent years.

The government did not make much of an effort to explain to the people the military and international political significance of being in the American bloc in a bipolar world. Nor did it dwell on its meaning for political idealism or ideloogy. Rather, it adopted a policy of the separation of politics and economics. That is, it sought to justify the "value" of the security arrangements in terms of its economic benefits. Specifically, it aggressively pursued an economic policy of high growth. It adopted a "mercantilist" policy of restricting imports and stimulating exports by means of proper administrative guidance. It encouraged the growth of industry and trade, which depended on raw materials and energy obtained from abroad. All this was done in the context of security provided by American forces, and of such international organizations as the IMF and GATT, which depended greatly on the American economy. In this way, Japan penetrated deeply into the international economy by means of foreign trade.

By contrast, the government adopted a very passive stance toward international politics. It sought to keep its involvement to a minimum. But it did seek to raise its international standing by being active in the United Nations, in which the United States exercised strong influence. For instance, Japan served as a non-permanent member of the Security Council. But in decisions affecting international relations, such as those related to the Middle East or Africa, Japan has followed the American lead.

Being inconspicuous and passive has been the Japanese approach to international affairs. Thus, when Japan, which today is an economic superpower, is asked to assume global leadership and responsibility in a world that is threatened by trade friction and economic conflict, the Japanese do not know how to act. This has led to criticism from other countries.

Reverse Course

It is not true that both the government and the LDP have always been on the receiving end with regard to relations with the United States. In order to put these relations on a more even footing, the Hatoyama Ichirō administration sought to revise Article 9. As a means of attaining this goal, it tried to change the electoral districts from medium to small districts. But the proposed change was so blatantly self-serving that journalists ridiculed it as "Hatoyama mander," with the result that the effort failed.

The Kishi Nobusuke government worked to revise the Security Treaty of 1952 to make it more equal. It achieved this goal, but had to resign as a result of the 1960 antitreaty demonstrations. The LDP has incorporated the proposals of the pro-Constitutional amendment group in its platform. In addition to amending Article 9 in order to increase the SDF, it has proposed to correct the "excesses of democratization achieved by the postwar reforms." Some examples of such proposals are: revival of the old Civil Code relating to family law, such as the rights of the head of the family, and inheritance rights of the eldest child; strengthening of the power of the police to maintain "order"; and revival of laws on public security.

These measures, referred to as "reverse course," have invoked the resistance of those groups that are beneficiaries of the postwar reforms. They are also resisted by the opposition parties and journalists. The 1960 demonstrations represented the high point of resistance.

The Ikeda Hayato government that followed came out with the income-doubling plan, and built a consensus around economic growth. Since then, the LDP has given up reviving the prewar political system and has become a conservative party that accepts the influx and spread of mass culture and Westernized modes of social life.

Radicals and Conservatives

Emergence of the Left

The Occupation revised the Constitution as a first step in reforming Japanese politics. But in order to assure the development of parliamentary politics, it was important that the proper political forces should operate in the halls of the Diet. GHQ very quickly got rid of the Peace Preservation Act and released political prisoners. As a result, the liberated Communist Party and organizations under its control reappeared on the political stage, and gained some influence. The old ruling groups, including the military, were purged. Many people in politics, government service, finance and business, media, and academia were forced out, creating vacancies. In many organizations, new faces filled these vacancies, resulting in a new leadership structure. New democratic forces were created that would seek to defend the rights they had gained by virtue of the postwar reforms, and would oppose the return of militarism. These were organizations and movements of workers, farmers, and women.

The mass media was used to promote "civilization and democracy" and foster opposition to feudalism and militarism. With the revival of general-interest journals and literary circles, the influence of intellectuals and writers increased, and some of the individuals undertook to tell about American practices, economy, society, and culture, and to help with the transfer of technology and scientific knowledge. Others became progressive intellectuals and writers, and revived the tradition of Marxism as a "system of knowledge." They became followers and supporters of the Communist and Socialist parties and joined the "progressive" and anti-American forces.

There was among these people the firm belief in the Marxian principle that a socialist economy would be established everywhere in the world as a historical necessity. They were also engaged in a practical mission; that is, they had to help the Soviet Union, which was the spearhead of the socialist movement, in its struggle with the United States.

A great many new faces thus appeared on the political scene, and numerous political parties were formed. But the number of parties rapidly declined due to elections and amalgamations. By 1955, there were the conservative Liberal-Democratic Party (LDP), and the Socialist and Communist parties.

As Japan struggled to revive its economy after defeat, it was confronted by two problems. The first concerned defense and diplomacy. The United States controlled the air and sea in and around Japan, and it also held bases in the country. The question was what stance to take toward this situation in terms of Japanese defense. Should Japan make use of the American presence, or should it try to get out from under it?

. The second problem concerned the economic situation. There was the pressure of population, exerted by the presence of people repatriated from overseas possessions, demobilized soldiers, and population increase caused by the baby boom. But the GDP per capita was small, given the restricted domestic market. In order to control inflation, stabilize prices, and achieve full employment, what kind of economic system should the Japanese adopt? Should it be a free capitalist system, or a socialist system?

With regard to defense and diplomacy, the conservative LDP definitely opted for maintaining the American-Japanese security system. Eventually in 1960 the LDP worked to amend the Security Treaty signed in 1952 to make it more equal.

As for the economy, the LDP chose a guided growth economy as its target. That is, although it was to be a capitalist economy, it was not to be completely free. Rather, the government would set guidelines, and by controlling investment, monetary policy, and tax policy would push the economy toward growth. The leading roles in this growth economy were taken, not by professional politicians, but by economic technocrats. Accordingly, although there was a good deal of political strife within the LDP, which had recently been formed as a result of the 1955 merger of two conservative parties, it did not affect the economy very much. In the 30-year period between 1955 and 1985, eleven LDP politicians have held the position of prime minister. If we exclude Prime Minister Satō Eisaku, whose tenure of eight years was exceptionally long, the average tenure of ten prime ministers was two years. It may be said that parliamentary politics has provided an open door and equal opportunity for the highest government position. But neither strong administrations nor strong leadership have materialized.

By contrast, the Socialist party, which has been in opposition since 1955, has stood for the abrogation of the Security Treaty with the United States, and for unarmed neutrality. The party is appealing to the initial Occupation policy of an unarmed Japan, as embodied in Article 9 of the Constitution. It was a kind of appeal that would strike a responsive chord among the Japanese people, who simply do not want to get involved in international disputes.

The Socialist position raised a number of questions that remained unanswered. Could Japan easily get rid of the Security Treaty? If it were abrogated, what effect would this have on the confrontation between the United States and the Soviet Union, and on world peace in general? If Japan were to abolish the Self-Defense Forces as advocated by the Socialists, would Japan be able to maintain unarmed neutrality? Since the Socialists could not provide answers, the voters, who tend to be practical and want freedom and economic security, refused to give the Socialists their strong support.

As for the economy, the Socialists naturally came out for a socialist economic system. But as knowledge of the poor economic performance of the Soviet Union became widespread, socialism as a way of achieving an affluent society lost its credibility. Thus, when the LDP under the Ikeda government launched its income-doubling plan in 1960, there was already a national consensus in favor of it. The Socialists had managed to secure enough seats during the Occupation period in 1947 to form a coalition government for a short while, but it has gradually lost its strength during the 1960s, 1970s, and 1980s. It was the victim of declining support and the graying of the population.

LDP and Economic Growth

Meanwhile, the LDP, maintaining its monopoly of power, succeeded in making the economy grow through the expansion of exports. This provided sufficient financial resources to enable the party to follow a policy of distributive politics. Constituency service was provided by appropriations that were poured into the election districts. This in turn enabled the party to secure a majority of seats in the National Diet and thus perpetuate its rule and maintain the Security Treaty. In this way, a stable system that linked politics and the economy came into being.

Continued LDP dominance was greatly helped by the imbalance in the allocation of seats that has already been mentioned. Since the party is strong in the rural areas, which are overrepresented, it enjoys a definite advantage.

In response to this, the Socialists and other opposition parties that were always in the minority in the Diet took to political activities outside of the parliamentary hall with the help of journalists. The journalists particularly like issues relating to diplomacy, defense, and public security. As the international situation unfolded, these issues increasingly divided the conservatives and the progressives.

Also, mass demonstrations and marching in the streets, mostly involving labor union members who had been mobilized, became the way the leftists showed their political strength. An example of this would be the 1960 mass demonstrations against the revision of the Security Treaty. This occurred in the capital city and involved the mass media, intellectuals, and writers, all elements sympathetic to progressive politics.

If leftist and conservative politics were to become completely at loggerheads, parliamentary politics would be in trouble. Therefore, conservative political forces have sought to reincorporate the leftists into the parliamentary arena, while the leftist camp, which has many legislators who come from labor unions, also sought to work together with the conservatives in order to provide constituency service. This was because they wanted to increase labor's share of the economic pie. Like the conservatives, the leftists began to become more practical. But radical politics still exists today, because it remains the symbol of the Left.

In this way, the long-term monopoly enjoyed by the LDP and the system of constituency service, in which the opposition parties also seek to share in the distribution of the benefits, tend to make politics be concerned with how to gain from government appropriations. In short, it is a politics based on calculation. This leaves no room for passionate politics—the emotional, impulsive kind that releases one from the humdrum everyday existence. The lack of interest in politics among voters and the low voting rate, which are what institutionalized politics usually produces, and which are often noted by the press, lead to demands that people should take more interest in political matters.

Political Confrontations

Amidst all this, a small minority of people, who are not satisfied with the drama of conservative and progressive confrontations featured in the press, become radicalized. They then forsake the halls of parliament, and step beyond the confines imposed by progressive politics. An example of this would be the activities of the New Left in the 1960s and 1970s. The New Left movement became the object of countermeasures by the police forces concerned with public security.

A phenomenon that one often sees in the radical New Left and in leftist and opposition politics is the Yankee-go-home type of anti-Americanism. According to many public opinion polls carried out in Japan relating to attitudes toward foreign countries, America ranks first among those "one likes." Most Japanese are pro-American. This is not surprising. Since the Meiji Restoration, and especially since 1945, the influence of America on the life and thought of the Japanese has been very great: science and technology, food, clothing, housing, movies, television, the arts, baseball, and democracy as a political ideal are some examples.

On the other hand, there were tensions and conflicts between victors and vanquished, occupiers and occupied, and there are not a few people who harbor thoughts about unpleasant experiences. Also, the Japanese people represent a mass society, comprising a market of 120 million. Since there is a common language that forms the basis of a national culture, the people have a sense of national pride and satisfaction. Individuals who take part in political movements sometimes are turned off by American involvement in international power politics, or by the nature of domestic politics under the LDP, which has monopolized power over a long period. Against this kind of psychological background, anti-American feelings can be touched off, sometimes in a violent fashion, depending on time and circumstances. In addition to this, intellectuals, writers, and journalists who are influential in public opinion have also expressed anti-American sentiments from time to time.

The Occupation led to the revival of intellectuals and writers as interpreters of "civilization and democracy," as exemplified by America. But with the coming of the Cold War with its military confrontation between America and the Soviet Union, the shift of Occupation policy from "idealism" to "realism," and the change after the peace conference to mutual security, some of the intellectuals and writers, and their followers, became disillusioned with the America that had been held up as an ideal. Disillusionment turned into hostility, and they came to judge American reality, which stressed military might and power politics, against the ideal of "civilization and democracy" that the Occupation had preached. The critics' position was that America suffers from racial discrimination and corruption and violence, as evidenced by racial riots and President Kennedy's assassination. American diplomacy was not aimed at peace, but was imperialist and warlike, as shown by the Cold War and Vietnam, and so on. In constrast to this indictment was praise for the British parliamentary system, French art and culture, and the social welfare programs of north European states. Europe and the Third World replaced America as the countries to identify with. As part of the psychological detachment from America, the so-called progressive intellectuals and writers joined the anti-American leftists forces and engaged in a war of words.

Behind the pacifist sentiments of Japanese people are prayers that there will be a peaceful world based on American-Soviet cooperation, the kind that existed during World War II. But the reality is that both sides feel that the other is a military threat, and so they both strengthen their defenses, mostly on the basis of nuclear capability. Given the fact that Japan is an ally of America, it was natural that those political forces who would view America as a military threat and the Soviet Union as a force for peace should take part in movements that would reduce the effectiveness of American policy in Japan. An example of this would be the armed struggles engaged in by the Japan Communist Party between its 4th conference in 1951 and the 6th in 1955.

Even after the Communist Party abandoned the policy of extreme left-wing adventurism, direct action continued, mostly by New Left students. They tried to obstruct the work of the American forces in Japan, and as a result clashed with the police, whose job it was to prevent such tactics. Sometimes they also tried to interfere with the work of the Self-Defense Forces.

The "anti-American progressive" opposition forces believed in the victory of socialism as taught by Marxism and performed the function of providing openings and opportunities for the Soviet Union, China, and other socialist countries to make diplomatic moves toward Japan. This was done through visits of missions to each other's capitals, meetings with high officials, joint statements, and the press reporting of these efforts. Moreover, they argued that it was the United States, rather than the Soviet Union, that posed a military threat, and thereby appealed to the Japanese wish "to be friends with everyone." In this way, they sought to abandon the Japanese-American security system, or to prevent the gradual build-up of Japan's defense forces. As a result, the politics of "conservatives vs. radicals" became intertwined with controversy over foreign policy. The LDP's monopoly of power and the Japanese-American security system became linked. The existence of an opposition that strongly opposed the Security Treaty strengthened the bargaining power of the government, which sought to hold defense spending increases to a minimum. The LDP believed that the United States would not wish to see the opposition win.

Meanwhile, there occurred a change in the Soviet bloc. Soviet-Sino relations evolved from extreme friendship following the establishment of the People's Republic to disagreements between the two in the 1950s, and conflict in the 1960s. In 1969, there was fighting along the Russian-Chinese border. Then in 1971, the United States made overtures to China, followed by Nixon's visit in 1971. It was in this context that the United States agreed to the return of Okinawa.

Also in 1973 China entered into negotiations with the Japanese government, which it had previously attacked for its alliance with the United States. In 1978, a treaty of amity and friendship that included the hegemony clause was signed. The changes in Soviet-Sino relations affected the left-wing opposition parties in Japan that had believed in and wanted a monolithic socialist camp. There developed within the Socialist party a conflict between the pro-Soviet and pro-Chinese factions; it became a house divided. Moreover, the military confrontation between the Soviet Union and China, and the war between China and Vietnam demonstrated to the people that the achievement of a socialist economy at home, and the attainment of international peace are two different things. It weakened the appeal of socialism.

Growth Economy

The Japanese economy was in ruins at the time of surrender. Crop failure in 1945 led to near famine conditions in the cities, which were alleviated by food provided by the Occupation forces. The Supreme Commander was not a conqueror, but a liberator, and a lifesaver, to whom the Japanese were indebted. Occupation policy was to remove Japanese war potential. Toward that end, SCAP decreed the dissolution of the zaibatsu, and removed, as reparations, machinery from factories. Some of the demobilized soldiers, war disaster victims, and those repatriated from the colonies were sent to the farming areas, where they undertook to reclaim farmland under difficult conditions.

Despite this, the economic reconstruction needed for survival got underway. In 1946, funds were made available for coal and steel production, which were given priority. The Occupation also provided funds to import cotton, food, and other raw materials. But in relation to the work force, there were few factories, and the economic outlook was not rosy. The appeal of socialism that preached equality of poverty and social welfare carried some weight. In the ensuing decade, the tug of war between capitalism and socialism ended in the victory of the former. With the emergence of a bipolar world and the Cold War, the goal of Occupation policy shifted to making Japan economically independent, through the export of manufactured goods. This policy persisted even after the signing of the peace treaty. American assistance for that purpose included financial and material aid, export of industrial technology and capital, and the opening of the American market to Japanese goods. The Occupation also allowed the resumption of foreign trade. On April 1, 1949, it set the rate of exchange of the yen at 360 to one dollar. In 1952, an independent Japan joined the IMF and GATT. Thereafter, starting about 1955, the country began its economic growth as an industrial and trading nation.

In the context of world trade that was growing in the 1950s and 1960s, Japan, which is dependent on other countries for much of its raw materials and energy, based its prosperity on the profits it made from converting raw materials into finished goods. The development of new technology, both imported from abroad and home-grown, and the investment of large amounts of borrowed capital to utilize this technology raised both productivity and the ability to compete in exports. As a result, domestic production rose, and Japan became a country with a large GNP.

During those twenty years of economic growth, exports shifted from textiles and other products of light industry to steel, consumer electronics, automobiles, and hi-tech items, such as semiconductors. This has led to friction with the United States and the European Economic Community. However, thanks to this high growth, the economy, which was characterized by surplus labor because of slow growth, began to experience labor shortages in the 1960s. But the government, with the support of Sōhyō,[4] persisted in its policy of not importing workers from neighboring countries; instead it did encourage labor saving, including the use of robots, and in this way increased productivity. Furthermore, domestic buying power rose, due to full employment. Many people came to experience prosperity and affluence in their everyday lives.

The Income-Doubling Policy

Economic growth, which began about 1955, became an official goal of the Ikeda government, with the adoption of its income-doubling plan in 1960. In order to restore calm after the 1960 demonstrations, the Ikeda regime used the plan to double month-

---

4. Abbreviation of Nihon Rōdō Kumiai Sōhyō Kaigi, (General Council of Trade Unions of Japan), a federation of labor unions whose members are mostly in the public sector.

ly income as a political goal. It used economic growth as a means of promoting national consensus. For two decades after that, political debate focused on economics, that is, whether it would be better to have high economic growth, or more stable growth. With regard to foreign policy, the government maintained its conservative stance, that is, the perpetuation of the status quo. It maintained the Security Treaty and engaged in a gradual build-up of military strength. In domestic affairs, the government continued its policy of providing entrenched interest groups with economic benefits.

The government's contribution to economic growth was to provide easy credit and invest in public works. This had the effect of expanding the domestic market. Good examples of this would be the Tokyo Olympic games and the building of the bullet train. Providing benefits through government appropriations meant that cultural uplifting spread throughout the land. The government's financial situation, which automatically improved with increased tax revenues as a result of economic growth, made possible the flowering of conservative politics that depended on the distribution of wealth and culture through government appropriations to the electoral districts of professional politicians.

Thanks to full employment, both the income and expenditures of the people rose. When it came to food, clothing, housing, and leisure, there was a trend toward Westernization because of the example set by America and the influence of television programs. Regional differences in these matters also declined, and the time lag in the spread of new fashions from one region to another also decreased. Because the mass consumption of consumer goods required its mass production, the social norm of "be frugal" was replaced by "be rich," and "use and discard." All this was readily accepted by the younger generation, who had large disposable incomes.

Moreover, with the spread of television, the spoken language became increasingly more uniform. In this way, in the period since the Meiji Restoration, for the first time all the people began to share in common lifestyles in terms of consumption patterns. This has led the great majority of the people to perceive of themselves as "middle class." They feel that they are all equal, share common characteristics, and are alike.

It is also true that in 1964, because of surplus dollar holdings, restrictions on foreign travel were lifted. Every year several million people travel to neighboring countries and to Europe and America on honeymoons or organized group tours. Foreign travel, television programs, American influences on consumption patterns, and the importation of mass culture have not only transformed lifestyles but have also "internationalized" the kinds of things people think about.

The Distribution of Wealth

The increase in productivity did not occur in every sector of the economy. Those in farming and fishing in the primary sector to small businesses in the tertiary were left behind. So long as these differences in productivity were not done away with, and differences in income were not reduced, not everyone could be said to have participated in income doubling. In order for everyone to become affluent, it was necessary that those who remained disadvantaged in the low-productivity sectors be given funds through political measures. It was also necessary that the level of social welfare benefits be raised for those who did not or could not participate in economic life. If one were to describe this distribution system in detail, it would be as follows:

First, workers get their wage levels raised through their unions. This process starts with the annual spring offensive. Employer associations and the unions negotiate against the background of pressure from striking transportation workers. The Socialist Party, which is the political spokesman for Sōhyō, officially or unofficially supports the unions. The agreement following the spring offensive sets the standard, and workers in all sorts of enterprises, large and small, as well as white-collar workers, get wage raises commensurate with prevailing standards. These raises are also given to civil servants.

Second, for farmers, the determination of the price that will be paid for rice is the equivalent of setting the wage level. The Agricultural Cooperative, whose work depends on the price the government will pay for the rice it buys from farmers, lobbies for an increase in the price. The method of calculation was changed from compensation for production costs to compensation for production costs plus the differential between farmers' and workers' incomes. In the meantime, the legislators who depend on the farm vote will politically back the Agricultural Coop. As a result of these pressure tactics, the price of rice is, by international standards, very high, and the government incurs huge deficits. As wages and the price of rice go up, everything from railroad fares and taxi fares to entrance fees to public bathhouses, all of which are regulated, go up every year or once every two or three years in order to provide income to pay for high costs.

Various social welfare programs will also raise their benefits. Between the time that the first wage increase goes into effect and the welfare payments go up, there may be a time lag of one year or more. The distribution of wealth in Japan does not take place evenly; there are time lags. There are also wage differences between large enterprises and small firms. The distribution of wealth is not done fairly. However, over the years, starting pay has increased because of labor shortages, and this has increased the buying power of young people, who do a lot of buying. At the same time, this has lessened the differences in income between young and older workers.

A number of conditions had to be met before economic growth could be sustained and the added wealth that resulted could be distributed to the nation. One was the maintenance of the ability to export, which rested on increased productivity. So long as the distribution of wealth depended on both wages and prices going up in tandem, it was hard to avoid yearly increases and inflation. In order for industry to keep its ability to compete in the export trade, the increase in export price or the wholesale price had to be kept low in relation to rises in wages and prices. It is a fact that in the 1950s, Japanese wage levels, when compared to those in the United States and Europe, were low. But increases in wages and prices were held down chiefly by rationalization and personnel reductions, leading to increased productivity.

As a result, hard-working, dedicated workers and quality-control circles came into being. Also, there was strong pressure for efficiency and rationalization in social life, and a "busy" life-style was established. On the other hand, there were farmers who seasonally migrated to the cities to work on construction projects for labor contractors, who used fringe labor with low productivity. Employers in the tertiary service industries, which provided unstable jobs for unskilled workers, hired students and housewives as part-time labor.

However, economic growth, the distribution of wealth, and rising consumption standards were not obtained without costs, such as pollution of the environment, and broad changes in the traditional way of life found in collectivities such as villages and towns and families. The mobilization of the entire nation for economic growth has lured people away from villages, led to over-crowding in cities, and resulted in the breakdown of collective life in traditional groups. Also, high economic growth has resulted in a highly pressurized, busy lifestyle, leading to the disintegration of family life. Intense competition to place their children in good schools has deprived the defenseless nuclear familes of their "family qualities," giving rise to such pathological phenomena as refusal to go to school and violence within the family.

Trade Conflicts

For more than 40 years, the government has planned, managed, and controlled the economy by means of administrative guidance and laws. Exports were encouraged and imports discouraged. The government put higher priority on national security and nationalism than on the principle of free trade. It either prohibited or limited certain foreign imports or levied customs on them. This was to protect those industries that were weak compared with those abroad. Sometimes this was also done to avoid deficits in the foreign exchange account.

Restrictions were also placed on foreign capital coming in to buy or establish companies. Moreover, there was a tendency, given the curiosity of the Japanese, to take industries from all over the world and duplicate them in their own country. The kinds of goods and industries to be protected were very extensive. The import of foreign workers was also prohibited in order to preserve jobs of Japanese.

By contrast, when it came to exports, the government made use of the principle of free trade, and provided subsidies and tax breaks to stimulate it. In short, the government adopted a "mercantilist" policy aimed at increasing foreign exchange reserves to back up increases in imports of raw materials, energy, industrial machinery and technology, which were necessary for economic growth. In the 1960s, the foreign exchange account got into the black because of the Vietnam war and the rise in exports, leading to an increase in foreign exchange reserves. At that point, it was argued both within Japan and abroad, that the value of the yen should be increased, but the government maintained it at 360 yen per dollar until the so-called Nixon shock in 1971.

Flood of Exports

In order to maintain export competitiveness in the context of the distribution of wealth, it was necessary to prevent increases in wages and prices from being reflected in export prices. This was done by rationalization and increasing productivity, which was achieved by building new production facilities using new technology. This resulted in increased overall production and more pressure to export. In addition, enterprises seek larger market shares than higher profits and dividends. As a result, various manufacturers that make similar products will compete aggressively in favorable foreign markets rather than cut back production. If more goods are shipped than can be absorbed by the importing countries, it is bound to lead to friction.

Now the ability to absorb imports depends first on the state of the economy, that is, prosperity or recession, and on purchasing power. Even if the importing country does not produce goods that compete, if the economy is shrinking and buying power is declining, then imports will not sell. The second element in the ability to absorb imports is the competitiveness of the goods that the importing country produces. If they are not competitive, the domestically produced goods will not sell, their manufacturers will go bankrupt, and their workers will lose their jobs.

There will be political problems when this happens. It will be necessary for the importing country to limit or cut off imports, or for Japan to limit or adopt a policy of "orderly exports." And it will be difficult for Japan not to accept this in principle so long as the country itself protects domestic industry. Thus, export stimulation through increasing the volume of exports may end in self-limitation of exports.

This tendency appeared as early as 1956 when restrictions were put on the export of textiles to the United States. This spread to steel and automobiles in the 1970s. After all, national economies are based on individual nation states. So the principle of free trade cannot ignore national security and nationalism, as can be seen in the policy of the Japanese government to restrict imports.

In both the United States and the EC there is a strong tendency to limit imports and protect their own industries in the case of steel and semiconductors, which are vital for national defense, and automobiles, which are a cultural and national symbol.

It is natural that there was a strong reaction when Japan entered the American market. It had managed to achieve a high level of productivity after it had protected its own market for a long time and then it invaded the U.S. market when American productivity and quality had declined. Thus, as the Japanese economy grew, and the volume and yen amount of exports rose, trade friction became more intense.

The policy of the government to resort to the separation of politics and economics within the framework of the Security Treaty, to avoid involvement in international politics, and to participate aggressively in the world economy was most successful. It brought prosperity and wealth to the people. But as a result of the economic success achieved after 30 years of effort, Japan has provoked intense friction with the United States and Europe, and, in addition, faces a number of problems. It has to do something about assisting in the development of the Third World in order to expand its export markets; it must provide for the security of the sea lanes over which its large volume of imports and exports are transported; and it must deal with issues in international politics, despite its inclination toward isolationism.

Decline of America
Among the international conditions that enabled Japan to attain economic growth was the security that the United States provided for the world, and the IMF and GATT that are based on the American economy. As for security, Pax America, based on a nuclear monopoly that overshadowed the strong Soviet land forces, lasted until about 1957, when the Soviet Union launched *Sputnik*. After that, the Russians, while maintaining large land forces, acquired strong capability in nuclear weapons, and in about 1970 achieved parity with the United States in terms of nuclear arms, and today it is said that the Soviets are even stronger. Furthermore, detente guaranteed the status quo in Europe, but not for the rest of the world. It cannot prevent political change in the Third World, which the Soviet Union supports. Even though we have seen the Sino-Soviet split and better relations

between the United States and China, the Soviet Union has improved its position in Southeast Asia, the Middle East, Africa, and Latin America. The Soviets have reduced the military superiority that America once had. As the balance in the bipolar world has shifted toward equality between the two giants, the United States has put pressure on the Europeans and the Japanese to increase their defense efforts and assume a greater share of the security burden. The Japanese people now have to reexamine the mutual security arrangements with the United States and the policy of the separation of politics and economics.

Conditions for Economic Growth

After the end of World War II, the United States supported the system of free trade based on the IMF and GATT with its enormous economic power, and helped Japan attain economic growth. But inflationary pressures built up in the United States as a result of the Vietnam war. In 1973, it had to abandon the system of fixed exchange rates in favor of floating rates. The devaluation of the dollar added to inflation, investment for new production facilities lagged, and social exhaustion and disorder worsened. Then Japan threatened the market for steel and automobiles. At that point America demanded that Japan, as an equal partner, liberalize imports as proof that it stood for free trade so that the United States would not have to resort to an isolationist policy of cutting off imports.

Now there were several systemic factors that contributed to Japan's economic growth. The first was that raw materials and energy were cheap and freely available. The 1973 oil crisis revealed another aspect of the system that had worked for more than 20 years. Oil was not only an economic commodity; it was also affected by military and international political considerations. It also became clear that the separation of politics and economics could not be applied to oil. In order to assure access to oil, the Japanese government, which previously followed America in supporting Israel, altered its policy toward the Israeli-Arab dispute. Second, in order to improve productivity by controlling inflation that accompanied the oil crisis, efforts were made to conserve energy and many workers were fired. This threatened the system of permanent employment.

Third, friction with the United States and Europe over foreign trade revealed some truths about the Japanese economy. Despite the self-image the Japanese have of their country as isolated, small, and weak, it is an economic power with a tremendous export capability. It forced a reexamination of the basic assumption once held that the volume of Japanese exports was negligible in relation to the world economy, and so international markets could absorb Japanese exports in unlimited quantities. It became necessary to study and determine how much of the yearly increase in production could be sold abroad without creating problems.

Lowering Temperatures

Changes in the conditions that sustained economic growth are also reflected in social conditions. The intensity with which all the people pursued economic growth and income doubling has declined. It would appear that the body temperature of the economy has come down. The population is getting older, and the proportion of those in their productive ages is declining.

The ethos that sustains economic life is changing. Traditions that date back to the second half of the eighteenth and the first half of the nineteenth centuries, such teachings as *Sekimon Shingaku* [Ishida Baigan] and *Hōtokukyō* [Ninomiya Sontoku] that provided "the spirit of Japanese capitalism," are entering a period of decline.[5] For example, today one finds intergenerational change. Mass culture and American consumption patterns have come in; instead of frugality and production, we now have affluence and consumption; instead of hard work, we have desire for more leisure. The proportion of urban, second- and third-generation white-collar workers is increasing, and they are more interested in themselves and self-fulfillment than dedicating themselves to their work. Furthermore, social movements aimed at fighting pollution, protecting the environment and nature are increasing. Doubts are being expressed more and more about the national religion that puts the ultimate objective in economic growth. These tendencies signify changes in the ethos.

5. Ishida Baigan (1685–1744), a Kyoto merchant and philosopher, founder of the Shingaku (Heart Learning) movement, which defined the work ethics of every class on a religious basis. Ninomiya Sontoku (1787–1856), an eminent administrator-manager of feudal fiefs, promoted from the farmer class. Also a very religious-minded propounder of the doctrine of work ethics.

Chapter Two

Political Paradigms and Processes

In Chapter One we briefly described both the institutional structure of Japanese politics and some of the basic policy decisions that emerge from that structure. We could take the conventional approach and delve more deeply into the executive, legislative, and judicial branches of the government. But the purpose of this book is somewhat different. Our goal is to introduce the reader to the actual political process and how it works on a day-to-day basis. To be sure, the formal, legal institutions provide a kind of framework for politics, but the more dynamic processes represent the working out of many informal, although partly institutionalized, common understandings that are shared by those who participate in the political process.

A number of items make up these informal, common understandings. First, there are basic articles of faith and varied secondary belief systems, both of which pertain to the meanings, values, goals, and purposes of human life in general, and of political life in particular. Second, there are myriad symbols and signs that represent these belief systems and evoke emotional responses from various individuals. Both speech and body language are included here. Third, there are a variety of expected patterns of behavior. These patterns relate to the questions of what, how, and when.

A thorough and systematic exposition of these informal understandings is something that is to be desired for a fuller understanding of Japanese politics. But we will not attempt that here. Rather, our approach is to take these common understandings and classify them into primary units, which we shall call codes. These codes can be fairly complex. At one level, they consist of a set of principles or rules that are to serve as guidelines for individual behavior. They specify what, how, and when. But at a deeper level, codes also contain basic articles of faith and related belief systems, and also symbols and signs.

We can observe, in the political process, a sequence or pattern of behavior that represents the working out of these codes. Some examples would be the elaborate rituals that are carried out in connection with the inauguration of presidents or the coronation of monarchs. We call this sequence of behavior a paradigm. If we were to use the analogy of a drama, it would be the script. Thus, our introduction to the Japanese political process begins with the discussion of several codes and paradigms.

The political processes in many countries, when viewed from afar, appear to be rather similar in their broad outlines. In particular, countries that belong to the so-called free democracies share many characteristics in common. But, as one gets closer to these countries and examines them in greater detail, differences among them become more apparent. Since the formal political institutions are fairly similar, if not the same, these differences are often attributed, quite rightly, to variations in cultural traditions. The codes and paradigms that are the subject of this chapter may be viewed as abstract constructs extracted from Japan's cultural traditions that extend into the past. Hence, we will deal with the relationship between cultural traditions and the political process in the section that follows.

Codes and Paradigms

A simple report that Party B won a general election in Country A has pragmatic value in international relations. Ordinarily, inhabitants of other countries do not pay too much attention to the nature of elections or the winning party in Country A. They assume that elections and parties are pretty much the same everywhere. Much of the news pertaining to international affairs these days consists of reports on individual events. However, some people who are curious might wonder what elections are like in Country A, and go to the library or even go to that country to find out. They will then discover that elections in Country A are different from what they have been accustomed to. Differences might cover such things as voter eligibility (age, sex, literacy, etc.), voting system (single-member districts, proportional representation), voting place (private home, school, public halls), voting method (writing in names, marking ballots, voting machines, with or without curtains), and so on. There is one way to understand these differences. It is to take a simple event like an election and connect it to a series of other events. What one would be doing is to look at, over time, the flow of politically relevant events that are connected to the working out of the formal political institutions. The result is the study of the political process.

Some examples of the kind of approaches that political scientists use are: "who gets what, when, and how," or the political struggle process, policy decision-making process, policy implementation process, and the use of analytical categories that can be applied internationally.

It is also possible to use a more oblique approach rather than one that is strictly political. For example, let us take general elections, which we have been discussing. Elections in Great Britain may be characterized as one between the ins and outs, in which the outs are Her Majesty's loyal opposition. By contrast, in continental European countries with proportional representation, one often gets unstable, if not ever-changing, multiparty coalition governments. These differences might be attributed to variations in political traditions. Since tradition represents a part of culture, one could attribute these differences to general cultural traditions and not just to political culture. One can take an approach that asks, what happens when political institutions that are internationally relevant—that is, can be imported or exported—are combined with the cultural traditions of various countries? Particularly, when the formal political institutions stress personal freedom, cultural traditions are more likely to be retained and function well, and the special characteristics of the political process in these countries are likely to be highlighted. These aspects are often stressed in comparative politics.

Now, how does cultural tradition work in the case of Japanese politics? I will give one example. During the 1973 oil crisis, Japanese drivers were not as restricted in their use of gasoline as their counterparts in the Western world. In the West, the use of oil by general consumers was strictly restricted in order that industries would have ample supplies. By contrast, industries in Japan were restricted in their consumption of oil. As a result, industries invested in the development and use of energy-saving devices, and

in later years they were able to become more competitive internationally. But, at the time, the government did not adopt long-
term policies with that goal in mind. One explanation is that
there was a cultural tradition in which the public expected the
government and the politicians to coddle them like a doting
mother. In this crisis situation, this tradition worked effectively.
By contrast, one gets the impression that in the Western world,
there was the expectation that the government should act like
a stern father. Thus, cultural traditions can exert a strong influence on policy choices.

There is one way in which cultural traditions affect the political
process, and that is by providing scenarios for the sequence of
events. For example, in drama, the situation, plot, dramatis personae, the spoken lines, etc., are provided for in the script. The
play unfolds on the basis of this script. In the same way, one might
think of the political process as unfolding on the basis of the script,
which is cultural tradition. We will call this script a political paradigm. As a paradigm, cultural tradition is not limited to the
political process, but affects various aspects of one's life. From
among these various paradigms, we are interested in those that
are politically relevant, and these will be explained in more
detail as we go along.

What is necessary for a paradigm to be effective is a code book
that will set for individuals the definition of the situation and the
roles they are to take. If the situation in which one is placed can
be deciphered by means of the code book, that person can retrieve
the proper paradigm from his or her memory, and take proper
action in accordance with that paradigm.

By knowing the codes and paradigms that guide the behavior
of people in other countries, we can get a better understanding of
their politics. And this knowledge also has pragmatic utility. Since
the cultural tradition is self-evident for those individuals who
grew up within it, it is easy for them to take for granted that these
traditions are the same everywhere. They tend to apply their own
cultural tradition to other countries with different traditions.
When we observe the behavior of people in other countries, there
is the danger that we will assume that they are acting on the basis
of our own paradigm, when in fact such people may have different paradigms. Such errors can lead to international misunderstandings. In this situation, if one knows what paradigm the other

party is using, it should be easier to predict that party's likely behavior than if one did not have such knowledge. Also, it is possible to avoid needless collisions caused by misunderstandings.

Three Codes

The Collectivity Code

In Japan, as elsewhere, people live in a web of social networks, some of which are more lasting and important than others. Often these social networks provide the basis for group life. It is also true that group membership can, in turn, help create social networks. In any case, the Japanese penchant for group affiliation of various sorts is well known.

Among important social groups are such collectivities as family, village, firms, and one's own country. These collectivities have in the past and in the present continued to exert a powerful influence on the behavior of their members. Accordingly, we will begin the discussion of politically relevant codes by taking up what we shall call the collectivity code, a set of principles and rules relating to collective or group life.

A code is a set of principles or rules. The first politically relevant code would be the collectivity code, a set of rules relating to collective or group life. For the sake of convenience, the subject has been divided into a series of subcategories, which are listed below.

THE SITUATION: This is when individuals are aware that their behavior is being guided by their membership in certain collectivities, namely, family, village, firm, or country.

TRADITIONAL BACKGROUND: As a result of Japan's industrialization and urbanization, the requirement that individuals in their behavior should conform to the code governing such traditional collectivities as family and village has become weaker. But, especially since the 1920s, the rules governing family and village have come to be applied to those who are employed in large companies. Today, large companies are the most representative collectivity for these codes.

Between 1889 and 1945, the code that related to one's country served to legitimate political power, and was the basis of behavior for Japanese as subjects. However, as a result of defeat in World

War II, the religious beliefs that formed the underlying basis of the country code have been eliminated. But it is true that one's country remains most important, and the element of national egotism is recognizable in many instances.

According to the traditional articles of faith that many Japanese accept, a collectivity is something that organizes the communal or public facets of their lives and controls their behavior with respect to these facets. The collectivity does not pertain to their individual, personal, and private lives. The three collectivities, family, village, and, until 1945, country, are protected by ancestor-guardian deities. Both collectivities and their members identify with the eternal being through these deities. Accordingly, those who belong to collectivities, by doing what is expected of good members, can become ideal individuals. That is, they must negate their personal and private lives, and assume the communal and public roles that are expected of them. In this way, they can realize the ultimate meaning of their lives. These are some of the traditional beliefs of many Japanese.

ROLE TAKING: With regard to collectivities that one belongs to, one must make a distinction between those who are members and those who are not. In one's own collectivity, one must assume the role that is expected of members. Toward collectivities that one does not belong to, one must take the proper role, which is one of noninterference. As a member of a collectivity, one must be cognizant of one's position and act accordingly, that is, whether one is an officer and official representative, an influential, or a rank-and-file member.

ACTION: For its members, the only legitimate goal of the collectivity is its continuance and prosperity. So members must be selflessly dedicated to it, render it service, and make sacrifices for it. Officers and influentials can act on their own judgment. Rank-and-file members must take orders from above and be obedient in a hierarchical system. Examples are the decision to surrender by the Emperor in 1945 and bravery shown by Japanese soldiers.

All members must act to maximize the unity and harmony of the collectivity. The origin and prototype of unity and harmony are to be found in drunken orgies in connection with festivities. Accordingly, company members often get together over alcohol after work stops at five o'clock in order to facilitate informal communications so that unity and harmony can be achieved. Even if the collectivity engages in unreasonable and irrational decision making, because of collective subconscious emotions and impulses, its members must accept that policy for the sake of unity and harmony of the collectivity. An example is widespread acquiescence to the government in World War II.

One must always distinguish between members and non-members of collectivities. Fellow members are brothers-in-arms. Non-members are outsiders and aliens. A non-member's voice is meaningless noise, and need not be listened to.

NOTE: When a collectivity's continuance and prosperity are the common goal, inner schism is avoided in a stable, slow-changing society, thus making unity and harmony possible. However, in fairly rapidly changing societies based on Western-style industrialization that began in the late nineteenth century, there will normally be differences of views as to how to achieve prosperity. As a result, political conflict between past-oriented, locally minded, centripetal views, and future-oriented, global-minded, centrifugal views cannot be avoided. If non-endogenous goods, technology, and institutions are adopted from the outside in order to better, enrich, and complement the collectivity's condition, they may produce an identity crisis in a tradition-bound collectivity. There are cases when after positive and active adoption, there follow negative restrictions after partial incorporation. There are such examples in Japanese history. Moreover, it is an article of faith among the people that active adoption and self-imposed metamorphosis does not harm the collectivity's identity. An example would be Westernization since the Meiji Restoration.

The status of a collectivity as a religious entity is connected to the ancestor-guardian deity and lineage. An example is the Imperial Family. There is no Judaic, Christian tradition in Japan. There is no belief in a god of creation. There is no instance of god the creator having given ethical commandments to human beings, and entered into a contract with them. There is no belief in human beings rebelling against god and thereby committing sin. There is no case of Jesus being crucified and resurrected by god the savior to absolve human beings of their sins. There is no belief that after that episode, history is proceeding in a unilinear fashion toward the ultimate historical goal of a new heaven and new earth.

Accordingly, in Japan there is no tradition that, eternally, human beings are responsible to a transcendent god, and, therefore, that their individuality will live forever. Therefore, according to tradition, after death, individuals will merge into and be absorbed by the ancestor-guardian deities and thereby lose their individuality. In Japan, both Buddhism and Confucianism have given commandment ethics. But the collectivity code does not contain commandment ethics. Also, individuals do not have eternal lives. This has led to political opportunism, extroverted realism, and pragmatism.

In periods of stability, collectivities are dominated by traditionalism, and possessed detailed codes of behavior that specified when, where, who, what, and how. These codes of behavior are well known to the members, and those who fail to act according to the codes are laughed at and ridiculed by their fellow members. Being laughed at is a very trying experience. Thus, a smart way for a collectivity member to carry on one's daily life is to make sure to behave in such a way as to avoid being the subject of ridicule and being put to shame. Thus, the shame principle is a way of maintaining order in a collectivity without commandment ethics, and a form of social control based on strong psychological pressure.[1]

The Possessed Individuals' Code

From the standpoint of a common, normal person, other people are classified cognitively in terms of such characteristics as intelligence, emotional intensity, will power, vitality, etc., into three categories—namely, subnormal, normal, and supernormal. The other people are reclassified evaluatively into two categories, that is, ordinary, who are normal, and the exceptional and/or deviant, who are either supernormal or subnormal. In the feudal system under the Tokugawa, there was an understanding that "to do what other people do not do is punishable." Traditionalism was strongly enforced and practiced. Although there were many, if minor, inventions in farming, textiles, pottery, etc., excellence did not involve originality and creativity. Rather, it involved an intensive outlay of energy and hard work according to the tradi-

1. Cf. Ruth Benedict, *The Chrysanthemum and the Sword* (Chicago: Aldine, 1946).

tional pattern. It was important for the ordinary individual to behave in the traditional manner and not strive to be exceptional or irregular. To be common and mediocre was strongly encouraged. This meant that in daily life one should be a good member of the collectivity. Those who were gifted and outstanding were expected to stay in the village and, like ordinary people, work for the unity and harmony of the village. Or they had to move to big cities like Edo, Kyoto, or Osaka, or to Buddhist temples where their talents were somehow accepted or tolerated.

Japan has modernized since the Meiji Restoration, but the value system of preferring to be common and normal has survived, as noted in the collectivity code. The value system also has survived in modern corporations and government offices in the form of a mentality that prefers to follow precedent and avoid the new. On the other hand, those who are intellectually gifted, are enterprising and ambitious, and have vitality can leave the tradition-oriented collectivities, such as the family and village. Now they can try to put their talents to work in new urban environments, or even in foreign countries. Eventually, many of them become the top and middle-range leaders of an industrialized and modernized Japan.

People who are normal and those who are exceptional have had to live together. In the parliamentary system, party politicians are drawn from the political activist groups and are marked with an exceptionally strong ambition and lust for power and/or with an extraordinary sense of mission. Hence the possessed individuals' code. The common people, who are the voters, want to lead ordinary lives, avoid sticking their necks out, and refrain from getting into trouble.

Typical examples of exceptional individuals are the heroes of folk tales, who are notorious for such characteristics as their gargantuan appetites or promiscuous sexuality. In a modernized, affluent society, such exceptional people are not troublesome. Other examples would be those who are emotionally unstable and frequently lose their tempers. Ordinary people are supposed to be, and really are, calm, polite, and well balanced. If ordinary people lose their tempers it is considered an anomaly.

Often in Japanese folk religion, such anomalies are attributed to the work of some numinous power that is alien to the collectivity and the ancestor-guardian deity that protects it. Those who are bent on behaving in ways that are not approved, or show signs of having some emotional disorder are thought to have been possessed by some known or unknown numinous power. Since political leadership with a strong sense of mission often comes from such individuals who are believed to be possessed with a vision of an ideal society, we will take up the possessed individuals' code as the second politically relevant code.

THE SITUATION: This is a code that operates when two people meet, one who thinks that he or she is ordinary, and the other who thinks that he or she is not regarded as ordinary but as exceptional and/or deviant.

TRADITIONAL BACKGROUND: According to the traditional articles of faith that govern many Japanese, in many things including human beings and events there reside numinous powers. This is a world of numen. The human spirits and these numinous powers are communicable, and the stronger can control the weaker.

The spirits of the common people are, if minimally, numinous. For example, if one dies in a strange place, and/or dies in an untoward manner, also if after death, proper memorial services are not performed, the spirit of the dead will be angry and could bring disaster on the living. Accordingly, it is necessary to give the spirit of the dead a proper funeral or memorial service. For example, every year the Ministry of Welfare has sent, at its expense, delegations of relatives to visit the graves of those who were killed in action on foreign shores in World War II. It is necessary in this way to appease and placate the spirts of both the dead and the living.

People who are not ordinary but deviant are better judged as bewitched or possessed by some numen. It is safer for ordinary people to deal carefully with deviant individuals.

ROLE TAKING: One can conceive of two categories of individuals: ordinary or self-possessed, and not ordinary, deviant, and numen possessed. If one's behavior is consistent with the rules of the collectivity or the narrow world[2] that one belongs to, that person and other people observing that person will think of themselves as ordinary. In the event that one's own self-categorization

2. The original term is *semai seken* for which there is no standard translation. Ezra F. Vogel in his *Japan's New Middle Class* uses the term "the narrow world" which includes acquaintances, benefactors, and friends; see pp. 117–38.

is different from the categorization that others make, one follows self-categorization.

ACTION (A): Those who consider themselves ordinary must observe the golden mean and preserve a sense of proportion, and must avoid excesses in both work and play. When it comes to impulses and desires regarding money, liquor, and sex, one must avoid self-indulgence and practice abstinence and temperance. One must be diligent in one's work, and avoid getting involved in other people's business. One must follow conventions and act conservatively and traditionally, and not create problems for others. Whether it is for good or bad, one must not be socially conspicuous. It is all right to have political opinions and cast one's ballot in elections, but one must not be an activist and get deeply involved in politics. When dealing with deviant, numen-possessed individuals, one must be respectful toward them, but not get involved with them nor committed too deeply in their activities.

ACTION (B): Those who consider themselves to be exceptional and who seek to promote the welfare of ordinary people must be prepared to go to extraordinary lengths to devote themselves to their work and must be willing to sacrifice themselves. Although now it is time-worn and outmoded, a popular saying among party politicians went as follows: "All my activities are for the benefit of the people and society. Nothing is intended for myself." In the early period of the parliamentary system, this reflected the mentality of the party politicians. One must not forget that the only ground on which others, that is ordinary people, will accept what one is doing is visible evidence that one is making daily sacrifices for the benefit of the people through asceticism. In the case of religious mystagogues, it means that the practice of asceticism has resulted in a religious rebirth, so it signifies that one has achieved magico-religious power to control various numen. For that reason, because of that power, the mystagogue is now useful to the ordinary people. To remain useful, every day one must show his believer-customers that he is undergoing ascetic practices without fail.

Specifically, let us take the case of socialists, communists, and political radicals, who, on the basis of revolutionary creeds like Marxism-Leninism, seek to achieve an ideal society on this earth for ordinary people. In order to demonstrate that they are not driven by the lust for power, but are working for the welfare of ordinary people through their selfless, rewardless dedication, such individuals will display for the benefit of voters, a personal life-style that is ascetic, clean, and poverty stricken. They must take particular care not to engage in bribery, become drunk, or have affairs. In the case of scholars who are enchanted with the pursuit of scientific truth, they must work hard and have a lifestyle that is ascetic, clean, and poor. In this way they can show that they are working for the benefit of ordinary people.

NOTE: Sometimes outlaw organizations emerge from groups which are made up of people who feel that they cannot engage in ordinary occupations, with ordinary discipline, in an ordinary society. There are also examples of members of such organizations engaging in assassinations and terrorism in the political arena. There are some ruffians who lead self-indulgent and lavish lives among those activists that engage in direct action.

Equality Code

During the Tokugawa period, Japanese society was composed of four basic strata: samurai, farmer, artisan, and merchant in that rank order. Each stratum was further subdivided into many categories. After the Meiji Restoration, all Japanese were de-clared to be equal. Equality under the law is now explicitly stip-ulated in the Constitution of 1947. There have been political and social movements aimed at getting rid of unjust discrimination and securing equality of treatment. But cases of discrimination based on gender, and others based on historical tradition continue to be reported. But, by and large, after a period of more than one hundred years, the feeling that all Japanese are equal has come to be widely shared. The strong belief in equality underpins the popular demand that benefits provided by the government be distributed equally throughout the country.

If people believe in the essential, ontological equality of human beings, it inspires many types of political and social movements that seek equal treatment. But the belief also inspires, supports, and justifies individuals to seek power, income, and prestige. The inspired individual can become "more equal than others" (George Orwell's *Animal Farm*), or even the "most equal among others." As already explained, those who are gifted and exceptional can gain the support of the common people by showing that they are dedicated selflessly to the welfare of the ordinary people. But ambitious, exceptional people also need the inner support that legitimates their activities, which are not shared by the common people. Hence the equality code.

THE SITUATION: This code has to do with exceptional individuals with intellectual gifts, enterprise, ambition, and vitality, who, on their own initiative, pursue goals they aspire to, but find that their goals are not approved nor shared by either their own group or their narrow world. Nevertheless, they still seek to pursue their goals as if by divine calling.

TRADITIONAL BACKGROUND: There is in Japan, in addition to popular beliefs in the numinous world, a very long tradition of trained experience in mysticism, and the Chinese tradition of Buddhist-Taoist metaphysics or ontology that has been transmitted and has become deeply rooted in the intellectual world of discourse. Based on these teachings, there are traditional beliefs in a plenitude of the eternal being in the cosmos. That is, every phenomenon in the cosmos is a manifestation of the eternal being, variously called the Great Life Force, the Way, Nature, or a variety of deities. Behind these beliefs are a thousand years of history, and they have been popularized in the period beginning with the Tokugawa period in the seventeenth century and extending to the present.

According to these beliefs, all things and events ontologically participate in the eternal being. Accordingly, although everything is separate and distinct, at the same time, they share a common, ontological quality. As a corollary of this, all human beings are ontologically homogeneous, and in this regard are equal. In the secular, relative world, all people are alienated from the eternal being. If one succeeds in getting closer to the eternal being through his endeavors, he becomes "more equal than others." In the religious tradition, the mystic unity with the eternal being is an end in itself. But, on earth, by becoming more equal, one becomes superior to those who are alienated. Thus, it is legitimate for that person to govern others. The question of what facet of the eternal, cosmic being is the object of ontological participation is of practical importance. The following table suggests a classification scheme:

Individuals	Cosmic Being
1. reason in mind	eternal law, natural law
2. art, skill	the Way (*tao*)
3. energetic vitality	life force

ROLE TAKING: One can take one of the following categories as pertaining to himself or herself: (1) Scientists, scholars, intellectuals: those who think that reasoning is the most important activity for them; (2) Men of arts, crafts, and skills: those for whom improvement and refinement of art and skills is most important; (3) Men of affairs: those whose capital is energy and vitality, and who want to go out into the macrosociety and attain power, income, and prestige.

ACTION (A): Those who think of themselves as scientists, scholars, and intellectuals believe that there is in the universe, natural law and laws of society and history. They also believe that because human reason participates ontologically in this eternal law, human reason can know eternal law. For them, the results of scientific research are not tentative, artificial constructs developed by human hands, but represent self-revelation of eternal law to human reason. Also, they must believe that ultimately scientific research will result in the self-revelation of eternal law, and that human reason and eternal law will result in final, mystic unity. In this way, scientific research confronts mystery.

To the extent that all human beings have reason, they are equal. However, there are differences in the degree of training in the use of reason. The use of reason is to have the highest value for human beings. Accordingly, scientists, scholars, and intellectuals must educate and enlighten individuals to reason more effectively. Thus, enlightened despotism by professionals composed of scientists, scholars, and intellectuals is legitimated. The same thing is true of bureaucratic autocracy led by LL.B.s and B.A.s. The popular superstition that supernatural, numinous power is effective is most inappropriate for individuals who use reason. One must use education to combat superstition and replace it with a belief in science and scientific knowledge.

ACTION (B): People who feel that improving and refining their arts and skills are most important never think that the work they do, which is based on their role in society, their position and status, and their occupation and specialty, is onerous or that they are doing it so that they can eat. Even while they are improving their arts and skills, they must pursue the Way or *tao*. Ultimately, they must strive in the belief that they can achieve a mystic union with the Way (*tao*), and thus become a divinely skilled human being. From the point of view of such a mystical experience, work is holy, and tools used in work are also holy. Accordingly, they regard their work place as consecrated, and their work tools as embodying their lives and spirits. In Japan there are many examples of arts and skills that contain the word *dō*, or Way, as in judo, fencing, archery, tea ceremony, flower arrangement, incense burning, poetry, and the world of theater.

NOTE: Because of the belief that improving one's skills and increasing productivity represents a form of religious pilgrimage, the motto that "work, that is, prayer" has become established in Japanese factories. This is important in understanding industrial relations in modern Japan.

ACTION (c): Those who seek to go out into one's narrow world and become successful, using their energy and vitality as their capital, must perceive themselves as a personification of the life force. They must not hesitate to satiate their desires for money, liquor, and sex and become hedonistic. They must look down on and, if they can get away with it, violate all forms of rules and discipline as inhuman impediments to self-indulgence. When they are forced to bear the high pressure of discipline in their collectivity every day, they must go somewhere else on their days off, or after work they must seek some form of orgiastic relaxation in order to regain their human qualities. All facts and events represent an unfolding of the life force, and that fact makes everything legitimate. Usually, a fait accompli represents good and "might is right." In the Japanese language, there are no equivalent expressions for "lost cause" and for "fairness." Thus, when it comes to competition in the society at large, one must constantly engage in struggle and seek to win. In the struggle for expanding and maintaining market share, one must pursue a policy that is unrestrained and unlimited in terms of expansion. The expansionism by the Japanese army during the 1930s is one example of "might is right."

In the event that one cannot win, one had better try to get close to a winner and become part of that person's entourage.

In this way, one shares in that person's income, power, and prestige, which is the materialization of the life force. One must behave naturally and unartificially, putting trust in Mother Nature, even if it means a succession of myopic, passive responses. Also, one must not forget valor, which represents life force having gone berserk. For example, following the attack on Pearl Harbor, Prime Minister Tōjō explained the decision to go to war to the members of the Imperial Diet by saying, "Sometimes human beings must be brave enough to jump [several hundred feet] off the deck of the Kiyomizu Temple [in Kyoto]."

It is youth who most typically personify the life force. Thus, even if there are excesses in the activities of youth who are full of energy, such activities must be treated leniently, and even encouraged in order to assure their future growth.

Three Paradigms

The Sin and Punishment Paradigm

So far we have dealt with codes, which are sets of rules to be observed in proper situations. Next we turn to paradigms, of which there are also three. These paradigms describe the unfolding of processes. They are stated in the form of scripts found in dramas. These paradigms may be viewed as modules or constituent elements in a longer script for a much more complex play, which is sometimes the political process, but more often the social process that lies behind the political process. The first paradigm describes the moral framework on which social and political processes are based. The drama of guilt and responsibility is explained.

Human beings are imperfect and cannot achieve perfection. Human beings also have the capability of doing evil. These perceptions have been held for many thousands of years in both the Orient and the Occident, and, therefore, have a long history. They also form the foundation of the legal order in the West. Modern Japan has adopted this legal system from the West. The result is a three-tiered court system for both civil and criminal cases. But Japan does not use the jury system. In criminal cases, the public procurator has considerable latitude in deciding whether or not to bring charges. The criminal code specifies that in "murder cases, penalties will be execution, life imprisonment, or imprisonment for three years or more." Thus, it can be seen that judges also can exercise a good deal of discretion in sentencing criminals. The granting of discretionary power is a convenient and effective way to bring about an accommodation between the Western legal system and Japanese traditions.

If one goes against the rules of the group or one's narrow world, that transgression is dealt with according to the following script.

THE STAGE: As was explained in the section on the equality code, according to the traditional Japanese articles of faith, the cosmos in its essential meaning is full of divine excellence of the eternal being. Moreover, this metaphysical reality is perfect and eternal. Concrete objects at the depth level of phenomena share in this reality. Thus, all things have the potential of attaining perfection and eternity. Evil cannot exist, ontologically speaking, in the phenomenal world, and human beings, as part of that world, have yet to commit the first sin.

Education in Japan has taken these articles of faith as its basic premise. That is, when the goals, meaning, and norms of life are taught, the first thing that has to be taught is the belief that there are no individuals who by nature are evil. Human beings by nature are good. Second, on the basis of the foregoing, people should be taught that human beings are to be trusted unconditionally, and not that they are untrustworthy. This basic belief has been the foundation for political socialization beginning at the elementary level to post-elementary education in contemporary Japan.

Even though instructors may teach in their political socialization courses that human beings are by nature not evil, it cannot be denied that evil does in fact exist. Thus, the existence of human evil can be explained as follows. It is assumed that infants and children represent the true uncontaminated nature of human beings before the Fall. Their purity and innocence are assumed. All doubts about this assumption are prohibited. Evil comes from selfishness, greed, and passion. As children grow up, selfishness, greed, and selfish desire, and self-interest come into being. If selfish desire, desire for goods, and passion succumb to the temptations of evil put forward by society and culture, then one becomes evil and violates the rules and taboos of the group. But even in this case, the real nature of human beings is good. No one is evil by nature. Criminal behavior represents excesses of youth and is a passing phenomenon. In this way, evil and chaos are characterized as something that is happenstance, comes from the environment, and represents an aberration from true human nature.

If it is assumed that no one is evil by nature, then if in some way evil and chaos that come from the outside can be cleaned out, one could return to the true nature of human beings before the Fall. Chaos can be removed by the process of the "regeneration of time," as explained below.

Chaos will surely intrude upon the group and disrupt its order. With the passage of time, order will deteriorate. In the light of this, it is essential and also useful to regenerate time with the help of the ancestor-guardian deities that protect the group. As M. Eliade has explained,[3] in the "sacred time" that is represented by religious rituals, the time of the creation of heaven and earth, the time of the early myths, and time of one's early ancestors are re-created. "Profane" time and history that has been soiled by chaos are done away with, and the clock of time is set again at zero. Everything gets a new start. "Profane" time starts over again from this point, and so time is regenerated.

In this process, starting over again by returning to the beginning are stressed. However, historical reality that exists only once has no ultimate meaning. The past is swept away, there is no reflection or repentance about the past, and what has happened in the past does not provide materials for analysis or self-enlightenment.

In the case of religious rites described here, the clock of time returns to zero for the group and its members. History that has been sullied by evil and chaos is nullified. If we apply this process to the case of an individual who has engaged in evil deeds, the clock of time will be set to zero every time such rites are performed, thereby nullifying the evil. Like a dirty mirror that has been wiped clean, his true nature will shine again.

THE PLOT: If guilt is the result of defilement by evil, then the restoration of the good will be achieved by getting rid of personal greed in order to become one with the eternal being.

3. Mircea Eliade, *The Myth of the Eternal Return*, translated by William Trask (New York: Pantheon Books, 1954).

But there is one step that needs to be taken before this. That is, the victim of the wrong doer must be able to determine the true state of mind of the wrong doer. This means that the wrong doer recognizes that he had done wrong and that he apologizes. In this way, when the wrong doer objectively perceives the evil and chaos that have attached themselves to him and deals with his past misdeeds, the time that had been defiled by evil and chaos is turned back to zero, when everything began. In the beginning of time, the true nature, which was pure, innocent, and good, is revealed.

The leading figure in this mythical drama, the secular manifestation of metaphysical reality, and one who teaches this paradigm is the mother. This is the forgiving mother, who, to the crying child that says, "I am sorry," responds with tears in her eyes, "I'm the one who should be blamed." The wrong doer regains the pure qualities that infants possessed before the Fall, and finds refuge in the tolerance and broad-mindedness of the mother. There is reaffirmation that the wrong doer was not cut off from the "mother" (the reality), and that by nature he was not an evil person. Then everyone will say, "he has apologized, he says he is sorry," and any thought of punishing the wrong doer will be abandoned.

With this reaffirmation, a new life, dedicated to promoting the public good rather than personal profit, will begin. By saying, "I am sorry," and taking responsibility, time is turned back to the beginning, and a new person is born.

There are others who can play the role of the tolerant and broad-minded mother. There are wives, and those who occupy a superior position in personal relationships, that is, teachers, one's boss at work, and such authorities as the police and courts and the government. If we resort to an explanation derived by Jungian psychology, the maternal principle—wherein one returns unconditionally to mother or the *magna mater*, and wrong doing that has not been atoned is permitted without punishment—is the basic principle that underlies the social order and the political system.

NOTE: Even in the case of those accused of criminal behavior, admission of guilt and expressions of regret are expected by many people. Such expressions are taken as signs of repentance, and, depending on the discretionary powers of the judge, it could work to lighten the sentence. In this way, Japanese tradition and the Western legal system have made an accommodation.

Also, after the defeat in 1945, the sincere reorientation of the Japanese people from militarism to democracy followed this paradigm. At the same time, some foreign people who did not share this paradigm interpreted this reorientation as a camouflage.

Paradigm on Decision Making Based on Atmosphere

People encounter all kinds of situations and conditions regarding decision making in their group life. If the behavior expected of them within the group is institutionalized and every member knows what it is, there is no need to decide what to do. But there are not a few instances where the group is confronted by a new situation or condition, and where there are no explicit rules to deal with it. That is, first, the details of the kind of behavior that is expected may not be clear. Second, the details may need to be worked out, but the procedure to be followed may not be evident. The development of an industrial civilization has forced changes in the traditional decision-making system, and so the instances where the system cannot provide guidance tend to increase. As was explained in the section on the collectivity code, with regard to the decision-making procedure within groups, it is likely to be as follows. The rank-and-file will follow the decision made by a great person or someone in an influential position (a government official, a rich individual, or an elder). As to what will be decided will likely to be of a conservative variety, either the maintenance of the status quo, or the perpetuation of tradition. Moreover, if the number of new situations increases, the ability of members to make effective decisions will decline, and the feeling of insecurity on the part of members will also increase. As a result, what is decided and the decision process will be unstable.

If we use the analogy of a drama, decision making under the circumstances described above may be likened to a plot. Another plot would be the *nemawashi* paradigm that will be described later.

THE SITUATION: All kinds of organizations, including small groups, trade associations, and groups formed to support professional politicians, are confronted by changes in the balance of power among their members, and by technological change, such as new developments in high technology and office automation. In response to this, it is possible that efforts will be made to maintain the status quo, or perhaps changes will be made. No one can predict the future.

DRAMATIS PERSONAE: The influentials. They do not have the knowledge, firm opinions, nor principles that could provide the basis for making judgments. They are mostly concerned with avoiding trouble and unrest within the group, and in maintaining group unity and harmony. They have the power to depend on group unity. Moreover, they feel assured that no matter what decisions are made, groups and organizations will not collapse.

The rank-and-file. As was explained earlier, the views of these people most of the time will be for the status quo or in the traditional vein. Because day-to-day life revolves around the individual, and he or she is at risk, it is natural for a safe course that avoids risk and produces the expected results to be preferred. Many people are reluctant to speak up. It is risky to stick their necks out in a group situation, because they might find themselves isolated, might invite attacks, and sometimes be censured.

The young innovators, sometimes, the young valiants. They believe that change is essential for groups and for organizations. They sometimes look into and think about pending problems and plan new strategies. Some are zealots who have neither studied or given much thought to problems, but feel that change is needed. They are concerned about pending problems and their solutions, but they have not given much thought to such matters as the effect on the balance of power within the group, the psychological uncertainty that change would impose on group members, and the resistance that such members have toward change.

THE PLOT: Groups wishing to maintain the status quo and tradition. There is a consensus that following precedent is important. In group decisions, the system known as *nemawashi* is important. In this system, the action plan is outlined to the members in order to give them the psychological satisfaction that they have been consulted. If the young innovators should make a proposal for action that is not in keeping with tradition without first making use of *nemawashi*, ordinarily no one, other than those who made the proposal, will support it. The proposal will get an icy reception, and will die without further ado. The person who makes the proposal may refuse to give up and persist every time the group meets, perhaps three or four times. But the proposal will die for lack of support.

It is, however, possible that the situation will change dramatically. Rather than highlighting the positive features of the proposal in order to support it, there will emerge a consensus, almost like giving in to a noisy child who wants to have its way. "If he is so insistent, let's let him try it." From the point of view of the influentials, group unity and harmony is most important. They want to avoid having unrest within the group. They also feel that the group will not disintegrate even if the young innovators are allowed to have things their way. Thus, the influentials will become supporters of the innovators, given the balance of power situation among the members. As was explained in the section on the possessed individuals' code, it is important to appease and placate the spirits of the living members. In this way, the change of opinion that started among a few influentials will spread quickly to the obedient rank-and-file members, and unexpectedly there will be a consensus.

When this plan is carried out, and so long as it produces good results (or appears to), support based on the consensus will be sustained. But if the results are not favorable, or if the prospects do not appear to be good, or if there is fear along these lines, then support will fade. Looking back, people will say, "We were influenced by the atmosphere at the time," and there will be a split into a conservative faction and a splinter group. After that the conservative faction may make a comeback and abandon the proposal that had been adopted, or the splinter group may prevail and push it despite opposition, or the struggle may continue. Thus, there are three possible outcomes.

NOTE: Examples of decision making consistent with this paradigm have been reported. For instance, there is the invasion of China by the Japanese military, especially the army in the 1930s. Another one would be a few military operations during World War II. There are also examples of this kind of decision making in connection with organizational change caused by rapid social and technological change.

But this paradigm would not apply to many Japanese organizations that are autocratically controlled by the top leaders, nor to organizations where young innovators are given a free hand to expeditiously carry out their own ideas.

Submission and Resistance Paradigm

As was explained in the section on the collectivity code, political opportunism is the rule of behavior in collectivities. This may sometimes result in influential members of collectivities engaging in irresponsible management, and being selfish and corrupt. For this reason, they may not have the respect of the members of the collectivity. If the influentials should demand selfless dedication on the part of the rank-and-file, the latter may not be able to comply because they are physically tired, psychologically pressed by other worries, or in a financial bind. All these situations will bring about a power struggle between the leaders and the followers. The script that will delineate this power struggle is the submission and resistance paradigm.

THE SITUATION: There are two codes that define people's roles and behavior, and they are contradictory. To begin with, according to the collectivity code, the group ranks higher than its members and can ask for their dedication. But according to the equality code, both individuals and the group share equally in the eternal being. Both the group and its influential members and its common members are ontologically equal. If we look at the relationship between the small group and its members, from the point view of their legitimacy, it would be as follows: The group could rank higher, or could be equal; the members could rank lower or be equal.

In this situation, the arguments that the influentials will use to try to get the rank-and-file to submit will be *tatemae*, or form. The rebuttal by the rank-and-file will be the *honne*, or substance. Accordingly, the relationship between *tatemae* and *honne* will also be like that between the influentials and the rank-and-file, that is, *tatemae* could be either higher or equal to *honne* or *honne* could be lower or equal. In terms of their contents, *tatemae* could give expression to the public interest, and *honne* could express individual spontaneity, decisions, and responsibility.

It will be useful at this point to digress and explain the terms *tatemae* and *honne* in some detail. Literally, *tatemae* is the wooden framework of a house. When one builds a traditional wooden house, the carpenters start by setting corner stones. They then place pillars on these stones and connect them with horizontal beams. When the ridge pole is put in place on top of this framework, the house is, in a sense, finished, because later the roof, walls, and floor are attached to or fill in the empty spaces in the framework. This wooden framework is called *tatemae*. At this point, the carpenters will have a ceremony that marks the completion of the *tatemae*, and this ceremony, celebrated with *sake*, also came to be called *tatemae*. Later, the word *tatemae* came to mean, metaphorically, an official or officially professed principle or doctrine that will serve as the goal or target of the collectivity, and provide guidance for its members in managing it.

Although in a collectivity, the rank-and-file are not expected to have a voice in running it, except perhaps to simply echo the orders that come down from above, usually, as a matter of fact, they have their own voices that might contradict the orders from the leadership. The term *honne* literally means true tone or pitch. It is the true voice that has to be kept secret because of several considerations. It is not wise for an ordinary member of a collectivity to be marked as one harboring some *honne* that is dissonant with orders from above. Pressure will be applied for him to express his *honne*. Nor it is safe for the content of the *honne* to be known by those in power. It would be dangerous if the kind and amount of dissatisfaction, ranging from discontent to subversive thoughts, were to become known. Pressure may be applied not only to himself but also to members of his family to make him change his mind.

Thus, metaphorically, *honne* stands against the *tatemae* when *tatemae* refers to a principle, doctrine, goal, or purpose of a collectivity that is enunciated by its leadership. The term *tatemae* can also refer to bureaucratic red tape, that is, official rules and procedures that are bypassed to expedite matters. When officials do not follow the letter of the rules, they might say, "The *tatemae* is this and that, but we will overlook it . . ." in order to impress the client that a favor is being done.

Hence, by definition, *tatemae* refers to the communal and public facets of the common interest of the members of the collectivity as articulated by the leadership. In that event, *honne* refers to the fulfillment of the desires of the individuals that are not in accord with the official line, at least in the eyes of and, perhaps, in the interest of the leaders.

DRAMATIS PERSONAE: The influentials will use the *taemae* to demand that the rank-and-file submit. The rank-and-file will reject this demand for submission. They will try, if possible, to get the demand withdrawn.

THE PLOT: The influentials, who demand the submission of the rank-and-file in the name of *tatemae*, will argue in terms of the public good vs. the private good, and demand that the rank-and-file admit the superiority of the public good and stop demanding the attainment of the private good. Within the small group, this position would be considered a legitimate one.

In response to this, the rank-and-file, who normally are expected to be obedient, will show their displeasure (something they are not supposed to do) and appeal to another code of behavior. As was explained in the section on the possessed individuals' code, the rank-and-file will resist by resorting to deviant behavior. When this happens, the influentials, trying to maintain their control, will also use non-routine measures. That is, instead of demanding compliance, they will try to accommodate the rank-and-file by either explicitly or implicitly retracting the demand that the private good be sacrificed for the public good. This is one possible outcome. It is often seen in Japanese politics, which is sensitive to the needs of everyone from babies to pressure groups.

Another possible outcome is where the demand that the private good be sacrificed for the public good is not retracted. In this instance, the influentials will say they, too, are sensitive to the reluctance of the rank-and-file but will in effect demand submission to the *tatemae* position. If, in response, the rank-and-file quietly submits, the case will be closed.

If the rank-and-file continues to resist, it will argue against the *tatemae* position, saying that it is unrealistic. The rank-and-file will argue that their interests must be respected. If the influentials agree to this, the case will be closed. If the influentials do not agree, the two sides will continue to argue on their own grounds, and in the end the dispute will be decided by a power struggle.

NOTE: Since these two systems of legitimacy exist, the resolution of the conflict between the public good and the private good will often depend ultimately on power relationships. Now, the peaceful, democratic system established by the Constitution states the basic principle of respect for individual rights. As a result, the demand that individual interests be sacrificed for the public good is heard less often. Individuals rights (*honne*) are now forcefully asserted as legal rights, and the authorities have a tendency to feel that they must give in to these assertions. Accordingly, many people now support the view that we have now entered a period when *honne* is being asserted shamelessly. People also feel that those who are going to assert their rights should also assume their obligations.

Chapter Three

Politics as Drama

In Chapter Two, we likened the political process to the performance of a play. Political codes and paradigms were extracted from the daily unfolding of politics and viewed as the equivalent of constituent elements in the script of a play. One finds all kinds of dramas in the theater: some are short, others are long, some are simple, others are complex. Often, long complex plays are divided into several acts, and acts, in turn, are composed of scenes. The political process, too, can be so divided. The three paradigms introduced in Chapter Two not only were part of the political process but also pertained, in many instances, to social processes. They were relatively short and simple. In this chapter we will take up political paradigms that are more complex.

For the sake of convenience, we will divide the analysis of the political process into two parts. The first will focus on the inner sphere, where participants try to manage and administer the groups to which they belong, particularly as in the case of domestic politics. In the second case, we will deal with the outer sphere, where participants will try to assure the existence and prosperity of the groups to which they belong, as in the case of international politics. The first group of paradigms will be called the collectivity paradigms, and the second will be called the battlefield paradigms.

The Collectivity Paradigm

Here I will choose and explain those paradigms that are most important politically from among those that are used to maintain and manage life through collectivities. Groups and organizations that are not collectivities will also use these paradigms depending on need. Since the script is well known to many people, it is used by political pressure groups, government agencies, and the mass media, and the script also influences their interaction. Thus it guides the political process.

The Esprit de Corps Paradigm

In order for a collectivity that organizes individuals to become an entity and influence the behavior of its members, it must convey a sense of identity to its members and strengthen their sense of esprit de corps. In collectivities, such as family and villages that are developed naturally, traditional festivals have performed that function. In the case of the country, from the middle of the nineteenth century until 1945, there were various measures, including education, to strengthen the sense of patriotism. It is a well-known fact that companies also take various steps to promote esprit de corp. We will discuss these steps in more detail below.

THE PLOT: *Introduction to historical identity.* Examples of measures used to promote identification include the dedication of a shrine to the spirits of the founder, the erection of a stone tablet or bronze statue of the founder, and the naming of a building in honor of his memory. The founding day is a holiday, and all employees are expected to participate in the programs scheduled on that day. An official history of the firm is written and distributed to outside dignitaries and to employees.

Encouragement of employee involvement in the company. Meetings of the entire force every morning, or perhaps once a week, in which someone read aloud the company creed, or perhaps all repeat it in unison are ways to promote involvement. A company house organ is distributed to keep all informed employees about recent developments in the industry, changes in the company's market share, how well the company is doing, and about new products. All members of a company are expected to be involved in the activities of other members. The lives of the employees rest on the system of the division of labor. In order to strengthen the sense of unity within this system of the division of labor, one has to be able to put himself in the position of others, who have to play different roles, and try to understand how other people feel. Also, there is training to put yourself in another's position and understand how that person feels. For this purpose, oral explana-ations are given, and there are discussions of printed materials on company matters. Finally, there is on-the-job training that gives one first-hand experience in performing other duties. Newly hired employees are often put through this on-the-job training by being assigned to different positions for a period of as long as one year.

Employees are made to compete collectively against employees of other companies. Just as a country has a national anthem and a flag, there are company songs and flags, and they are used during the morning meetings. The company logo will be dis-played on buildings, company cars, and stationery. Company badges, uniforms, and hats are provided free of charge. Television commercials are used to promote a public image of the company. Just as Japan sends teams to the Olympic games, so companies sponsor athletic teams in such sports as baseball, basketball, volleyball, football, and track and field. Company employees will serve as cheering sections in these athletic contests. This is also an efficient form of company advertising.

The exclusion of those who belong to other groups. When distinctions are made among groups, members of other groups will be ex-cluded. This happens in the case of villages, companies, and coun-tries. Among groups, we and they, kin and non-kin, buddies and strangers, and insiders and outsiders are distinguished. And those who belong to the outside world are carefully excluded from the inner world. The traditional tendency of villages and business communities to exclude outsiders and to keep to themselves is well known. The same is true of firms that remain internally unified by shutting themselves off from outside in-fluences. In the case of Japanese policy toward immigrants, it stands in contrast to the United States, whose basic policy is to let immigrants come in to live, become naturalized as citizens, and to become Americanized. In Japan, one had to inherit the status as a Japanese. The regulations regarding citizenship until 1984 and treatment of refugees are examples of this exclusion of outsiders and isolation from outside influences.

In contrast to the American cultural tradition that is epitomized by the words *e pluribus unum* inscribed on currency, according to the Japanese tradition, members of a collectivity should be as much alike as possible if it is to enjoy esprit de corps. This tends to result in uniformity among members. In concrete terms, it produces people who see things alike. One way to get people to see things alike is to start from the outside—appearance. Children are dressed in identical clothing, and adults participating in festivals wear identical *happi* coats. In many instances, in schools and companies, uniforms are the rule. Moreover, not only in outer clothing, but in one's inner feelings and thoughts, the denial of individuality and the need to cooperate within the group are stressed and taught at every opportunity. Within a collectivity, the principle that one is an individual, that he or she should be valued as such and should behave as such, is not stressed. This pressure for uniformity has become particularly strong under democratic politics since 1945.

The rejection of excellence. In group life, such as that in stable villages, precedent, custom, and tradition are valued. Traditionalism—meaning repeating what one's ancestors did—remains strong. There is a tendency to deny the future, which is an "outsider," and to reject change. As the proverb "a child that does not look like the parents is a devil's child" suggests, being ordinary and simply repeating what had been done before is valued. By contrast, it is not good to excel because it could bring about change in the group. As a result, non-conformists, mavericks, and those who want to excel go to the towns and cities and even abroad in search of self-fulfillment. This lies behind the dynamics of Westernization since the Meiji Restoration. This Westernization involved the importation and adaptation of industrial civilization from the advanced countries. The originality of the Japanese has been manifested in their superb ability to adapt advanced technology.

NOTE: From what has been said above, the reader has probably gotten the impression that collectivities have naturally strengthened the tendency toward isolationism. But groups depend on the outer world in various ways. There are worldwide markets, empires, and military systems. In a time when Japan has become an industrialized country, families, villages, firms, and the country as a whole must trade with and interact with the outside world. It is impossible to maintain self-sufficiency, and not seek resources, energy, and information from the outside.

Moreover, because Japanese civilization was for 2000 years

in the periphery of the Chinese cultural sphere, and that the outlying areas within Japan were also in the periphery of the cultural sphere of the center, the Japanese have a strong sense of depending on the outside world. As a result, there is a practice of establishing reputations within the country, based on reputations established abroad. Families, villages, firms, and the whole country are compared with outside reference groups and ranked. When it comes to companies, ranking in *Fortune* magazine's top 500 corporations is very important. Information from the outside world about these rankings greatly influences the ratings of the individuals, leaders, and groups that are involved. The ratings of members and subgroups also depend on the outer world. That is, if one's reputation in the outer world of strangers rises, then that person's ratings among kin will also rise. For example, if a scientist is awarded a Nobel prize by the Swedish government, that scientist will be given the Japanese Cultural Award even if he does not have the seniority that would normally be required. The opposite would be true if one's reputation should decline.

Then this kind of "intellectual" dependence on the outside takes the form of the notion that "the outside world has a higher cultural level than the inner world." We have what the ethnologist Yanagita Kunio has called "city and country mentality." Cultural subordination of the hinterland to the prosperity of the West and the metropolitan cities is thus added to the political submission of the hinterland. As a result, political submission and cultural imitation become intertwined.

Intellectual dependence on the outside world results in collectivities working hard at importing information. Japanese civilization has been likened to a radio receiver (Umesao Tadao) and while it exports a good deal of manufactured goods, it is mostly an importer of information. For more than the hundred years that Western civilization has been imported, information from abroad has come into the country through ports and has been disseminated first to the large cities, and from there to the towns and villages. The movement has been mostly in one direction, and little has gone from Japan to the outer world.

It has become commonplace in an industrial, high-consumption society to spend lárge sums for advertising and public relations. However, as a result of the tendency toward isolationism noted earlier, collectivities are not very happy about unfavorable information getting out. The bamboo curtain has not exactly disappeared. Information that could bring shame and impair the reputation of the inner world in the outer world is not allowed to go out. It is taboo for insiders to expose wrong doing in a firm in order to attack it. A firm's secrets and the secrets of the industrial world are supposed to be strictly guarded by everyone. It is customary to reject the mutual exchange of information on the ground that "even if we explained what is going on within Japan, they [the foreigners] would not understand."

The way in which foreign civilization is imported affects the power struggle within the collectivity. The new civilization that the inner world imports and spreads gives authority to those in leadership positions, and serves as psychological and economic capital. In this instance, it makes a great difference whether the existing authorities will exercise leadership, or upwardly mobile groups that are vying for leadership with the old guard will emerge victorious. In the case of the former, the authority of the old leaders will be strengthened. In the case of the latter, their authority will be demolished, and a change in civilization will occur. If the old leaders give a negative valuation to the newly imported civilization, advocate the complete retention of tradition, criticize the additional expenditure of funds for importing culture, and launch a political attack to bring it to a halt, then anti-foreignism will be the result.

This power struggle can occur in families, villages, and firms, but in the case of the whole country it occurs on the largest scale. Since the Meiji Restoration, the country experienced both a change in leadership groups and a transformation of civilization. The old civilization represented by Confucianism and traditional Chinese medicine lost its authority. A new civilization represented by Western science and medicine became established, spread throughout the land, and found roots among the people. This led to political demands that those areas that had been left behind also share in enjoying the fruits of Western civilization. It also gave rise to the advocacy of restraint on luxurious living, and the practice of frugality, which was produced by actual economic poverty. Today, the effort to make the importation, diffusion, and establishment of American and Western civilization a reality is a central problem that confronts parliamentary politics.

Decision-Making-Based *Nemawashi*

Even within such groups as families or villages, conflicts among individuals engendered by the struggle for existence are sometimes inevitable. Still, group unity remains the ultimate goal. The right of veto of all individual members is recognized, but the outward display of conflict must be avoided. Under these circumstances, if something must be decided, taking the conservative course of maintaining the status quo with conflict lurking beneath the surface is easiest.

Any decision to change the status quo must be one of two types: a decision based on power play or on consensus, which requires, for creating the proper atmosphere, a good deal of time. Such decisions are those that are based on group unity and peace. It is a passive decision designed to preserve what exists. One seldom finds aggressive actions taken under the guidance of a forceful leader, as one might find in combat units. When something happens and the details are exposed by the mass media for all the group members to see, it is easier to achieve a group consensus than before the occurrence of the incident. Thus, one way to get the decision made is to wait for a consensus to form after something has happened. Of course, there is the risk that the decision may come too late, resulting in harm. There are political strategies based on this principle of waiting for a consensus to crystallize. In such cases, preliminary work needs to be done, and sometimes contingency plans are made in secret.

THE PLOT: There is a traditional way of arriving at group decisions. All members are given an equal right to participate, and all have veto power. In taking a vote, the appearance of conflict or a split into majority and minority factions should be avoided as much as possible. Accordingly, unless an advocate or a leader uses power to overwhelm the members, time and care must be taken, using *nemawashi* to arrive at a consensus. There are various aspects and steps in this *nemawashi*. First, there is organization and participation. As has been explained before, feelings must be shared. Those in leadership positions must go around to the members and talk to them at length in order not to give the impression that they are ignoring the complainers and other members, and to show the members that they are important in the eyes of the leadership. The advocates and leaders must personally meet and talk with each member, or talk to them on the telephone. In these conversations, the leaders must allow lots of time and speak earnestly. After chitchat, the leader must turn to the topic at hand, and speak with great care so that the other party will understand that he is important in the leader's eyes.

There are situations involving conjecture and communications. When someone within a group expresses definite opinions, that is, takes clear-cut positions on issues, and commits himself to a policy line and thereby assumes responsibility for his actions, there is a danger that the open conflict that is to be avoided will take place. There is also the risk that irreparable harm will be done to that person as well as to other members. Accordingly, in a group situation, one is very careful in what one says and makes only ambiguous statements in order to protect oneself and avoid conflicts. The traditional wisdom is that silence is golden. Thus, leaders have to fathom what the other party's true intentions are, particularly in conflict situations. From the point of view of the latter, this may produce outcomes that are advantageous. Success in this operation lies in common sense and judgment, but errors cannot be ruled out.

Nemawashi also relates to the matter of "nerve" (*hara*). Decision leaders must draft a proposal. In drafting the document, one must have the courage to take risks. The proposal might be turned down, amended, or if approved, it might be undermined. Even if the original proposal is agreed to by individuals, say by a leader and a follower in face-to-face meetings, since such agreements are arrived at in secret, there is no assurance that this agreement will stand up later. If one were to infer that the other party agrees with the proposal even though he has not stated it explicitly, and if one hints that an agreement has been reached and the other party does not explicitly deny it, then one can assume agreement and go on to the next step. This would be an example of *haragei*.[1] Also, if two different interpretations of what was said are allowed to stand, and it is made to look like an agreement had been reached, when in fact it had not, it would be an example of *tamamushi-iro* [from an insect whose color varies depending on

1. Literally "stomach art," a form of non-verbal communication in which one person can read the other person's mind although nothing explicit has been said about the matter or problem that has come up. Robert Butow in *Japan's Decision to Surrender* (Stanford: Stanford University Press, 1954) gives some interesting examples of this.

the angle from which one views it]. The ability to take this kind of bold action depends on the confidence one has in human relations and one's judgment in balancing different interests.

The final step is the formal decision. All the while that the decision leaders are going around talking to people, making guesses about where others stand, making changes in response to the opposition, and so on, there will be an atmosphere that suggests that a majority in favor of the proposal is in the making. Thereupon, in view of the atmosphere, the leaders will urge and pressure the opposition minority by saying, "Since everyone is in favor, why don't you also join in?" and bring about an unanimous decision in which some whose hearts were not in it are forced to agree. If this agreement is approved in a meeting of the group, called to show approval by acclamation, the decision process comes to an end. If the minority in opposition hardens its position in the face of majority support for the proposal, there will be a move to get the minority to agree to let the officers decide how to reach an agreement. If this is agreed to, then an agreement on the procedure, but not the proposal, will have been reached. Thereupon the officers will take the proposal, which has the backing of the majority, as the official proposal and adopt it. The decision to surrender in 1945 was an example of this procedure. Political parties often use the same procedure. And it is common practice to make adjustments to balance the interests of the defeated minority.

However, if the resistance of the minority is strong and an agreement to "let the officers decide upon the procedure" cannot be obtained, then the decision leaders, out of respect for maintaining harmony within the group, may abandon the proposal and accept the status quo. This will be the defeat of the majority.

If the original proposal is not abandoned and an effort is made to push it through, there will be open conflict between the majority and the minority. There will be a militarylike confrontation between friend and foe. Thus, when the formal decision by vote becomes violent politics, there will necessarily be a residue of hard feelings among the group members. For this reason, those who put a premium on unity and harmony will work hard on *nemawashi* to arrive at a concensus and to avoid a repetition of open conflict.

Leadership Failure and Violence Paradigm

It is a rule that a collectivity should have as its goal the unity and harmony of its members. But, of course, there are exceptions to this rule. There are cases where members, in opposing their leaders, have rioted. The script on riots does not consist of rules. Rather, it may be viewed as a process wherein the leaders can avoid provoking such riots. However, there are in fact some cases that proceed as if according to script, so it is necessary to go into this question.

The dramatis personae are oppressive leaders and the weak and oppressed. Within collectivities, there is an image of an ideal leader against which such leaders can be measured. Accordingly, we will now turn to this matter.

DRAMATIS PERSONAE: *The ideal leader.* In deciding anything in a collectivity, someone, an advocate of a policy or a leader, must make a proposal. However, leaders who stress the general good and demand that personal sacrifices be made to attain that good must have an appropriate standing, that is, institutionalized authority. As in the case of the Emperor system, this authority is legitimized by tradition. In villages and other closely knit groups, family status and age and seniority confer authority. But in Japan, where there is rapid change in the amount of wealth people possess, it is rare for families to remain distinguished for many generations.

For this reason, there is another traditional system that determines authority according to personal merit rather than family status. As has been explained in the section on the equality code, all individuals are believed to be manifestations of the eternal being, that is, the life force in the universe. So they are entitled to pursue life and prosperity, wealth and power on an equal basis. Now, if one becomes like a bodhisattva, who is on his long pilgrimage to become an enlightened Buddha, and is selfless and dedicated to promoting the salvation and well being of other commoners, one would gain authority as an exceptional individual. Specifically, one can gain authority as a leader by doing certain things: working for the public good at personal expense, showing that one would not personally profit from engaging in public employment, and impressing others by being a model of personal sacrifice.

Such dedication and self-sacrifice were virtues that were taught in village families that were influential and assumed leadership positions. Those who were in a position to spend their own money on community projects were obviously people of means, such as landlords in olden days. Such individuals contributed funds to shrines and temples, an act regarded as for the public good. They supported charities, provided, on behalf of the village, facilities for entertaining official guests, picked up the tab on community projects, provided funds for schools and village offices, and they were even willing to give their lives in the event that they were chosen as leaders of peasant revolts. Such were the norms for this group of people. Of course, if one followed such norms, large sums would have to be spent, and there was the danger that it would result in the dissipation of family wealth. Accordingly, in old families there were rules designed to promote frugality and modesty in daily life.

As a result of rapid modernization after the Meiji Restoration, and also after 1945, the old families declined. However, this image of an ideal leader still remains in people's memories. It also serves as a standard whereby professional politicians are measured today.

The weak and oppressed. It is not necessarily the case that there are no conflicts and complications among group members, and that peaceful coexistence is always possible. There are not a few instances where human existence itself is threatened. In addition, modernization has legitimized the struggle for existence among individuals. Thus, in the inner world, conflict is latent, and, depending on circumstances, it surfaces in many forms. Sometimes it is like a living hell.

A certain kind of education becomes necessary. If group members are to avoid becoming victims in a scene of carnage, and are to assure the survival of the group itself, they need to be taught to be prepared to sacrifice themselves. That is, they need to be made to understand that "the small fish will be eaten to let the big one survive." They must also be taught to be prepared to face the consequences if chosen as the small fish that must give up its life. In many instances, education that teaches traditions is required. As we have explained in the section on the possessed individuals' code, "unless an adult dies with the satisfaction that he has lived out his allotted span of life, his death will be an unnatural one that will bring a curse." Death does not pertain only to physically dying. Being expelled from the group is also a form of death. When a person quits his job because he has reached the mandatory retirement age, this is a form of death that he readily accepts because it is based on an unambiguous condition, namely the attainment of a certain age.

In this way, those individuals who have been classified as "small fish" will be among those that will be obliterated. This raises the question of who, using what measure, will do the classifying. With regard to who, there is, on the one hand, the group consensus, and, on the other, the high-handed choice made by those in power. An example of the former is staff reductions in a company. The company seeks voluntary resignations. There is usually an agreed-upon ranking in each workshop based on ability, and those ranking lowest will take it upon themselves to ask for separation. Under this system, staff reductions in the entire company proceed smoothly. By contrast, separations that disregard the consensus and are arbitrarily put into effect by the employer often give rise to bitter disputes. As for the second item, namely what measure to use, there is the degree of (1) *en*, a relationship by blood or of friends, and (2) vitality or energy.

The oppressive leader. Most people would rather live than be killed like a "small fish" and be employed rather than fired from a job. Thus, the stronger party will tell the weaker, in a domineering way, "at least be thankful that you won't be killed like a small fish," and forces the weaker side to abjectly agree to the demands that are being made. This would be an example of tyranny and oppression. For example, during the 40 years since labor unions were legalized, there have been a large number of unfair labor practices, including measures on the part of small businesses to prevent the formation of labor unions in their enterprises.

With Japan's modernization, many of the old families have disappeared, resulting in changes in leadership and influentials. The leaders who have come from new families were never trained to exercise self-restraint, and were dedicated to the pursuit of lust and greed. Luxurious living replaced restraint and frugality; arrogance replaced modesty; the pursuit of personal gain replaced service to others. In many places, changes of this kind were considered to be illegitimate and not to be respected. In this way, upstart leaders, who surround themselves with an entourage and hangers-on, took the view that "if I have money, I can do anything." Moreover, the struggle for existence led to the spread of this kind of "upstart" behavior. Accordingly, in groups, power that lacks respect, and oppression and tyranny that rests on it, have become a familiar sight.

THE PLOT: The weak, who are not strong enough to resist the demands made upon them by the powerful, have no alternative but to submit. They have been told by those in power that "you ought to be glad that you are at least alive." The result is the establishment of norms that prescribe that one ought to be prepared to do anything to avoid being pressured or hurt. Individuals adopt an opportunistic policy of indiscriminately doing whatever they are told to do. They can, as hangers-on to an influential person, be sychophants. The function of language becomes flattery rather than the transmission of information; the influential person is consequently cut off from the flow of information, a price that has to be paid.

Also, other weaklings will join the influentials in attacking the weak. It is an act of betrayal. The saying "break the strong and save the weak" refers to chivalry, where someone defends the weak against oppression by the strong. But contrary to this saying, "break the weak and save the strong" seems to be the way for the weak to avoid being destroyed. Sometimes kin and close friends are left to their fate. When one contemplates this kind of cold behavior, one appreciates all the more the warmth that sometimes comes from people who are not our kin nor friends.

In group life, the roles that leaders and the roles that the followers are to play are set by tradition. The leaders, according to ideals, are supposed to sacrifice their personal interests, and work for the perpetuation and prosperity of the group. Like the loving mother, they are supposed to protect their followers and provide for their welfare. The followers are supposed to respond by submitting to the leaders and work for the general good at personal sacrifice. In this way, the two roles complement each other, and constitute a system. But, the oppression and tyranny we have been describing go against the basic understanding and expectations.

When the collectivity code is violated in this way and loses its relevance, group members become angry, and the possessed individuals' code comes into operation. The followers, betrayed by their leaders, feel that they cannot put up with it, and now the worm turns. Their passions are aroused and there is violent behavior. There are riots that will have behind them all the energy that can be mustered. Some examples are urban riots, peasant revolts, and *abare-mikoshi*. [This is the case where young men carrying a portable shrine in the annual festivals enter the house of an unpopular person, such as a money lender, and cause damage through their violent actions. But these men cannot be blamed for their actions because presumably the deity in the portable shrine ordered them to act that way].

On the one hand, this outburst will indicate the power of chaos that will destroy the existing order, and, on the other, it will revive the group. This is because the upstart leaders, the target of the violence, will restrain somewhat their pursuit of self-interest, make an effort to protect and satisfy the demands of the followers, play the role to some extent that is expected of them, and restore the system. For example, after the Rice Riots in 1918, the zaibatsu donated money for hospitals and other social welfare programs, even though such actions would not result in immediate profit.

If the violent outburst, the sign of resistance, is not to end as a kind of diversion, organizational activity with long-range planning and goals must be undertaken. Here outstanding leadership, the kind that is legendary in peasant revolts and labor movements, was displayed. When these riots are transformed into political resistance through outstanding leadership, for upstart leaders it is a serious omen of their impending defeat. Accordingly, the power holders and the influentials seek to divide those in resistance before they can get organized. They take advantage of the jealousy that is prevalent among the weak and destroy the support and sympathy for the rebels that exist in the society. Then, they buy off the troublemakers, and the leaders. The political resistance quits the stage once people's minds are bought by tangible rewards. Finally, they divide the resistance by sowing seeds of doubt by treating the resistance leaders less harshly. In this way, those in power destroy the resistance by a policy of divide and rule.

The Battlefield Paradigm

Individuals cannot live solely within groups and organizations, that is, collectivities. They cannot do so economically, socially, or psychologically. They must get outside of the group and interact with and have transactions with others within the society at large. In contrast to the unity and harmony that exists within the group, the world outside has been perceived traditionally as a battleground where the struggle for existence goes on. Accordingly, the political process paradigm differs, depending on whether one is inside or outside of the collectivity. We will call the relevant paradigm for outside of the collectivity the battlefield paradigm. We will take up three facets: namely, a military base and battlefield as the scene or setting, competition and cooperation as the strategy, and the roles of leaders and followers.

Base and Battlefield Paradigm

As was suggested in the section on the collectivity paradigm, family, village, firm, and country make up the list of collectivities. From the point of view of individuals, one can have a series of concentric circles, with the individual at the center. The four collectivities mentioned above, and other groups and organizations will fall into different circles.

Social relationships can be classified into four types, depending on the relationship between the individual and the other person. If one ranks these relationships according to closeness, with oneself placed at the center, we end up with four concentric circles. The smallest circle in the center depicts one's relatives. Its size will vary. The smallest contains the mother and child. As it grows, there are parents and children, the nuclear family that is common today. Even larger would be the traditional family or house, with three or even four generations living under one roof.

The next circle includes one's "buddies" (*nakama*), whom we can identify by name and face. Siblings and relatives might be in the smallest circle or in the next one. Friends, colleagues, and others who are close would belong in this second category. These are neighbors in a village, town, or city. There are also coworkers, especially those employed in the same division of an office or factory, that is, those with whom one spends the most time. For self-employed individuals, there are their fellow businessmen, customers, and fellow members of business associations. Buddies would not be kin, but would identify with each other and make up one's narrow world. It is the world of give-and-take, where behavior is influenced by such things as memories of past incidents, and reports and rumors of current actions.

The third larger circle includes strangers, society at large, and the Japanese nation. It is an anonymous world where no one cares what you do. It extends from the big cities to the far corners of the country, and is the world whose happenings are reported by the mass media. Politically, it is the national stage where the drama of politics is carried out. The largest circle includes the whole world beyond the borders of Japan. The people who live out there are not even Japanese. They are cut off because they speak a different language and have a different culture, often quite the opposite of Japan's.

THE STAGE: The world of family is characterized by the fact that its members commonly eat the meals prepared by the housewife. Its canon is a world featured by unity and sharing. The manifestation of this unity and sharing is the mother, representing the *magna mater*, and embracing and protecting her child, and the child utterly dependent on the mother and seeking her love. Thus, the world of family is governed by the flow of emotion and warm love.

In addition, there is the complete trust that comes from the sense of unity and sharing. So, in this world, there are no secrets and privacy; indeed, there must be none of that. Because trust makes it unnecessary to be on one's guard or put up defenses, there is security and peace of mind, rest and relaxation. As a result of this, interpersonal relationships among family members are characterized by self-willed behavior, impertinence, and rudeness. If in one's family life, one is taught to have good manners and dress properly, you will have the middle-class lifestyle. In order to maintain this world of family, its members, particularly the housewife and mother, must be prepared to make significant personal sacrifices for the good of all.

By contrast, one's narrow world is a civilized world ruled by good manners and courtesy. It involves interpersonal relationships among those who know each other's backgrounds. It is a more formal relationship that requires polite etiquette and company manners. The principle of human relationships, unlike that among family members based on dependency and protection, is mutual obligation based on the relative social standing of the principals involved. There are two systems, depending on whether or not one has achieved adulthood. There is the case where the buddies are still living in dormitories and other quarters, which serve as a training ground for entry into the mutual obligation system of adulthood. Second, there is also a strong tendency where in adult relationships buddies are likened to family members and the interpersonal relationships of obligations transformed into relationships of emotion and warm love.

In the wider circle people are complete strangers. So long as you do not speak to one another and exchange business cards, you are mutually anonymous. In a crowd of people, no one pays any attention to the others. One does not need to mind his manners or be polite in a crowd. This wider circle is the battleground for those who seek fame and fortune. If you are not aggressive, you feel left behind. One is taught to be strong, and push ahead without regard for others.

This is the world beyond Japan. Here there are two contradictory attitudes: open and closed. This stems from national isolation during the Tokugawa period and the Westernization of Japan during the last one hundred and twenty years. On the one hand, there is the reluctance to set out to see a world where one cannot speak the language, and where customs are different. On the other hand, particularly with regard to the West, there is a desire to visit it because it is the source of civilization and the focus of infatuation. Korea and China were regarded as areas that Japan could dominate and exploit. In contrast, there is the desire to be tranferred to, visit, or study in the West as a means to furthering one's career. Well-known foreign visitors coming for short-term stays are welcomed and entertained, but those who wish to stay for the long term were treated as *gaijin* (outsiders). Also, foreigners employed by Japanese firms abroad are treated as "locals" and are never able to be treated as buddies.

Running through the four-fold stage of interpersonal relations is a line that extends in opposite directions. One line runs in one direction toward the "family," and the other toward "strangers" in the opposite direction. The first runs from outer concentric circles toward the center. This indicates the movement toward unity and sharing, or non-kin being treated as family. If one lives abroad, he feels friendly toward other Japanese he meets there because they are countrymen. If one is in business and thus is in the larger circle, he feels some affinity to other businessmen, and so on. In this way, individuals try to get the benefits that accrue to those who are in the center circle. In this way there is a system of turning buddies into kin.

The second line runs in the opposite direction, from the center to the outer edge. This signifies interpersonal relationships that are competitive, and those who are related become like non-kin. It suggests a fierce competitive world that lies in the outer circle. That is, siblings compete with each other for warm love and material advantages from parents and relatives. Buddies compete to become successful, or compete with each other within their own firm. In the society at large there is struggle to survive, and in the world there is competitive nationalism.

DRAMATIS PERSONAE: It is ambitious people, those who liken themselves to soldiers, who occupy these four stages and move back and forth among them. As a result of modernization since the Meiji Restoration, we now have the model of these successful soldiers.

Since the Meiji Restoration, it has become legitimate to try to better oneself and gain fame and fortune by winning out in the competition. There have been those who have a lifetime plan to be successful. These ambitious individuals, full of energy, with the help of their families and villages, may seek their fortunes elsewhere. In that case, they are given a warm sendoff. Or they may sneak away at night, headed for the battlefield of competition in the towns and cities. Eventually, people in the competitive environment where individuals are at risk, tire and deplete their supply of energy. They then return to their native villages to savor the natural surroundings and human warmth. After having regained their energy and power of spirits, they return to the battlefield. Thus, the native village, protected by the ancestor-guardian deities, functions as a base for rest and recreation. In this way, people in the course of their struggle to survive and to succeed make many trips between the battlefield and the base. Many end up failures, but some are successful, and bring honor to their places of birth. The reputations of these successful ones are sustained by their generous contributions to the village temples and schools. Stone tablets and bronze statues are erected in their honor to inspire future generations. These trips between battlefield and base still occurr several times a year for millions of people even today.

But, as a matter of fact, this going back and forth can also be figuratively applied to everyday life. If we go back to the concentric circles, the inner circle may be thought of as the base to the outer circle, which is the battlefield. That is, the world of kin, buddies, and Japan would be the base, while the world of buddies, Japan, and the outside world would be the battlefield. The family is always the base collectivity, while the battlefield would be the outer world, that is, foreign countries. The in-between circle, buddies, village, place of employment, and the wider circle, one's country, Japan, can sometimes serve at times as a base, and at other times as the battlefield.

THE PLOT. To the soldier who replenishes his energy and spirits at the base, then discharges it at the front, and becomes exhausted, the base must provide something like the following:

The struggle for existence that has come to prevail since the Meiji Restoration has given rise to the saying that "when a householder leaves his house, he faces seven enemies." If the battlefield requires one to be on his toes and always alert, it also makes one tired. Thus, the base must be able to provide relief from always having to be on guard, as well as relaxation and rest. Such a carefree atmosphere is free from the pressure of the battlefield and of the burden of obligations that are found in the smaller circle. Relief must be provided from the pressures imposed by social taboos and the need to be on one's best behavior by means of substitutes for the religious orgies where men and gods became one. Examples of these substitutes are taking hot baths, drinking *sake* at night, and playing mahjong, etc. Compassion and warm support must be provided for those who have suffered reverses in the battlefield and who have been buffeted by the cold treatment received on the battlefield. These forms of relief will be provided so long as there are kinsfolk, buddies, and Japan.

In the base, the world of kinsfolk, and particularly in the family, the role of the housewife is very important. She is expected to provide children with unlimited protection. For her husband, she must be his wife, and she takes care of the children and in general serves behind the lines. As a substitute for his mother, she must provide him with unlimited protection. Of course, the wife also expects her husband to protect her. The protection that the husband expects from his wife may not necessarily be forthcoming. Husbands who want to lighten the burden on their wives and families might seek this unlimited protection in bars and eating places specializing in "mother's" cooking.

The soldier who has proceeded from the base to the battlefield must fight his own battles. In a battlefield that resembles the state of nature described by Hobbes, what is required to win are, in military terms, realism and practicality, and in political terms, opportunism. Many examples of this may be found in popular culture. Books, novels, movies, television programs, popular songs and the like have taken up the lives of the heroes living in the Warring States period (fifteenth and sixteenth centuries) as well as the end of the Tokugawa period, a time of political turbulence. These works have attracted large audiences.

The development of an industrial civilization has forced many firms to become large in size, and as interfirm competition has intensified, these large organizations began to take on some characteristics of military organizations. Thus, the company has come to have a dual character, as a collectivity and as a military organization. The military in World War II tried to reorganize the whole country into a combat unit. But even when military-like structures are created, whether in the case of firms or nations, the individual struggle for survival goes on. So while lip service might be paid to sacrificing personal good for that of the collectivity, realism and political opportunism continue to be the guiding principle for many people. In that sense, hangers-on, sycophants, war profiteers, and black marketeers are the successful ones.

Even though one may sally forth into the battlefield, not many attain success and fame and come home in triumph. Quite a few fail and remain obscure. Some quietly return to their native villages, never to move out again. Others, after being revived by the ancestral spirits, migrate again. There are also some who manage without returning home to gain the sympathy of others and replenish their energy. In this way, mass culture was formed during the period starting early in the twentieth century, extending until today on the theme of failed victims in the struggle for existence. The ballads and stories of those who failed and who, like war refugees, wandered about the battlefield aroused the sympathy of many. It also satisfied the sense of narcissism of those who achieved success. The amusement districts that developed in the cities served as a stage for those songs and stories. The base and battlefield are depicted below.

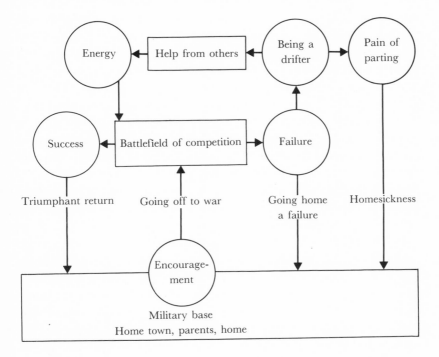

Competition and Cooperation Paradigm

THE SITUATION: The world is a battlefield for the struggle for existence, like a jungle where the strong devour the weak. No matter what one does, there are no rules to cover it. For an individual to take part in the struggle for existence and be a winner, that is, to succeed in acquiring wealth and fame, is to become a personification of the life force. As was explained in the section on the equality code, since the Meiji era, not only was the realization of one's latent ability to become a successful person approved, but the struggle to attain success was also approved and made legitimate. The maintenance of harmony and the avoidance of conflict has been stressed in the group, while, by contrast, in the world outside of the group, competition and conflict were emphasized. Moreover, constant struggle and progress through the achievement of victory was considered the motive power of progress and enlightenment. As seen, in the four concentric circles, there was a tendency for the inner to become somewhat like the outer, and vice versa. That is, the principle of harmony tends to spread from the kin group to the middle circle, the larger circle, and to the outside world. By the same token, the principle of struggle infiltrates from the outer to the inner. Harmony and conflict are not isolated in two different worlds.

THE STAGE: Individuals are not the only ones to seek victory in competition. Those in the inner world also engage in competition by forming one unified group. Among families there is competition to improve their relative standings in the town or city. There is competition to increase family wealth, expand the family business, make home improvements, educate sons and daughters in better schools, and enjoy leisure through travel, and the like. In villages, in shopping districts in towns, and in cities there is competition for achieving a higher level of civilization. There is also competition for transportation facilities, such as railroads, freeways, and airports, for communications facilities, such as telephones and television stations, and for public institutions, such as schools, government offices, hospitals, libraries, museums, parks, and urban facilities. In the business world, intercompany competition involves capitalization, revenues, market share, profits, reputation and industrywide standing, and domestic and overseas activities. Among nations, it involves relative ranking, whether a nation is one of the big three or five, or is a superpower and so forth. The people are reminded that after defeat and Occupation, Japan re-entered the international community, has joined the United Nations, attends summit meetings, has the third highest GNP in the world, and is an economic power that ranks second in the free world.

Groups also engage in competition. First of all, there is a tendency to liken the group to a combat unit with military organization. Today this is particularly strong among firms and large corporations. As a result, knowledge of operations research and other military matters are being applied to corporate management. The mass media reports victories and defeats in the business world in the same manner that it might write about wars. Personnel matters, market share, and intercompany rankings are like zero-sum games and lend themselves to this kind of reporting. In this way, information about how the struggle for existence is going, and its outcome, is transmitted through business newsletters, local newspapers, and the national press, that is, the mass media. Since the media itself is a competitive business, they try to write in an easy-to-understand and interesting way. Thus, the mass media gives the relative rankings, which are based on success or failure in the competitive game, and thereby influence the reputation and prestige of the firms in the competition. When the results of the first round in the competition are announced and the trends become known, it is time for the second round to begin.

THE PLOT: Competition will proceed on this stage, but it is not always the case that the competition will continue until the competitor is defeated. Sometimes competition will give way to cooperation. In the case of businesses, competition involves risks. There is the danger that if competition gets too intense, they may all fail. So, firms formally or informally get together, exchange information, reach an agreement, and form cartels. This reduces the cost of competition, assures monopoly profits, and avoids mutual destruction. This choice is always available to firms.

As has been explained, the outer world is a battlefield, but it is a base of an even larger outer world. Accordingly, there is pressure for kin, buddies, and firms and the business world, from both within the group and the outside environment, to make their relationships more intimate in order to avoid conflicts. The formation of cartels is thus supported and legitimized both within and without. Mutual adjustments involving individuals, such as brotherly quarrels being patched up and mediation of conflicts between individuals, as well as business enterprises, for mutual survival, are quite common. This is another aspect of the battlefield of the struggle for existence.

There are three ways of making adjustments. First, there is arbitration and mediation by those with seniority and authority, such as parents, relatives, supervisors, influentials, and the elders in business and financial circles. Second, there is mutual agreement arrived at by the principals themselves through negotiation and compromise. An example would be collusion in submitting bids. Third, there is administrative guidance on the part of government agencies. There are times when arbitration and mediation, negotiations and bargaining will not produce the desired adjustment and results. On those occasions, administrative guidance will be used. When a substantial number of parties of about equal size are competing, administrative guidance will be accepted without much resistance. Those agencies that are anxious to use administrative guidance like to intervene in cases where there are many small firms engaged in competition. But when a few powerful corporations are dominant, it is difficult to get them to accept administrative guidance that is unfavorable to them.

In many lines of business, there are business associations and other organizations that have been established either voluntarily or as a result of government intervention. These associations are organized to facilitate communications and liaison among firms and also between associations and government agencies. In many cases, after mutual adjustments are arrived at by methods already described, these understandings are communicated to the administrative staffs of the business associations, who, in turn, formally inform the smaller companies. This becomes the basis of "order" among these enterprises. When this order becomes established and respected, excessive competition will be lessened and a system of mutual survival will be established. Individual firms, out of a domestic need to maintain internal discipline and morale, always take the position that the outer world is the battlefield of competition and that one must always be on guard against sudden attacks. Hence, everyone will be prepared for competition even after they have arrived at mutual understandings. If order within the business community is broken, either because of the appearance of an outsider who refuses to submit to the informal understandings, or a member refuses to cooperate, intense competition will be revived.

Order within the business community involves the positions that individual firms and associations hold, and their rankings. These rankings will be recognized and endorsed by the government agencies. The awarding of titles before 1945 and of decorations today reflect the outcomes of the competitive struggle, and provide a hierarchical ranking system that cuts across the business community. These ceremonial proceedings are reported in the mass media, and a large segment of the society is made aware of these rankings. If the system of free competition to achieve success is to be effective in getting recruits, it must provide free access, promotion on the basis of merit, and a clear-cut position at the top of the ranking order in the end. The hierarchical system of ranking with the Imperial Court at the top had an important function in this regard.

Moreover, the recognition and endorsement of the rankings within the business community outside of the political realm means that the autonomy of the business world is socially recognized. It also means that the Emperor system serves as a source of authority and prestige apart from the business community. Today, there are many more awards, prizes, and honors in the business world and in the area of cultural activities that are independent of the government. These systems endorse the system of free competition and the rule that ability counts, and have the function of giving recognition to those who are successful.

Leader and Follower Paradigm

Most of the competition in the larger society takes place among firms and groups of firms, or among leaders, each at the head of their followers. There are two important considerations concerning leadership. First, there is the question of whether those in leadership positions fulfill the conditions expected of them. Second, does the leader lead his followers properly? These two conditions will affect both the survival and prosperity of the group, and the success of the leaders. Because competition also takes place among individuals within groups, and at the same time, among groups, for followers, too, the survival and prosperity of their groups are important. Many people take part in the competition among groups as followers, and as individuals competing within their own organizations for personal advancement.

THE SITUATION: There is an official system whereby in the government agencies, and many other organizations, the top leaders actually turn over most of the decision making to their subordinates, bureau chiefs, and division chiefs. On occasion, they turn matters over to those who are even lower in rank on things that are in their jurisdiction. Hence, in many cases, ministers, vice-ministers, and bureau chiefs are like portable shrines that are carried around by their subordinates. Or these leaders may be merely acting as official spokesmen for their underlings. This is an extreme example of where subordinates are trusted and everything is turned over to them. At the other extreme are those who insist on deciding everything themselves, the so-called one-man rule. Thus management of subordinates lies somewhere between the portable shrine and one-man rule.

DRAMATIS PERSONAE (A): Such leadership conditions as temperament and virtues, which serve as standards of behavior, have been specified in textbooks and in the mass culture. If, as has already been explained, those who go to the battlefield may be likened to warriors, individuals in leadership positions are generals. As for the conditions that go with being a general, they have been taught in schools, in social ethics, and language and history textbooks. Outside of the classroom, they have been featured in popular literature, movies, and on the stage, both affirmatively and negatively. For the sake of convenience, these matters will be explained, according to three traditional categories: wisdom, virtue, and courage.

Wisdom: Given their position, leaders are surrounded by their fawning hangers-on, and consequently do not communicate well with their other subordinates. As a result, they often fail to get information about their inner world as well as the outer world. By contrast, wisdom constitutes "knowing both the strength of the enemy and one's own strength (*Sun Tzu*)," that is, to have precise knowledge of what is happening, and then having the knowledge to proceed to the target in an appropriate way. Wisdom consists of a sensitivity for inputs of information. One collects unbiased, detailed information about a wide variety of matters. This provides acute powers of observation, which will be used later for intellectual activity.

Wisdom consists of thought processes, that is, analyzing information. The ability to think precisely and logically makes it possible to project trends on the basis of the present, pick out the more likely scenarios, and compare and contrast them. There is also imagination, which is related to how one uses information. In both the inner and outer worlds, human behavior is not based solely on cold, rational considerations. They are strongly affected by urges and impulses. As is true with thought processes, it is important for leaders to have the imagination to figure out the direction and strength of pressures that orginate from the urges and impulses of individuals who are placed in a certain situation. Insight, or ways to use information or data, is another form of wisdom. Insight enables one to grasp the totality of things. Insight enables one to see more than what is discerned through our senses, that is, what is hidden from view. This discernment provides a framework for sorting out materials that are in a state of disarray, and shows how information should be used. In this way, data analysis becomes an intellectual enterprise.

Of course, among individuals there are differences as to their aptitude and their potential to use these factors. It is not always the case that leaders are competent to use them equally well. In order to make up for their shortcomings, in many cases, there are staff people that work with the leaders.

Virtue: An often idealized form of organizational activity is one where a leader directs his subordinates by giving the right orders at the right time, and the subordinates all fall in line, and the group operates as one unit, like a kind of military parade. Moreover, for a long time a policy of rewarding the good and punishing the bad has been the respected tradition. As a method of maintaining or improving submission to rules, appropriate rewards are given to those who follow the rules, and strong punishment is meted out to those who disobey them. Rewards and punishment are to be given out fairly without favoritism.

Now, there is an unavoidable tendency to be overly strict in punishing those who violate these rules. There is a need to correct this tendency. Leaders must not be cold-blooded tyrants. They must be gentle, tolerant, and broad-minded. They are expected to lessen the severity of punishments to the degree compatible with the attainment of organizational goals.

Formal authority and the institutional system come in between the leader and the subordinates. As a result, from the point of view of the subordinates, the distance between them and their leaders widens, or sometimes they feel cut off from the leaders. Also, communications between the two sides tend to become more bureaucratic, another tendency that needs to be corrected. Leaders are expected not to be cold-hearted, but rather warm persons, kind, astute, and personable individuals who get rid of bureaucratic formalism, and who establish a human relationship between themselves and their subordinates.

Leaders are expected to be good teachers. The reason for this is as follows: Spontaneity and self-respect are basic qualities of human beings. If the behavior of the subordinates is minutely regulated by orders, rules, and specifications in manuals, making them into robots, their morale naturally weakens. Their submission inevitably becomes mechanical. Moreover, it is impossible to prepare for all contingencies in the rule books. In order to encourage spontaneity and self-respect among subordinates, it is normal practice to give them some degree of freedom of action.

Human beings do not like to be used as tools by someone else. If subordinates are given some degree of freedom of action, they may become more interested in giving play to their spontaneity and self-respect than to the pursuit of organizational goals. As a result, the behavior of subordinates may become somewhat more independent, given centrifugal and deviant tendencies. Accordingly, it will become necessary to control indirectly the freedom of action of subordinates in order to attain organizational goals. As a good teacher, the leader must explain the goals, meanings, and norms of the organization, so that the subordinates will understand them, so that they can exercise some self-constraint over their freedom of action.

If the subordinates are given some freedom of action, and allowed to act spontaneously, there is no guarantee that their judgment and behavior will be appropriate on every occasion. Accordingly, leaders must aggressively engage in education and training of their subordinates. To do that, leaders must show leadership by example and be a model for their followers. Leaders must show their faith in the ability of their subordinates by turning jobs over to them. If they succeed, you praise them and try to bring out their potential abilities. Even if they fail, you accept it in a broad-minded and tolerant fashion, and do not criticize or punish them. This kind of teacherlike behavior is expected of leaders. And as management begins to incline more toward education, and becomes less enthusiastic in rewarding the good and punishing the bad, there is a tendency to pull away from the latter. But when subordinates begin to expect that mistakes will always be tolerated, organizational discipline will deteriorate and work standards will decline.

Courage: Generals sometimes take part directly in military engagements. If, on that occasion, they are cowardly, their subordinates will not obey them, so bravery is essential. However, since olden days, there has been a distinction made between physical courage and spiritual courage, the kind that generals and leaders need. The first characteristic of courage is judgment and resolution. That is, the ability to compare the various alternative scenarios and take the one that is most appropriate according to one's standards, even though that course of action may not be risk free, and thereby confront the unknown future. And it goes without saying that the ability to take decisive action at the appropriate time is the first requirement of a leader.

The second requirement is to have the courage to stay on the course once a decision has been made, even though the situation has deteriorated. If one changes course every time in response to altered conditions, it would be difficult to get the subordinates as a group to follow the course of action that had been set. The third requirement is to have the courage, willingness, and resolve to face defeat and failure. The traditional principle is to expect the worse. One must think beforehand what would be the worst possible outcome, which is ultimately death, and then act, with the final resolve to face up to whatever might happen. If a leader has this resolve, then he can be calm and collected, and his actions will be clothed in bravery. According to the equality code, when individuals die, they become one with eternity. So a good leader is expected to have the nerve to face death, which is the equivalent of going home.

Whether characterized as the portable-shrine type or one-man-rule type, the head of the organization, as the leader, must take final responsibility for failure. It is the leader's privilege as a final act to take responsibility and resign, even commit suicide, in order to bring about a political solution to the problem. It is expected, from the institutional point of view, that the leader will act responsibly and do what he has to. Those leaders who refuse to resign, or try to shift the blame on to their subordinates, will lose the trust of the public and of their subordinates.

The ideal figure in modern Japan who, while acting in the role of the portable shrine, nevertheless assumed final responsibility is Saigō Takamori. Saigō, who in taking his own life in defeat in the Satsuma Rebellion, established himself as the ideal of a selfless and magnanimous leader.[2] He has had a tremendous impact on the political education of the people.

DRAMATIS PERSONAE (B): When one participates in the competition on the battlefield as an individual who is at risk, what makes it possible for him to compete is, first of all, energy or spiritual power. Energy brings with it physical health and pyschological well being and gives rise to the desire to strive and compete. Thus, if one's spirit is high, he will be alert, and the first requirements on the battlefield, namely, circumspection and astute observation, are possible. At the same time, since the individual is in an alert state of mind, he will be resourceful and capable of coming up with an original plan. In addition, he will be very vigilant, and able to provide for various future contingencies. Moreover, he will not ignore common sense, which dominates the battlefield of competition, so will not be faced with unexpected failures. In this way, the soldier will march forward with determination. One cannot always count on clear sailing, and sometimes failure cannot be avoided. In that event, it is important that one endure the pain of failure and wait patiently for better times. Thus, energy provides the basis of competition on the battlefield.

From the point of view of character or temperament, it is paranoid-type individuals who have the appropriate energy and spirit to engage in competition on the battlefield. But, needless to say, not everyone is a paranoid type. There are hysteroid or nervous types as well. In addition, the system of *amae*[3] and protection that dominates the inner world, and particularly the world of kin, tends to create those who are "a lion at home, a mouse abroad." There are many individuals who are socially shy, the kind exemplified by the image of a youngster who looks out at the world with its cutthroat competition from under his mother's skirt.

The fear of shame caused by being ridiculed is included in the feeling of insecurity and fear of society that is the basis of shyness.

2. About 30,000 ex-samurai from the former feudal fief of Satsuma were angered by the abolition of the samurai class and rebelled against the new government in 1877 under the leadership of Saigō (1827–77). After six months of fighting, the government's conscript army put down the rebellion, and in defeat, Saigō took his own life.

3. A term that may be unique to the Japanese language, it roughly means "to seek and bask in another's indulgence." An example would be a small child whining because it wants to be picked up by its mother.

Such individuals are apprehensive that their own socially inept behavior might cause others to laugh at them. Those who are temperamentally not paranoid types or were brought up to be nervous types, must enter the battlefield of competition in order to support themselves and the family, and to find meaning in their lives. Thus, there exists a system to stimulate numinous powers to encourage shy and withdrawn individuals who must go out into the world. It is to have going-away parties, have sending-off delegations at the train station, etc. And as a going-away present intended to encourage the person who is leaving for greener pastures, there is the expression *gambare!* (carry on!).

There are not a few instances where a nervous-type individual is inspired to become a paranoid type. In such instances one will find certain characteristics. On their own, they will generate features found among the paranoid type, namely perseverance, using as their springboard their determination to overcome adversity. They will stubbornly maintain a high level of tension and self-control over a long period of time, and by trying again, they will eventually taste success. There are many popular stories about individuals who attained success in this way. Actually, in order to succeed, one needs, in addition to luck, persistent effort. However, in order to convert a nervous-type individual into a paranoid type, you need to revive the will to win. Thus, it is customary for nervous-type individuals to be exhorted by others, "Aren't you mad at yourself for losing?" Even when talked to that way, paranoid-type individuals may be unconcerned so that nothing much happens. Nervous people may be hesitant. Those who are upset when losing are the hysteroid types.

Let us take the case of people as individuals or as representing groups. Suppose that A, a hysterioid-type individual, puts forward an aggressive policy, saying, "How can you be such a weakling," and beats out B, also a hysterioid type of individual. In that event, A gets the upper hand. Individual B, also being a hysteroid type, does not relish losing, so in order to put down A proposes an even more aggressive policy. Thus, competition between hysteroid types becomes one of escalation. In order to avoid being called a weakling, reckless policies like General Tōjō's advocacy of going to war with the United States get adopted. Moreover, in the psychology of hysterioid-type persons, there is a tendency toward hysteria, where urges and impulses overwhelm thought process and self-control. Hence, instead of calculated decisions based on objective assessments of both oneself and of the environment, emotions and personal opinions carry weight, or are likely to be adopted. In this way, belief in certain victory, a form of self-intoxication, alternates with mass hysteria and emotional instability, arising out of the fear and insecurity that had been suppressed. Out of this alternation, there will appear reckless valor that is blind to reality. This process was not something that was unique to the prewar Japanese military; it has always been part of the social system.

THE PLOT: Organizations allocate roles to members, who are forced to accept them unconditionally. Moreover, in carrying out their roles, as has been explained already, they must put the group welfare above their personal interest. That is, they must not act contrary to what their role calls for, and they must avoid actions that are not appropriate for the attainment of organizational goals. They are also asked to give their all in carrying out their roles. If the actions of the members are not to be mechanical but are to represent spontaneous devotion to the organization, their roles must be meaningful in terms of organizational goals, meanings, and norms. They must also be meaningful to the personal livelihood of the members or as a steppingstone to their success.

However, as already explained, in the equality code, organizational roles are also a manifestation of eternal being. Individuals, through their roles, secure a "meaningful niche" in the universe. To perform tasks faithfully in this niche is the "human Way," and is the Way to realize unity with the eternal being in individual life. If one completely abandons commenting on or criticizing organizational goals, meanings, and norms, and gives his whole energy to the fulfillment of his niche with his whole heart and soul, he will be well served.

Because niche has a ontological meaning, the determination of whether one has or does not have a proper niche involves each group member's spirit or numinous power. The distribution of proper niches to proper individuals is what makes one want to work hard, while failure to so distribute niches will lead individuals to give up making the effort. Sometimes the decline of morale will lead to outbursts of anger and the abandonment of group membership.

If one is not dissatisfied with his niche and devotes himself to his job selflessly and with a true heart, working for the good of all will be a daily occurrence. It goes without saying that the daily work that goes on in government offices, in business firms, and other organizations is sustained by the employees working for the good of all. And this system teaches employees the "beauty of gallantry." Every day the rank-and-file display gallantry when they often have to endure difficult situations without complaint and devote themselves wholeheatedly to the performance of their tasks. And this gallantry is a common theme in the popular literature. Moreover, it is well known that leaders sometimes have used this gallantry as steppingstones for their own success, and that it has been taken advantage of.

However, if such gallantry comes to be ignored, not understood, or is not rewarded by the leaders or the general public, then the only thing that remains for the employees is self-satisfaction. If self-satisfaction and, presently, self-intoxication become important, the goal of carrying out one's duties will be affected. Personal satisfaction will become more important than pursuing organizational goals. The result of all this will be the spread of sectionalism and conservative traditionalistic tendencies in the organization.

The growth of an industrial society has produced a situation where many people have no alternative but to work for large organizations. In workplaces of large firms, the tradition of gallantry is still visible. But for many people who are assigned to petty jobs, or are forced to work in places where sectionalism and conservative traditionalism operate, or are put under incapable leaders, declining morale is common. These days, instead of devotion to the good of the whole, desired by the organization, bureaucratic inertia is more common. The behavior of those who are employed is often the subject of jokes: "They are never absent, never late, and never work hard."

Chapter Four

Government and Benefits

Economic Growth and Benefits

Economic development centered on industrialization produced a
number of economic problems for the people. The voters, who
felt that the solution to such problems lay in politics, brought
them into the political arena. Rapid economic growth was fueled
by investment in productive facilities designed to take advantage
of the technological revolution produced by the importation of
new technology from the West, mostly the United States. It was
natural that this revolution should produce marked differences
in productivity among those corporations engaged in the competitive struggle. In turn, this produced sharp variations in the
incomes for those who were employed. Also, as a result of the dis-
placement of old production processes by the new, some industries, firms, and employees were forced out of the national
economy. This, and the anticipation of something like that happening, produced a great deal of insecurity as well as defensive
measures on the part of those affected. It became necessary to
find some kind of political solution to these problems.

Income Disparities

The largest disparities in income are those among the primary,
secondary, and tertiary industries, and particularly between
the primary and secondary. The best-known example of the
political use of government funds to deal with this disparity is
the price support program for rice, intended to augment farmers'
incomes. In addition, large amounts in subsidies are directed

toward farm families. Within the secondary sector, there are disparties between the rising and declining industries, which have led to remedial measures. A second type of disparity within the same industry has to do with the size of the operation: large, medium, or small firms. Wages in small and medium firms are about 70 percent of those of the large firms. Moreover, as subcontractors to the large firms, the small companies are often at a disadvantage with regard to prices they are paid, and the terms of the payment. To deal with this, various types of political solutions have been tried.

The third kind of disparity has to do with productivity on an international level. Japan's economic development proceeded with administrative guidance from the appropriate government agencies. All three sectors, in varying degrees, were shielded, by means of protective measures, from international competition. At the same time, Japan entered foreign markets with the help of export promotion schemes. Moreover, this kind of closed system, together with a system that regulated the employment of foreign workers, foreclosed the possibility of Japanese workers developing close ties with workers in other countries. (The system of enterprise unions, and the lack of unions in many small firms has impeded the growth of labor unity.)

Political Countermeasures

It was inevitable that people in local communities and business enterprises should take their economic problems to their representatives in the National Diet. The kinds of political measures that were taken in response may be categorized as follows:

Various steps were taken to import new technology. Delegations were sent abroad, classes were set up on how to use new technology, funding for new investments in technology was provided, special tax treatment was enacted, and markets were created for new products by such steps as government procurement.

Measures were taken to deal with disparities. One way to assist local industries to become more competitive was to help them acquire new technology. Providing the infrastructure, land, water, and roads to help local industries as well as entice new ones to locate there was an important step. Furthermore, as already noted, subsidies, in addition to price supports for rice, were provided to deal with income disparities.

Protection for existing industries was provided. Examples are the subjection of imports to inspection measures, quotas on imports, high tariffs, and other restrictions on imports. Another example is restrictions on competitive businesses coming into an area. A conspicuous case is the restrictions on the entry of large companies into the retail distribution system. Another example is assistance to declining industries.

Programs were established to help individuals who were forced out of the economy. These steps overlapped with other social welfare programs.

Policies designed to deal with recessions were set up. In times of recession, the central government was under considerable pressure to take fiscal measures, such as funding public works, and monetary moves, such as lowering interest rates. However, prosperity is something that is desired, not only by financial interests in Tokyo, but also by medium and small businesses in the local areas. Especially before elections, various policies to produce prosperity were usually tried.

A More Civilized Life

The Westernization and urbanization made ports like Yokohama and Kobe, and metropolitan cities like Tokyo and Osaka, distribution centers of the newly arrived civilization from the West. Western civilization was like a halo to those in power and served to enhance the prestige of the Imperial Court, the military, the government agencies, schools, and eventually business enterprises. Cities represented the battlefield of those who sought success. Cities were also the center of civilization. Thus, the disparty in civilization between the cities and the rural areas tended to increase. To combat this, civilization was distributed, through political means, to the local areas in order to reduce this disparity. It was also explained that "thanks to the benevolence of the Emperor, one can enjoy civilization even while living in the local areas." The purpose of this kind of explanation was to convince the public of the utility of the Western-style government that had adopted the policy of Westernization by guaranteeing the benefits of imported civilization to the people who were practical minded. The Japanese National Railways (JNR) best typified the political connection and the cultural link between the center and the periphery. What pushed the local dignitaries to fight for the extension of the railroad into their areas was the economic factor, the establishment and stimulation of local industries. However, there was also the psychological wish to overcome the feeling of isolation and become linked politically and culturally to the center. Incidentally, the problem of getting rid of the continued deficits of the JNR cannot be solved merely from the point of view of relieving the central government of the financial burden. It has become a serious political problem because it is also a part of "the world of meaning."

Facilities for Civilization
The blessings of civilization are distributed through new facilities, including buildings, equipment, and personnel. Not all of these facilities are owned and operated by the central government. There are many public facilities owned by local governments, and private facilities owned by business enterprises. However, in the administrative and welfare state, many aspects of life are under the jurisdiction of the central government. Cultural facilities, even if they are not government owned, in many cases receive government subsidies. As a result, bringing culture to the local area is an important job of the parliamentary politicians, who seek to provide constituency service. They use their influence to get government facilities built, obtain subsidies that have been authorized, or seek to have new ones created.

Health care is one of the most important forms of the blessings of civilization. Thus, the building of hospitals, clinics, and health-care centers means a great deal. Also, the problem of villages without doctors has become a serious political issue, and so government-supported medical schools have been established in every prefecture. Moreover, a national health insurance system that pays doctors' fees has been established. Excluding schools, which will be discussed later, various kinds of cultural facilities, such as libraries, repositories of historical materials, museums, art museums, cultural centers, and parks, have been established in local and rural areas. Finally, playgrounds, sports centers, auditoriums, and civic centers have also been built.

The blessings of culture are not limited to these various cultural facilities that are outside of the home. "Civilization" has also come into the everyday lives of the citizens. A notable example from the recent past is the diffusion of electricity that has dramatically changed our lives. The diffusion of electricity, gas, and oil has brought air conditioning and changed the way we do our cooking, ridding our kitchens of wood-burning stoves. Running water has made it unnecessary to haul water from wells. Kitchens in homes in the farming areas have been modernized and are no different from kitchens in the cities. There is widespread use of telephones, and electrical applicances have changed the nature of housework. The diffusion of television has brought information about living styles, and has encouraged the spread of Western lifestyles throughout the country. Shopping arcades and department stores that serve to introduce the new culture have been built in the smaller cities. Theaters, movie houses, and amusement districts help people spend their leisure time. Even while some are entertained by touring theatrical companies and movies that travel from one town to another, others, taking advantage of the availability of cars and highways, visit towns and cities to enjoy the goods and pleasures that can be had. Behind this diffusion of cultural life lie the various activities of parliamentary politicians, and the financial assistance of the central government.

Because the cultural connection between the center and the periphery is meaningful, the means of transportation and communication linking the two are important in terms of constituency service. Mail and telephone service, and living in an area that can receive television signals are important from the communications point of view. As for transporation, roads, freeways, bridges, harbors, and airports are important. It goes without saying that these links are vital for stimulating economic development in the region. At the same time, these links also symbolize "access to the center."

Schools are valued as symbols of cultural linkage. The building of schools became an important political concern for several reasons. Because of Westernization and industrialization, academic training is beneficial for securing jobs in the Westernized sector of the economy. Youngsters living in big cities and towns have a relative advantage in receiving this academic training. People in local areas began to demand an equal opportunity to acquire an education that would enable their children to succeed in life and enjoy cultural advantages. A significant form of constituency service was dealing with the strong pressure to build more schools in the rural areas. The demand for schools and academic training led to reforms in the educational system in 1918, 1944 (eight-year system), and 1947 (nine-year system). Finally, there were increases in the number of government-supported schools, with some being set up in the outlying areas, in schools supported by local governments, and aid to private schools in the form of subsidies.

Political Expectations of Voters

Locus of Political Authority

With the coming of the age of universal suffrage, the entire population, now having the right to vote, participates in the power struggle. In electoral contests, key factors are party labels, policies, and the political aura projected by the party leader, which becomes the focal point of political competition.

Elections are more or less regularly scheduled "internal wars" that are institutionalized and nonviolent, but they are as expensive as small-scale wars. Moreover, the party leader is the commander of the troops that fight in the internal war. The leader of the party that wins the election is the winner of the internal war, and receives the mandate of the people. In this way, the winner of the election secures the power to rule over the entire population. The leader also secures the charisma that goes with the position.

The system of parliamentary cabinets was established by virtue of Article 67 in the postwar Constitution: "The Prime Minister shall be designated from among the members of the Diet by a resolution of the Diet." Thus there came into being a political system whereby the party securing a majority in a general election, as the victor in the internal war, and backed by a mandate of the majority of the people, secures the power to rule the nation. The first winner to acquire power under this system was Yoshida Shigeru (later known as a one-man prime minister), who led the opposition Democratic Liberal Party to victory in the 24th General Election in 1949. However, Japan was occupied by the Allied Powers, and power lay with the Supreme Commander for the Allied Powers. In 1952, Japan regained sovereignty and independence. Since the unification of the conservative parties in 1955, the LDP has enjoyed a monopoly of power. The establishment of continuous rule by one party has influenced politics in various ways.

Because the system assures that the LDP will always get a majority in an election, the president of the party is never confronted with the possibility of a dramatic development. It is not a situation where the transfer of power from one party to another is commonplace, and where a party in a minority position can win power by virtue of a strong campaign, or where a party succeeds in staying in power by fending off an attack by the opposition. Not only that, the president of the LDP does not even perform the function of leading his troops in the internal war. In American politics, there is the phenomenon of "congressmen riding into office on the coattails of the president." By contrast, the popularity or appeal of the president of the LDP (to cite an extreme case, even if the president has died and the post is vacant) has no direct effect on the chances of the individual LDP candidates being elected or defeated. This is because under the one-party dominant system, the party's electoral fortunes depend on the election efforts of individual candidates.

The Electoral System
The main features of the electoral system are as follows: Unlike the Anglo-American system with its small single-member districts, in the House of Representatives election there are medium-sized districts with three, four, or five members being elected. In the electoral districts, LDP candidates or conservative independents, who upon winning will join the LDP, will conduct their own campaigns relying on their own support groups as their electoral base. At every election, a certain number of these candidates will be elected. Over the country as a whole, about 20 to 30 percent of the incumbents turn over, but the number of seats won by the LDP always comes to more than one-half of the total, so whatever movement there is, it is quite limited, and no dramatic change occurs.

In order to support this kind of localized campaigning, and to mobilize the elected politicians as troops for political struggles, the so-called big-shot politicians usually organize factions. Generally, a new party president is chosen as a result of political maneuvering that takes place toward the end of the term of the incumbent party president, and the backstage machinations of the various factions. The new party president will be chosen as prime minister in accordance with Article 67 of the Constitution, and he will thereby attain the seat of power. This, in short, is an outline of the system that has kept the LDP in a dominant position.

Thus, the prime minister, who is the president of the LDP, will govern on the basis of authority vested in him by law, but, unlike the American president, he did not achieve power by being a victor in the internal war and obtaining a popular mandate. Of course, professional politicians are aware of this. New party presidents want to be able to say that they have experienced the "baptism of an election." Hence they have always tried to opt for a general election. Others who do not want to have an election maneuver to prevent it.

Thus, the 1955 merger of two conservative parties did assure the LDP that it would enjoy a monopoly of power. But it also produced a situation where party presidents and prime ministers could not enjoy long tenure, leading to continued weakness in political leadership.

Role of the Party Politician

Political vs. Bureaucratic

The political system has a history extending back almost a century, and the traditional functions and authority of the Diet and its members are duly recognized. The Westernized state based on the Meiji Constitution was, in a way, a bureaucratic autocracy supplemented by a wide-ranging Imperial prerogative. The benevolent bureaucratic autocracy, sometimes felt to be over-protective, consisted of an elite of officials who had passed the civil service examinations after having been educated in a Western-style school system. It governed by means of a Westernized system of laws imported in order to bring Western civilization into the country. But from the point of view of those being ruled, this engendered a feeling of disharmony. This is because this rule was seen as an overly legalistic and oppressive kind that was being carried out by a different breed of outsiders, and thus represented a break with the traditional views of the social order.

But there were two factors that to some extent mitigated this feeling of disharmony and discontinuity with social tradition. One was the benevolent and compassionate image, particularly in social welfare programs, projected by the Emperor and the Imperial family, who were regarded as the descendants of the ancestor-guardian deity of the nation, which was in turn seen as a large extended family. The other was the activities of the parliamentary politicians who tangentially meddled with, modified, and adjusted the autocratic rule exercised by the bureaucrats who ran the country. As the expressions "party people vs. civil servants," "political vs. bureaucratic" suggest, the party stalwarts were the spokesmen and defenders of the nameless, poverty-ridden masses against the elite bureaucrats, who were a different breed of outsiders. In contrast to the bureaucrats who laid great stress on abstract law drawn from the West, the country bumpkin type of elected officials were more attuned to the everyday life that went on in the backwater towns and hamlets. Moreover, the anti-bureaucratic spirit played into the hands of the party politicians, whose function it was to frustrate the autocratic rule of the bureaucrats through political measures.

In any case, it is a fact that looking after the needs of the constituency is the traditional role of politicians as well as their source of power. It remains their role even under the present Constitution.

The Workings of the Diet

The postwar Constitution established a cabinet system based on parliamentary majority. However, as a result of the long-term monopoly of power held by the LDP following the merger of two conservative parties, the prime minister, who is the president of the LDP, no longer possesses the political authority to head the state and govern the people on the basis of securing a mandate of the people following victory in an internal war. Accordingly, even though the prime minister has the legal power to get the government and its agencies to comply with his orders, he does not have the necessary leverage to politically dominate the organs of government, which have the following characteristics: (1) retain bureaucratic power on the basis of traditional authority; (2) expand the administrative and social welfare functions which were under their jurisdiction; (3) maintain leadership in matters under their control; (4) maintain autonomy, resulting in a segmented administrative structure, which makes it difficult to bring about unified and coordinated policies. One example is the difficulty of achieving administrative reform.

Thus, because the power to guide the state and govern the people is pretty much in the hands of the government agencies, the activities of the parliamentary representatives, in intervening in the work of the bureaucrats and thereby providing constituency service by giving play to local conditions, has the effect of mitigating feelings of hostility toward bureaucratic domination, on the one hand, and satisfying the desire to secure financial benefits from the central government coffers, on the other. To this extent, even in the case of parliamentary politics established under the postwar Constitution, the general populace has accepted to a considerable degree the more traditional authority and functions of the bureaucrats and elected politicians carried over from the prewar system.

"The Government Will Pay"

The economy, which recovered from a state of disarray in 1945 and later enjoyed high growth, greatly enlarged the financial capacity of the central government, which engaged in constituency service. The distribution of wealth via the national treasury enhanced the buying power of the local communities and assured the existence of a domestic market. Moreover, the fact that the LDP monopoly of power rested only in Article 67 of the Constitution and the legal system made the elected politicians acutely feel the need of securing some kind of political backing from the voters in their respective electoral districts.

Accordingly, they became more active in constituency service, and they took on the role of serving as a pipeline for bringing the financial resources of the central government to their home districts. In addition, the traditional desire for equality that was legitimated by postwar democracy required that all areas of the country be treated equally. Thus there developed the notion of "let the government pay," that is, a willingness to take the benefits, sometimes free, sometimes secured at low cost, proffered by the central government.

Concept of the Great Mother

The notion of "let the government pay" ran counter to the more traditional values of independence and self-respect generally held by the voters, and so there was the problem of how to make legitimate the state of dependency inherent in the "let the government pay" attitude. The "dependency-motherly care" model was the answer. As has been explained in the sin and punishment paradigm, the person with the superior status in an interpersonal relationship is thought to be a manifestation of the eternal being. Parliamentary politicians, too, are expected, like a "mother," to embrace, protect, and nurture the voters, and in acceding to the pleading of their constituents with a mother-like feeling, they are to look after their welfare in an unlimited way.

The concept of "let the government pay" is thus given legitimacy. Of course, those people who are involved are perfectly aware of what is actually going on in this politics of benefits: the benefits to the constituents are being provided in exchange for votes.

The System of Amae

One of the models for interpersonal relations is the bond between mother and child that rests on protection and dependency. On the one hand, it is a relationship that draws on and symbolizes the mother's unilateral love and gives metaphysical expression to the infinite love that is inherent in the cosmos. On the other hand, the full satisfaction of one's wants as experienced by a spoiled child, who is always allowed to have his own way, is equated to life in paradise. Unlimited endearment, protection, and support become the true phase of eternal being. Accordingly, not just all mothers, but power holders, and those occupying superior positions in human relationships, have to act like the mother. Moreover, in this article of faith, motherly love, as the quintessence of being, enjoys utmost legitimacy, occupies a superior position, and is capable of overcoming numerous difficulties. However, when a child becomes an independent and autonomous individual, it means that he escapes from the mother's "tyranny." Accordingly, both mother and child psychologically are bound together, the mother reluctant to let her child become independent by prolonging the latter's dependency. As a result, the mother dominance permeates the social system, leading to the so-called mother principle society.

According to Ruth Benedict in her *Chrysanthemum and the Sword*, in rearing children in Japanese households, the young, instead of being strictly disciplined, are given free rein. Several decades have passed since the time Benedict made her observation. In the meantime, the permissive way of raising children has been imported from America, and so there has been no change in the traditional undisciplined way of rearing children.

Thus today, as in the past, socialization, that is, the internalization of civilization, is the responsibility of those outside of the family—the community, the government and its agencies, schools, other educational institutions, the police, and correction agencies. It used to be said, "If you love your child, let him go on a trip," "let him become an apprentice somewhere." As these sayings suggest, socialization in the past was experienced in the outside world, where one learned about social etiquette, acquired common sense, and obtained trade skills. In addition, the young nurtured feelings of independence by being removed from the immediate influence of the mother; learned to suppress feelings of self-indulgence and acquired patience; learned to become passive and cooperative; and gave up vanity and the idea of being omnipotent, thereby nurturing self-awareness and stimulating them to exercise initiative. However, in these days of labor shortage, live-in apprentices and apprentice training have disappeared. Moreover, in these affluent times, it is feasible, from the economic point of view, to sever ties with people one does not like and quit one's job, and come home to mother. As a result, socialization by working as an apprentice no longer prevails. Because of the lack of opportunity to acquire social graces, the number of children and adults who are ignorant of social etiquette and lacking in common sense are said by the mass media to be increasing.

Freedom
Ruth Benedict has also discussed "freedom." Child rearing entails training in the ability to discipline and control oneself. The end result is self-regulation based on conscious control of one's emotions and impulses. Freedom for an individual is the ability to lead an independent and autonomous life without hinderance to one's self-determination and self-control. Accordingly, adults

who are recognized by the social system to have the ability to assume risks and who by so doing have the right of self-determination are free. Children who are being socialized and trained because they are supposed to be uncivilized and hence are burdened with all kinds of restrictions are not free.

But sometimes freedom is said to be a situation where one gives free, unrestricted rein to one's emotions and impulses. This second form of freedom is an indulgent freedom that is undisciplined. The origin of this undisciplined freedom is the freedom experienced by babies who enjoy full protection and are able to act without restraints. According to the traditional Japanese view of babies, they are pure and innocent and partake of the essence ·of human life. The obvious way to raise children is to let them have their way without restrictions, since they are the manifestations of the eternal being. Accordingly, it is the children who enjoy indulgent freedom that are truly free, while the adults, burdened with obligations in social networks, are not free. The time adults regain the freedom of children is when they reach retirement age.

Regression

Ordinary parents who teach their children not to become a source of trouble for others are independent and disciplined individuals, and while they may not be given to asceticism, they are wise people who have a balanced perspective and avoid being impulsive. But there are many turns in one's journey through life, and there are those who go astray. Also, there are many obstacles in the competitive world, and one cannot always avoid hitting barriers. When that happens, adults sometimes want to regress, that is, they will seek a protector and revive the dependency they felt as a child when they were bound to their mothers. In many cases, this regression is fulfilled in the privacy of the home by either their mother or their spouse. But dependency has been traditionally recognized outside of the home in the world at large.

In the case of adult dependency, those who fulfill the role of the mother toward the child are known as "paternalistic individuals" and "magnanimous persons." Paternalism, in this context and in the following chapters, is used to mean motherly and unlimited compassion and generosity and is not used in the strict disciplinarian sense of patriarchalism. Rather than reject dropouts, they show sympathy toward them (compassion), accede to their wishes for protection (magnanimity), they listen to their wishes as unreasonable demands without getting angry (magnanimity), they forgive such misdeeds as addiction to wine, women, and gambling as passing phenomena—such is compassion and magnanimity. This is the popular view of benevolence with its unlimited coddling, unlimited protection, and unlimited support, and provides the goal toward which the paternalistic politician should strive.

The Drama of Supplication

Parliamentary politics today operates on the basis of politicians securing benefits given to local communities in exchange for votes provided by the electorate. And local benefits consist of the distribution of wealth and culture. As a result of this kind of distributive politics, vast sums are provided by the national treasury to local residents in the form of subsidies. Moreover, it is a fact that the decisions as to who gets what are not always based on rational grounds. However, interest democracy, which distributes wealth and culture, is a form of democracy whose basic principle is that it is open to the public. Distributive politics that appears to be giving away large sums recklessly must appear to be legitimate to third parties, who are not recipients of this largess.

Legitimacy

Whatever the government does has legal legitimacy because it is based on the provisions of the law. The payments of funds to aid local communities is also based on laws and budgetary appropriations, so they have legal standing. In many instances, basic bills to aid local communities or business enterprises are supported by both ruling and opposition parties, and are passed by the National Diet inconspicuously. In this sense, they are different from legislation pertaining to diplomacy, defense, and internal security matters, which provokes confrontations between the ruling and opposition parties and excites the mass media.

Once the basic law has been passed, subsidies are regarded as an indisputable legal right. Now the job of the politician is to make sure that the share that will go to his constituents will be as large as possible. Needless to say, just because there is a legal provision, or that legal procedures were followed, does not guarantee that the substance of these laws is legitimate.

By contrast, the present Constitution puts stress on popular sovereignty and self-government, and, by implication, on independence and self-help. Despite this, so far there has been no attempt to explain distributive politics as a manifestation of national unity and mutual help based on equity and fairness. As a result, distributive politics appears one way to the principals involved, and another way to third parties. In the former case, distributive politics is viewed as an activity designed to help constituents, and so it comes down to the particular situation in the electoral districts or within industries. The parties within the electoral districts, who feel that the government can afford to help them, may be likened to children, and the parliamentary politicians and the government agencies to mothers. This would be the way that paternalistic politicians would justify distributive politics to those involved.

Third parties, however, are given no explanation of the contradiction between independence and self-help, on the one hand, and paternalistic politics with their dependence on the generosity of the government, on the other. Hence, for third parties, the legitimacy of distributive politics has not been established. Since the principals interacting in such politics can only point to legal rights, the power relations that are involved stand out, and so third parties are dissatisfied. But, third parties, depending on circumstances, might become one of the principals, so they do not voice their anger. In this way, excluding those directly involved, distributive politics, while lacking legitimacy, has, in a de facto way, been accepted. The fact that lobbying efforts can take on a combative style stems from this ambivalent feeling.

Dramatis Personae: The Supplicants

Lobbying involves trying to explain setbacks and hardships. Since remedies depend on government appropriations, the purpose of lobbying is the passage of laws relating to local communities or to industries, and the payment of subsidies. Supplicants will seek the aid and support of their parliamentary representatives. Local delegations, armed with introductions from their representatives, will turn up at the offices of government agencies, present relevant documents, and make their case. What happens after that depends on bureaucratic response. The supplicants believe that the government has lots of money and so they have high hopes. If a budgetary allocation is made, and it is less than what they had asked for, they will be realistic and accept it.

In the meanwhile, the local delegation will have many meetings with their parliamentary representatives. From the point of view of the delegation, which might be thought of as the child, the responsibility for neglecting the situation that deserves sympathetic treatment lies with the government, which is like the parent. Accordingly, the delegation expects to get and seeks some expression on the part of the politician that he is sorry and feels apologetic. Such expression accords legitimacy to the work of the delegation, and confirms that this was a proper request for funds, and not an improper grab for money. Also, even though no one can figure out whether the sum of money being sought is an appropriate amount, the fact that it is being provided as a gift affords psychological comfort to the recipients. The parliamentary politician, who had to show his paternalism, must now utilize his political influence to provide more constituency service.

Now, sometimes lobbying can become combative and provide material for the media to report on. With some lobbying groups, this is a common occurrence. They perform for the benefit of press and television crews. Sometimes a combative style is adopted as a reaction to the knowledge that the general public is critical because it feels that lobbying is not legitimate. This style may be likened to that of a child who has put up with a problem for a long time and whose anger finally leads to an explosion. In that event, the lobbying delegation is likened to an unreasonable, self-centered individual who cannot distinguish right from wrong. Accordingly, one counters that there are no scientific or technical bases for the amount of money sought, that if like sums were given to everyone, the total would come to some gigantic figure and the amount sought so high that it would defy common sense, but such arguments are not accepted. There is an old Japanese saying that you cannot win against a crying child and the feudal tax collector. And now a crying child wins against the government.

Dramatis Personae: Parliamentary Politicians

In order for politicians to show their paternalism, they must, first of all, listen to the requests of their "children" with a "human-like heart" and sympathetic ear. Here being human-like or having a human-like heart indicates an ontologically common character which the eternal being and human beings, concretely all Japanese, share. When both the parliamentary politicians and the lobbying delegations come to an understanding, the situation where the mother and the demanding child are one is reproduced. Accordingly, when a demand has been made, if the recipient, instead of responding with a human heart, sticks to legalities, especially the minute provisions of the law, he will be criticized and rejected as formalistic and bureaucratic. Moreover, unless one indicates sympathy for the demands being made, one has not become the mother who forgivingly embraces the unruly child. So one will be called "inhuman." This is because the only one to have the right to determine, on his own, whether some action is human-like or not, is the the lobbying group, the child.

Another indication of paternalism is, as we have already mentioned, to acknowledge that one had been wrong in not taking care of the group for a long time and apologize for it. Paternalism is the expression of 100 percent sympathy, and assumption of the mother-child stance. Showing one's sincerity and agreeing to secure funds even though such action may not always be reasonable is being the mother who provides unlimited protection and love.

However, when the lobbying group (the child) adopts combative tactics, the politician, in order to show paternalism, must respond with a loving embrace. The politician must try to listen in order to calm the child's outbursts and be tolerant. An adult dealing with a child must not get angry, and if the child is agitated the adult must not join in. One must accept both the combative style and self-centered demands as a manifestation of an innocent form of *amae*, which one must listen to with unlimited tolerance. As an indication of sincerity, the politician must provide the minimum amount of subsidy that the lobbying group would be willing to accept. By so doing, one will acquire a reputation as a veteran politician who is understanding, mature, and calm.

Chapter Five

Distributive Politics

Methods of Distribution

Channels of Political Pressure

For parliamentary politicians who chose politics as their profession, getting elected over and over again is a basic condition of their work. To achieve this, the politician must maximize the vote that is committed to him. Japan uses the medium-size electoral district with three, four, or five representatives. Moreover, since the LDP enjoys a monopoly of power, those who want to gain power will try to belong to that party. As a result, from the point of view of the conservative politicians, electoral contests represent intraparty competition involving several LDP and conservative independents. Hence, elections take the form of contests, within the electoral districts, among several support organizations belonging to individual politicians. Accordingly, all sorts of activities designed to build up these organizations, such as group tours both in Japan and overseas, have been devised, and have been duly reported in the mass media. Voters, who are being looked after by their politician, give the latter personal credit for whatever he has done for them.

Channels and Contents
There are several channels through which voter requests and demands are tendered. One is through the staffs of the support organization offices in the local district and in Tokyo. Another is through be the local notables who, officially or unofficially, are

involved in the work of the support organizations. The politician himself can also be approached. Among those who make requests and demands are, naturally, members of the support organizations, especially the more influential individuals. There are, in addition, persons who are, officially or unofficially, members of lobbying groups. For instance, there are office holders, such as governors, mayors, prefectural assemblymen, city council members, and the like. There are officials of local organizations and local notables. Officers of local business organizations, such as chambers of commerce, junior chambers of commerce, and youth organizations, cooperatives, officers and leaders from bar and medical associations, organizations of retired persons, housewives, youth, and so on are also among those making requests. We have already noted that the basis of constituency service has been its exchange for votes at election time.

Among the demands made to politicians are those that concern individuals. Examples are assistance for sons and daughters seeking admission to schools, in finding jobs for those who have just graduated, in finding marriage partners, or attendance at engagement parties and protocol at wedding receptions, and intercession in medical and other social welfare matters. In a mass society where life is becoming more complicated, the needs concerning personal lives that are to be looked after keep growing.

There are also problems related to economic life. Specifically, there are matters connected with taxes, finances, and credit, and the need to contact the proper government office on behalf of constituents. By contrast, the most commonly held image of constituency service involves problems relating to groups and collective life. We have already discussed those aspects pertaining to the economy, such as development projects, and to cultural matters, such as schools and other facilities. Because there is intense competition among party politicians, local demands relating to economic and cultural concerns keep increasing. In response to this, all kinds of subsidies will flow to the districts of powerful politicians.

Looking after Business Interests
Constituency service naturally includes working for the economic benefit of local business and industry. At the same time, politicians will also look after the interests of business and industry that are

represented by national organizations, such as the Federation of Economic Organizations and the Japan Medical Association. Most people are not so aware of these interests. For one thing, because of the struggle to acquire votes at election time, politicians will try to take personal credit for their good works by publicizing their achievements among their constituents. It is also true that national organizations will sometimes provide campaign funds, so politicians may not wish to talk about such matters outside the business community. As for the local business community, there are channels for obtaining funds. Business people can go to their local business organizations, which in turn contact local assemblymen, and through them gain access to local governments. An alternative channel is to go through national business organizations, to party politicians who work for legislation favoring industry and for budgetary appropriations. Depending on circumstances, business firms will use one or the other alternative.

As already noted, the business community and business organizations have dealings with the appropriate divisions of the various government agencies. Party politicians participate in getting bills drafted by government agencies enacted by the National Diet and help agencies win their budgetary appropriations. Government agencies will try to accommodate particular requests by party politicians, and provide administrative guidance, which will benefit business, either through favorable regulations or financially. This is the so-called three-way alliance, involving politicians, bureaucracy, and big business.

Business, Bureaucracy, Parties

There are very close relationships between the relevant divisions of government agencies and individual firms and business associations. In terms of movement of persons, there are examples of personnel being loaned to government agencies by business establishments. There are also cases where business firms have taken over functions that were supposed to have been performed by government agencies. There are not a few examples where businesses have extended courtesies and help to government agencies. The practice of corporations hiring government officials upon their retirement from civil service positions is well known.

From the point of view of government agencies, this means that their seniors, superiors, and colleagues can be found in private firms and business organizations.

Along with this interchange of personnel, business also provides government agencies with reports. It is well known that business firms and organizations are required to provide all kinds of reports and statistical data in large amounts to government agencies and that a large number of employees are needed for the preparation of such documents. Agencies, on the basis of these reports, will draft new laws or plan budgetary appropriations, or issue administrative guidance on the basis of existing regulations. Thus, both individual enterprises and the business community have to put up with overprotection and the heavy hand of administrative guidance. As a result, it is said that the contemporary economy is a bureaucratically controlled capitalistic economy. This image of an efficiently controlled economy has given rise to the expression "Japan, Inc." Of course, in reality, politics, as attempts to deal with trade friction indicate, is not subject to unified, centralized control, but rather is featured by competition among sovereignlike agencies, which leads to a vertically segmented administration.

The scope of administrative guidance of business enterprise is rather broad. With regard to production, it embraces production planning, including controls through the formation of cartels, and production processes, including technical innovation. In terms of distribution, it includes price fixing of products and services, market adjustments through inventory and price control, and control of foreign trade. There is also regulation of financial services, such as banking and stock transactions. Those industries that are subject to regulation by government agencies tend to be those whose positions are secure, that is, are the main line industries for which laws have been enacted and budgetary provisions have been made. The more obscure, newer industries for which neither legal regulations nor budgetary provisions exist tend to be left alone. After some of the small and medium industries have reached a certain size as a result of their own efforts, they may become subject to a specific government agency and its guidance and control. Moreover, the large corporations are economically powerful and relatively few in number. Their social impact is great, and so they are likely to become the subject of protection and regulation. It is more difficult to bring the more numerous small and medium firms under control. On the other hand, in their case, financial assistance from the local governments, villages, towns, and cities is very important.

Bureaucracy and Political Parties

Normally, the relevant divisions in the government agencies will draft local laws and laws regulating business and work on budgets. Sometimes party politicians will first suggest these matters to the bureaucrats, or they might indicate their approval and support for actions taken by the bureaucrats on their own initiative. They will support passage of such bills through the National Diet. Generally speaking, in many cases the actual leadership in governing the country lies with bureaucrats and the bureaucracy. The LDP, the ruling party, takes a supporting role. The Political Affairs Research Commitee of the LDP has divisions that parallel the segmented administrative system of the bureaucracy. Government agencies will seek out these divisions, will brief their members, and engage in caucusing activities in order to get the support of the committee members. Thus, the segmented administrative structure will be directly reflected in the inner councils of the LDP, causing intraparty strife among groups of politicians.

Within the LDP, in addition to the Political Affairs Research Committee, there are various research policy committees, and leagues of Diet members. These committees concern themselves with legislative and budgetary matters. There is a great deal of contact between the government agencies and the relevant Diet members for the purpose of facilitating legislation. This provides opportunities for elected politicians to obtain funds for their own districts. They can then have the pleasure of being the first to report the good news to their constituents. When these contacts extend over a long period of time with good results, politicians will acquire considerable power in influencing policy making in the government agencies. They then become members of the *zoku* (tribe) who has developed specialized skill and power in a policy area and relations with the relevant agencies.

The factions in the LDP serve to facilitate the exchange of benefits that flow from the possession of such specialized skills and power. Because faction members are assured the influence to satisfy the wide range of demands made upon them by their constituents, the value of factions for politicians engaged in a struggle for existence is indeed great. When factions are able to aggregate the pressures being generated in all of the local districts and direct them against the government agencies, in reality they take on the characteristics of a pressure party.

It should be noted that constituency service is not something that is monopolized by the LDP. Opposition parties also participate in bringing benefits to the local communities and enterprises. It goes without saying that government agencies need the National Diet to enact their bills and pass appropriations bills. The ministries cannot be completely indifferent to "Diet operation" and "Diet measures" that are intended to avoid frequent interruptions in the parliamentary proceedings by opposition walkouts and boycotts. In order to facilitate orderly debate on legislative bills, also so that they will not be held responsible for interruptions in Diet proceedings, government agencies will take certain steps. Bureaucrats will explain the details of bills to opposition party leaders who are members of the standing and special Diet committees. They will also confer with both the LDP and opposition committee members about questions they plan to ask during the Diet interpellation period, and prepare answers for the cabinet members and government committee members who must publicly respond to the questions. In this way, there is usually a certain amount of interaction between the bureaucrats and opposition politicians. And in this interaction, opposition politicians also can find opportunities to perform constituency service.

Political Problems and Politicians

Constituency service provided by politicians takes the form of day-to-day activities on the part of many government offices. Every day, government agencies are in touch with local communities and businesses for the purpose of carrying out the law and the budget. Social life proceeds smoothly under administrative guidance. But, at one time or another, something will happen that will be reported by the mass media, thereby drawing public attention to it. It will become a political problem that requires the intervention of bureaucratic agencies and sometimes even of political leaders. There are all kinds of political problems. Some have their origin in the society, others in the political world itself. Once a political problem develops, Diet investigating committees might take up the matter. There might be questions raised in the Diet, or the issue of political responsibility on the part of those politicians that are involved might be raised. Accordingly, the problem will be studied and dealt with at the political level, which would bring in members of the Diet, cabinet ministers, party leaders, and the prime minister. Looking after the needs of the local areas and businesses, which we have already discussed, might also become a political problem and be dealt with as such.

The Solution of Problems
There are all kinds of problems that emerge from the society: natural disasters, industrial accidents, social strife involving opposing interests, and conflict among parties over violation of their rights and financial losses. Because there are variations in the numbers of people and in the scope of these conflict situations, they do not get uniform treatment in the mass media. There are also variations in who has to take political responsibility. As for problems that originate in the political world, many involve power struggles. Examples are conflict among agencies over turf, conflicts among ministries, conflicts over foreign policy and budgetary allocations, scandals and slips of the tongue. All kinds of considerations enter into the solution of these political problems: for instance, the need to settle conflicts relating to economic interests, as well as social interests, and the need to arrive at a political settlement of the struggle of power, and to clarify and settle the issue of responsibility. Thus, the matter will be taken up by the top-level leaders. For the party, it is the party president, the secretary-general of the party, and the chairman of the executive committee of the party, and for the government it is the prime minister and the relevant cabinet members. The problem is solved not administratively but politically. When the problem seriously violates an important part of the legal order, in order to deal with it, there is a political ritual, namely, the minister assumes responsibility and resigns.

Where the problem involves a serious economic conflict, and, for example, damages are sought, there may be no clear-cut basis for determining what amount of damages should be awarded, so its solution must rely on the politicians' opinions, determination, and judgment. In many cases, the mass media will criticize the monetary amounts that have been set on the ground that they are ad hoc unprincipled (add up and divide by two) decisions that are not based on long-term considerations. Actually, a series of short-term, ad hoc decisions appears to be a characteristic of human life, including politics.

Politicians

If a problem arises as a result of some mistake made by a government agency in the performance of its duties and the agency admits the mistake, someone, even high-level officials, depending on the authority they possess, is reprimanded according to legal provisions on supervisory responsibility. This system of being punished because one is responsible serves to maintain discipline in the bureaucracy and corrects violations of the legal order. The situation with respect to the politician is different. Whereas the bureaucrat is reprimanded, the politician has the privilege of resigning in order to show that he is taking responsibility for something having gone awry.

In the olden days, the Chinese emperor, the head of the empire, had a position that corresponded to heaven, the center of the universe, and assumed responsibility for anything anomalous that took place on this earth. Today, when things are much more secularized, the scope of responsibility has shrunk, but the parliamentary politician still has the traditional authority to preserve the order and participate symbolically in its restoration when it is damaged. This authority is the same as the authority to intercede in the work of the bureacracy to correct its errors. Thus, parliamentary politicians, regardless of whether they had previously been members of local assemblies, high-level bureaucrats, or journalists, must, when voters are watching, behave like politicians and not bureaucrats. That is, they must demonstrate that they are capable of participating in political decisions, and of assuming political responsibility.

The first thing in demonstrating that one is a politician is to interact closely with the voters, the nameless masses. He must live in his district with his family, use the local dialect and follow local customs in socializing with the voters, work with various local organizations, and become someone who understands the hearts of the local people.

The politician must pay attention to the local situation. He must learn to associate the names and faces of members of his support organization so that he will know them individually. He must call on them in their homes, talk with them in discussion groups in order to learn about personal conditions in the electoral district. He must not forget to write to them, send them newsletters, invite them for meals, and bring back presents for them from a trip abroad. It is necessary that one be sympathetic, fulfill all obligations, and follow the traditional norms of social intercourse, and thereby establish rapport with individual voters.

Demonstration that one is human, and not "bureaucratic" is also required of a politician. To be human means that although one may be in an influential position, one will be humble, not proud and arrogant, and be like one of the common people. Other desired qualities are that he is approachable, that he listens to requests from constituents, that he is interested in what one has to say, and, after listening, that he says, "I understand your position," "I will look into it," etc. This type of politician will have shown that he is a paternalistic type who will understand and respect the feelings of the local people as well as of all the people of Japan. If we assume that the people are sovereign, and that national feelings are the basis of order, it is natural that politicians who understand and respect popular feelings have the right to assume political responsibility.

Economic Costs of Democracy

Treating Everyone Alike

Given the competitive nature of elections, it is necessary for politicians to provide constituency service and respond to requests from the local people and businesses without questioning the merits of such requests. When these requests are taken up by the government agencies or the Political Affairs Research Committee of the LDP, if we set aside the question of the influence of the politician involved, there is no way of ranking the requests from, say, three different localities. If we assume that because of budget limitations, ranking on the basis of political influence is inevitable, there is no way but to give equal consideration to all requests of the same kind. For this reason, a policy of giving everyone equal shares is commonly used with regard to requests from localities. In this sense, paternalistic politics has the basic tendency to lead to bigger appropriations.

When the Japanese economy was in a high-growth phase, tax reductions and natural increases in revenues were both possible, so appropriations grew. Tax reductions, savings, investment in productive facilities, high wages, and expansion of buying power, as well as additions to income, distribution of cultural facilities, and development of markets were assured. All this came to an end with the oil crisis in 1973 and the onset of the worldwide recession. But the system of subsidies for local districts was imbedded in the organization, authority, personnel, and budgets of the various ministries and agencies, so any large-scale adjustment was difficult. In addition, the LDP continued to enjoy a monopoly of power. Hence, paternalistic politics and the policy of treating all alike led to large-scale deficit financing based on the issuance of government bonds. This situation led the big business community, which began to worry about the problem, to come out for sound finances and control of inflation. The result was the demand for administrative reform.

The Economy and Politics
Even though the economy is based on capitalism, it does not mean that all Japanese have economic ideas that are typical of businessmen. Even in the case of industrialists and parliamentary politicians, their attitudes toward money and the economy are quite different. First of all, industrialists and business people seek long-term stability of their enterprises and of their profitability. They are aware of expenses, such as interest rates, the cost of materials and wages, and try to keep them down. By contrast, politicians are engaged in elections, a form of internal war, and are not owners of enterprises. Politicians collect funds, in the form of political contributions, from a wide variety of sources, and use them for political purposes and for building up a following in their electoral districts. Such operations are not easily subject to cost-benefit analysis. Accordingly, as might be expected, they are not cost conscious like business people. Moreover, given the competitive context, it is important to outspend your opponents, so it is unlikely that politicians will engage in rational cost accounting methods.

The accounting systems in government offices are clearly

divided into revenues and expenditures. Expenditures are set, without regard to revenues, by adding incremental amounts for new projects on top of fixed items that are already in place. Consciousness of costs cannot arise in government agencies, which have no need to be concerned about revenues, and need only to worry about using up all the monies that have been appropriated. Thus, neither politicians nor bureaucrats, except for those in the Ministry of Finance, are as sensitive as are businessmen to the dangers of deficit financing. In order to win the support of voters, politicians welcome prosperity and some inflation. So far, large political contributions and deficit financing represent the cost of maintaining, through the system of paternalistic politics and LDP dominance, the parliamentary system and the governance of the people. It was an insurance policy for maintaining a stable, peaceful lifestyle.

Consequences of Distribution

Achieving National Integration

As a result of economic growth and paternalistic politics, the country has attained an affluent society and a level of consumption never reached before in its history. The growth of the distribution system and the advertising business, together with the spread of television opened up a large domestic market for goods. Of course, the distribution of wealth and culture does not mean that distortions and inequality have been removed. However, compared to the past, and to the experience of foreign countries, there is no question that wealth and the benefits of culture are now more evenly distributed.

Mass Consumption Society

Among the special features of this high-consumption society are the following: The lives and health of the people have improved. In contrast to the low nutrition levels that prevailed in 1945, now people are concerned about eating too much and having weight problems. Both the height and weight of young people have increased rapidly. The standards of public health have risen remarkably, while dramatic improvements in medical practice, and better access to medical care through the spread of the medical insurance system have lowered the death rate among children and youth and increased longevity. The reduction in the birth rate that accompanied this has led to a graying of Japan.

Educational levels have risen. The educational reforms carried out in 1947 extended the period of compulsory education to nine years. Now more than 90 percent of those of high-school age are attending high school, while more than 35 percent of those of college age are in junior colleges or universities. The spread of education went hand in hand with economic growth, and also stimulated growth and benefited from it. The attainment of widespread higher education by the younger generation, when compared to that of their parents, together with economic growth, produced tremendous geographical, social, and cultural changes. As is suggested by the fact that a large number of men now go to work dressed in suits, consumption levels reached by urban, white-collar workers set the standard for the mass consumption society.

The slightly Westernized lifestyles of the nuclear families of the urban, salaried employees has become the pattern for the whole country, thanks to the spread of television. As a result, there are all kinds of changes in the traditional mode of living. In terms of food, a Westernized style of cooking, starting from breakfast (bread) to side dishes at dinner time, has come to be adopted. Influenced by television commercials, and with encouragement from children, prepared and semi-prepared foods are now consumed. In terms of dwellings, many people in big cities live in large apartment complexes, and Western-style furnishings, such as beds and living-room and dining-room furniture, have come into vogue. In the countryside, there was a move to improve kitchens. Gas stoves and running water, first available in big cities, spread to kitchens everywhere. This, together with electrical appliances, such as washing machines, refrigerators, and television sets, have made the work of housewives much easier. In terms of dress, Western-style dress has become the norm for both men and women, and the fashion industry, which promotes frequent changes in apparel and accessories, has become big business. Changes in fashion take place almost simultaneously all over the country, and the time lag between regions has been greatly reduced.

In terms of leisure, rises in income and buying power greatly increased travel, both domestic and foreign, after the removal of restriction on foreign travel in 1964. As for modes of travel, all kinds are available, from package group tours to individual travel. Moreover, large-scale road construction and the rise in car ownership have made travel by car easy. It has also led to demands for more highways and roadside facilities. Increases in income and the availability of more leisure time have led many people, especially housewives, to use sports facilities and cultural centers for enriching their personal lives.

National Culture
The relative equalization in income distribution, the absence of a "leisure class," in the Veblen sense, which would show differences in the ability to consume, and the near standardization of consumption all over the country, have given rise to middle-class consciousness. More than 90 percent of the people classify themselves as belonging to the upper or lower middle class. Moreover, the standardization all over the country of the spoken language, also aided by television, has enhanced the feeling of national unity.

These three factors—consumption standardization, middle-class consciousness, and language standardization—have finally produced a national culture that transcends the traditional culture that goes back to the Tokugawa period. In terms of its contents, this national culture has pulled away from tradition in the sense that there is confusion in what is proper in social intercourse and manners. Also, in terms of lifestyle, the national culture no longer fits the traditional stereotype, but represents a mixture of Japanese and Western elements. In addition, the language that sustains this national culture has indeed incorporated a large number of words derived from foreign languages and written in *katakana* (a phonetic script used to transliterate foreign sounds).

Naturalization of Parliamentary Government

The Allied Powers that occupied Japan in 1945 brought about a complete change in the political system and also proclaimed the ideal of "democracy and civilization." Democracy, which was popularized by intellectuals and the school system, attracted a large following, especially among young people, as a secular religion that would fill the spiritual void left by the abolition of the old Emperor system. By contrast, ordinary individuals interpreted democracy as a principle for a social order in which everyone would try to live in harmony, and incorporated it into traditional views of the social order. As has been explained before, living in harmony refers to group cohesiveness, participation by all, decision making by consensus, and everybody being treated alike. Accordingly, it was natural that, in this context, democracy in practice should have merged with the traditional values of peace and harmony and resulted in a commitment to peace, in which Japan does not want to get itself involved in other countries' quarrels. Furthermore, in terms of contents, this kind of democracy did not always agree with Western-style democracy, which encouraged individual development, guaranteed freedom, and the protection of human rights, and stressed equality, popular self-government, and national unity.

Pressure Politics
Modernization institutionalized the struggle for existence and the drive for profits on the part of individuals. Groups and organizations also served as a means in the drive for profits. As a part of democracy, the Constitution guaranteed the right of workers to organize. In the course of economic reconstruction and growth, negotiations between management and labor were institutionalized, and, as a result, the fruits of economic growth were distributed to workers and became purchasing power. This was an important element in the emergence of an affluent society. However, labor unions, which every spring stage the spring offensive, a large-scale "struggle," are represented by Sōhyō, made up mostly of unions in the public sector, and Dōmei,[1] made up mostly of unions in the private sector. Workers in small and medium firms are generally not represented by unions. And, even if they are organized, they are usually not involved in these struggles because of their conditions of employment. In addition, strikes in the transportation system, which is a trump card in these struggles, cause many people a good deal of inconvenience. Accordingly, when the Socialist members of the Diet, who are

1. Abbreviation for Zen Nihon Rōdō Sōdōmei (Japanese Confederation of Labor).

negotiating with the government behind the scenes along with leaders of Sōhyō, support these strikes as a legitimate right of workers, those who are not involved feel that this is willful behavior on the part of unions that are using mass tactics, and reject all this as class struggle based ideological politics.

Another example where interruption of service to the public was used as a lever, which, in the same way, elicited a negative response, was the Japan Medical Association's threat to pull out of the system of health insurance. "Pressure groups," "pressure activities," and "pressure politics" were technical terms translated from English, but they now not only describe reality but also have acquired a negative connotation of the tyranny of numbers, as a result of these psychological responses.

The Politics of Distribution

Presumably, democracy means a system in which everyone lives in harmony and all are to be treated equally. So a way had to be found to replace the system characterized by pressure politics based on large numbers, and where those who have integrity and remain silent get left out, with something that would assure the participation of all the people and equity for everyone. The solution was for everybody to use the channels leading to politicians who provide constituency service.

With the passage of time, many individuals who sought to promote their interests came to take advantage of their access to politicians. Aside from the activities of parliamentary politicians working hard to fulfill the needs and demands of their constituents in order to build up a following, voters found ways to be heard. For instance, when they went to lobby at the local government offices or to central government ministries, they learned, directly or indirectly, the effectiveness of support from their parliamentary representatives. Also, they heard from their friends, colleagues, work associates, and neighbors how helpful political contacts could be. They were also introduced to the representative by members of his support organization. All this represents the maturation of paternalistic politics and of distributive politics, in which pressure politics has been fragmented and popularized. As a result, the cases where innocent bystanders are victimized have been reduced in number, and people have become more tolerant of those who defend the right of workers to strike.

The Utilization of Parliamentary Politics

Economic growth has given society wealth and prosperity. Through paternalistic and distributive politics, parliamentary politics has also provided those who do not participate in growth industries with wealth and prosperity. For most people who are practical minded and interested in the here and now, it is self-evident that parliamentary government is effective. Of course, in practice, in many instances, parliamentary government consists of exchanging votes for funds from the central government's treasury for the purpose of helping local communities and businesses. The relationship between the voters, who are ordinary citizens, and parliamentary politicians cannot avoid being like, on the one hand, business relationships based on strong bonds of mutual obligation, and, on the other hand, a free and easy one. The situation to date is that the people have shown real ability in using the imported parliamentary system. The maintenance and development of the system in the future will depend on the efforts of the politicians themselves.

Unresolved Problems

It is hard to avoid distortions in the allocation of representatives to electoral districts. How many voters should each legislator represent in parliamentary government in industrialized societies? As a result of industrial development in cities, or the growth of new industrial cities, cities will tend to grow in size, either from natural population growth or from immigration. If the allocation of seats is left undisturbed for a long period of time, city districts will become underrepresented. By contrast, non-urban districts will become overrepresented because of outmigration, especially of youth, and slower natural increases in population. This tendency is found not only in Japan but everywhere, as long as industrialization produces population movements. Hence, unless a reallocation of seats, if necessary splitting or combining of districts, is undertaken frequently, the right of voters to equal representation will be violated.

In the case of Japan, the discrepancy in both the districts for the House of Representatives and the prefectures for the House of Councillors has grown tremendously. The difference between the overrepresented and underrepresented has reached as much as three to one or even five to one. Despite several Supreme Court rulings declaring this situation to be unconstitutional, the legislature and the ruling LDP have not taken steps to correct it. At present there is no law that requires that the allocation of seats be adjusted as a result of the national census, and the enactment of such a law has not occurred. This is because the number of LDP representatives and the number of districts where the LDP is strong are concentrated in the overrepresented non-urban seats. What steps that have been taken to remedy the imbalance has consisted of limited measures to increase the number of seats, rather than to undertake a wholesale reallocation of seats. If a reallocation were to occur without increasing the total number of seats, some legislators would necessarily lose their jobs. Those who resist change are not confined to legislators that would be affected. Under distributive politics, the number of representatives may be likened to the diameter of the pipe through which benefits would flow. So the constituents would also not favor reallocation. Thus, the distortion in representation in the National Diet goes with continued LDP dominance.

Distortions in Burdens
The mass media has repeatedly noted that the income tax burden is not equally shared. That is, those who earn wages or salaries have their income taxes withheld by their employers, and they have no way to scale down their reported income. By contrast, owners of small businesses and farmers are required to report incomes. It is widely believed that such people greatly underreport their earnings. Partly because of understaffing in the tax bureau, tax collectors are not able to investigate this underreporting and collect the proper amounts. There are several estimates of the income that is subject to taxes. If 90 percent of the income of the salaried people is being taxed, small business owners are believed to be taxed on about 60 percent of their income, while farmers are thought to be subject to about 40 percent.

Moreover, for lack of data, there is no way of determining the distribution of employed persons, small businessmen, and farmers in each of the electoral districts. But there is a strong impression that in the metropolitan and urban areas there are more employed persons and fewer farmers than in the rural areas. This would suggest that income and corporation taxes are collected in the urban areas and, through the politics of distribution, given to the rural areas in the form of grants and subsidies. The rural areas expect the government to pay while the cities feel they are being victimized. Against this psychological background, so far no one has dared to explain paternalistic, distributive politics on the principle that everybody should share benefits and burdens equally. Parliamentary politics has distributed economic and cultural benefits without providing a clear-cut rationale.

The Future of Culture

National culture in the high consumption society has as its basis the lifestyle of the urban white-collar class. This lifestyle has spread to the hinterland as a result of the traditional tendency to look up to the capital, and of paternalistic politics. But the relationship between the traditional village way of life and the rapidly spreading urban way have not been brought into harmony. It is clear that this will be a problem when one contemplates the future of the national culture in the context of the political weight that is given to the rural areas. This problem was inherited from the Tokugawa period and has persisted as a chronic disease throughout the period of Westernization following the Meiji Restoration.

It was military fascism that put a high value on the rural way of life and denounced urban life and culture as evil. Under democracy and civilization proclaimed by the Occupation, this was changed, and the agricultural, rural way of life was criticized as a bastion of feudalism. It was as a result of LDP dominance that urban life was left to develop haphazardly, cities were built without adequate planning, and commuters in Tokyo were forced into a "commuter hell" that required individuals to spend from one to two hours traveling one way to work. The problem that remains for the future is whether urban attitudes, such as the freedom to be what one wants to be and also be creative, be more internationalist, and enjoy life more, will be encouraged and become the centerpiece of our national culture.

Bias Toward Self-Containment

At present, Japan faces international difficulties. As a result of the Japan-U.S. Security Treaty, Japan became allied with the

United States and was placed under its nuclear umbrella. During the intervening 30 years, Japan has gradually built up its defense forces, while depending on the United States forces for its security. Also, during that interval, the balance of military power between the United States and the Soviets shifted from one of American superiority to one of equality. This has given rise to conflict over defense regarding Japan's share in the defense arrangements.

Moreover, during this period, Japan, using the formula of separation of politics and economics, has taken a passive role in world politics, but pursued foreign trade aggressively. Through import restrictions and export promotion, Japan achieved economic growth at home, while becoming a giant in foreign trade. Economic development soon led to a powerful export offensive, resulting in a foreign trade conflict with the United States and the EC countries. These countries demanded export restrictions on Japan's part, and the opening of the market to their goods and services. Thus, economic conflict was added to disagreements over Japan's role in its defense. All this has added a sense of urgency for the people to become more aware and knowledgeable about their independence and security, their existence and prosperity, and the need to pursue a diplomatic policy that can guarantee the attainment of these national goals.

Domestic Considerations First
Given this situation, it is perhaps inevitable that party politicians, because of political competition, should devote their attention and efforts to their own constituencies. It is normal for such politicians to put first priority on paternalistic politics, and not pay too much heed to matters concerning the international order, of which Japan is merely one member. Of course, this is an internationally common phenomenon that is not limited to Japan. Even when politicians stress the need to protect local enterprises from the point of view of constituency service and insist on import restrictions, they are not necessarily advocating protectionism as a matter of general policy to promote Japan's independence, security, existence, and prosperity.

Of course, from the traditional point of view, it is clear that international society is a battlefield where the strong dominate the weak. It is natural that, in order to survive, one should use the existing rules to one's maximum advantage. International society is there as a given fact. It is not a world of buddies, where independence, equality, and mutual aid are the rule. Politicians who belong to this tradition are bound to be perplexed when they are asked to provide a blueprint of a world society that seeks mutual benefits for all. Of course, politicians used to constituency service, money elections, and money politics are familiar with the power of money. One cannot say that money is of no use in international politics. The need to provide foreign aid for some countries is understood and has acquired the necessary support in domestic politics. But this willingness to provide foreign aid is not based on the conviction that we all belong to the human race. Nor does this willingness square with the purpose of foreign aid, which is to encourage the indigenous people to promote self-help.

In the traditional social order, individuals tend to avoid explicitly expressing their ideas and principles, and in social intercourse try to arrive at an emotional feeling of oneness with the other party. For that reason, when Japanese engage in diplomacy, there are often cases where things are not explicitly stated, which is not always effective with Western-style diplomacy, in which things are stated explicitly. It is also true that Japanese politicians do not make sufficient efforts to clearly explain to their voters, using explicit language, the problems that Japan is facing in international relations. Today, Japan has the problem of what the politicians and voters, both of whom are unprepared, should do to avoid proceeding on a collision course, in both domestic and foreign policy areas. Accordingly, as might be expected, the research activities of the bureaucrats and the reporting of the journalists are of great importance to the party politicians, the voters, and the future generations.

Chapter Six

Political Criticism

Violation of Rules

Ordinarily people's lives proceed smoothly on the basis of the system. People are not aware that their behavior is being governed by various systems. But there are marked variations in the degree to which individuals have internalized the norms that are to guide their actions. As a result, sometimes there are accidents and incidents stemming from the violation of rules that harm the person in question and others. When that happens, people become angry, morally indignant, or anxious about the violation itself, or about the harm that has been done to oneself or to other loved ones. Of course, it does not mean that people are angered about all violations. An individual's definition of his role is derived from the norms that he has internalized, and that definition, in many cases, gives meaning to his life.

Accordingly, violations of rules and the harm they do, depending on their nature, go beyond monetary calculations of damages incurred and give rise to an emotional response. In that event, people react in anger because the mechanisms that control one's impulses and urges are affected. Another way of putting it is that when violations and the harm that results have only a marginal effect on one's definition of his role and self-image, he does not get terribly excited. Even if the harm is great for the principals that are involved, it is not necessarily the case that third parties will be concerned, so long as it does not have much meaning to them.

Today, among violations of rules that people become most angry about are those committed by individuals who are professionally involved in politics. The constitutional order proclaims that the people are sovereign. So they constitute the primary force that makes government agencies function. Politics has become nationalized. In this way, the people have become politicized and the object of political education. Hence, their roles as people and as voters have become important in terms of giving meanings to their lives. Accordingly, violations of rules on the part of those who are in politics professionally—party politicians, bureaucrats, political commentators, and journalists—have come to arouse the anger of the people, who are not professionals. Such behavior has become the target of political criticism. It goes without saying that the freedom to express political criticism is guaranteed by law.

The Self-Perpetuation of the Order

The standard that the people apply when they engage in political criticism is not limited to specialized knowledge of the legal codes. It includes unstated understandings that are self-evident to the people, as well as their view of the order, a view with a long tradition, widely shared by the people and defining the role and self-image of many individuals. Thus, political criticism on the part of the people is not a call to revolution. Rather, it seeks to reaffirm the system by going back to its beginnings. It tends to preserve the present system, and in that sense, it advocates conservatism. From this point of view, political criticism expressed by the people, the political professionals, and the mass media represents a feedback mechanism. As a move to reset the system, the responsibility of those in charge will be made clear, and as punishment, personnel will be dismissed at various levels.

For the politicians, who assume that the system will continue to exist as a matter of course, and carry on their political struggles within that set of assumptions, the preservation of the system is not a meaningful goal. For them, having to resign a cabinet position and withdraw from politics is a great loss that can be measured. It is understandable that those cabinet ministers threatened with dismissal should resist strongly, saying, "I was made a scapegoat to save the prime minister." But from the point of view of maintaining the constitutional order and the parliamentary system, it is important that, when violations of the rules do occur, they be dealt with efficiently by criticism and debate, that order be restored quickly, and that the people not be psychologically disturbed. If this is not done, it is possible that it will eventually elicit a violent emotional response from the people, and will lead to demagogic politics that could render a fatal blow to constitutional parliamentary politics.

Seiron

In the traditional order, the system is *tatemae*. The arguments that those in control of the system make to seek compliance are *tatemae-ron* (formal argument). The protests that those who are being ruled make against the formal argument are *honne*. Not only political criticism but arguments that seek to correct the violations of rules in general are those that seek the agreement of the other party on the basis of institutional legitimacy, and so belong to *tatemae*. An argument that is *tatemae*, no matter who its advocate is, is a valid and just argument that cannot be refuted so long as its premises and contents are not altered, and so it must be accepted. Thus, in addition to the *tatemae* arguments put forth by the authorities seeking compliance, other *tatemae* arguments put forward from the side by colleagues who are equal in rank, and from below by those who are being ruled are possible. Against the *tatemae* argument from above, it is possible to resort to passive resistance that appeals to *honne*. But, against *tatemae* arguments from the side and from below that cannot be refuted, there is no system that applies *honne* in a valid way and so there is nothing one can do. Thus, *tatemae* arguments from the side and from below are often called *seiron* (sometimes with a negative connotation).[1]

Freedom of Speech

Those whose definition of role and self-image has been adversely affected by violations of rules become critics. That is, they tell others that they are aware of the violations, disapprove of them, blame the offenders, and seek the support of others who are around them. They advocate the restoration of the order by correcting the violations and imposing sanctions, and seek the help and support of those around them. In this way, criticism of violations seeks to organize allies and to increase their numbers and influence. In this sense, it is a social and political activity. It is also

---

1. Composed of *sei*, meaning true, valid, and *ron*, meaning thesis, essay, or argument. Thus, *seiron* is an argument or advocacy that is based on high principles.

social and political movement in that it seeks the submission of the offender to punishment. Accordingly, violations of rules and criticism of them create disturbances even in such small group situations as families. In the political world, such disturbances end up as conflicts between contending political groups. For this reason, in status-organized societies, such as feudal regimes, individuals were forbidden to comment on what their rulers were doing. On the other hand, as a system of criticism, there was the "remonstrance" system within the ruling strata. By contrast, in a constitutional order, the freedom to engage in political criticism is guaranteed by law.

Assembly and Organizations

Political criticism starts with securing the approval and support of others, even if, for example, its purpose is to recall a prefectural governor, and is connected with a power struggle. When, after many meetings, the number of supporters increases, there is an organizational meeting whose object is to launch a political movement. A president, secretary, treasurer, and other officers will be chosen. This kind of organizational structure is used by pressure groups and many citizens' organizations. In terms of numbers, there are more pressure groups than groups engaging in political criticism. It is easier for pressure groups to sustain themselves over a long period of time because, under the system of constituency service, in which votes at election time are exchanged through politicians for benefits from the central treasury, the rewards are substantial. By contrast, organizations that engage in political criticism and seek the punishment of offenders find it difficult to make their charges stick, and so they have a hard time achieving results. Consequently, they often fall by the wayside. Some, like those that undertake a recall movement, will disband after their mission is achieved. Thus, there are not many organizations that engage in political criticism. When it comes to political criticism, the role of the mass media and opposition parties is important.

Today, political criticism more often takes the form of telephoning and writing to the newspapers and magazines than having meetings and forming organizations. Those in charge of letters-to-the-editor sections of the mass media choose the letters for publication according to policies set by the newspaper, by the department, or by themselves. They provide a forum for political criticism, and for criticizing violations of rules in general. Also, the media will publish articles that criticize what is going on in politics. Among such articles are those that alert their readers, or that preempt an issue before the readers have even thought about it.

Also, the opposition parties raise issues on behalf of the people, by speaking in the halls of parliament, where they enjoy immunity from prosecution for their remarks. Since the opposition parties are engaged in a struggle for power, political criticism becomes criticism of the government. They criticize violations of rules of government as a means of engaging in the power struggle. Hence, opposition parties are sometimes criticized by the people who support the ruling party for engaging in criticism for criticism's sake, or for having no constructive alternatives to make. Finally, as already noted, political criticism on the part of opposition parties and the mass media represents a feedback mechanism for correcting violations of rules and restoring the order.

Types of Political Criticism

Common Sense

When people engage in political criticism, they apply common-sense standards. A vision of the order based on the social system is commonly shared among the people. Included in this vision of the order is the behavior expected of those who are in politics professionally. It is convenient to look at the behavior of these professionals from two points of view: procedural norms and substantive or policy goals. The former might be called "clean politics" or ethics of the professionals, and the latter "good politics" or the distinction between good politics and bad politics. Of course, this distinction is for analytical purposes only. The two are not carried out separately.

Clean Politics
The first norm that is part of the ethical standards of the professionals is fairness or equity. Unfairness, partiality, and favoritism can be criticized as violations of rules. The demand for impar-

tiality, on the one hand, leads to an expectation of fairness and nonpartisanship, which is the stated policy of the mass media, and also to the dislike of and demand for the abolition of partisanship, which means a subtle dissatisfaction with parliamentary politics. On the other hand, the demand for impartiality also puts value on uniformity, and so it represents an implicit approval of the autocratic bureaucracy, which is supposed to be above partisanship.

The second norm of professional ethics has to do with "being selfless" and "clean." What is demanded is clean politics, conducted out in the open, where a professional does not use one's position as a means of feathering one's own nest. The abuse of power, promoting one's own interests, enjoying special privileges, corruption, and money politics are forms of violations of rules. The commonly shared understanding is the understanding of ordinary individuals who approve of *honne*. Thus, such understanding will not go so far as to condemn what is considered "natural" in politics, but will criticize and demand punishment of violations of rules that go too far.

The third norm is that a politician will devote full effort to the job. Strict observance of the rules is expected, and being habitually late to work, leaving before quitting time, absenteeism, playing golf on workdays, and going on sightseeing trips while on official trips are subject to criticism. Also subject to criticism are accidents, incidents, and problems that are evidence of laxness on the job, laziness, errors, and lack of ability. And if one does not accept responsibility for these misdeeds, that, too, will be criticized.

Good Politics

When it comes to policy outputs, there is the expectation that policy makers will avoid bad politics, and engage in good politics, which will bring stability to the people's lives. The first requirement is to guarantee the lives and security of the people. Policies that will assure the long-term independence and security, existence and prosperity of the entire nation, and policies that will guarantee the daily existence and comfort of individuals are not always compatible. For example, there is a problem as to whether industrial accidents and natural disasters are caused by human failure or not. If accident prevention measures are shown to have been inadequate, there will be criticism that devotion to the job was lax. If government agencies put too much effort into accident prevention, then it would lead to an excessively protective administrative state.

The second requirement of good politics is the assurance of prosperity for the people. When it comes to economic policies to produce prosperity, there is the connection between the Japanese economy and the world economy. Also, there is the relationship among big business and the small- and medium-sized enterprises. From the point of view of policy makers, too much is expected of economic policy to assure prosperity. But it is a fact of life that policy makers are expected to overcome recessions and unemployment and guarantee prosperity. Thus, bad times, depressions, and economic crises are a source of political criticism.

Laws and Common Understandings

Political professionals are expected to base their behavior and perform their functions in accordance with law. It is understood that the preservation of the Constitution and the legal structure are their professional responsibilities. However, acting according to the law and performing one's job in accordance with law cannot be approved unconditionally. For instance, the application of Article 14 of the Public Procurator's Office law to the 1954 shipbuilding scandal has been the subject of a good deal of political discussion since then.[2] Also, with regard to requests for reconsideration that have been filed in criminal cases, a certain number of them have had the support of the mass media and of the people. Another example would be doubts about the strict application of laws regarding prostitution, and drinking and smoking by minors. If laws regarding these matters are too strictly applied, it will lead to criticism that things are being carried too far. The widely shared understandings, and the news pages of newspapers that reflect such understandings, carry certain political weight in terms of the applicability of the legal system that incorporates elements imported from the West. In interpreting and applying the laws to cases, their applicability in terms of

2. A number of shipbuilding and marine transportation firms were suspected of bribing bureaucrats and some LDP leaders to secure large government loans. Among those implicated was Satō Eisaku, then Secretary-General of the LDP. Mr. Yoshida, the prime minister, used his authority under Article 14 to order the postponement of Satō's arrest for fear that such action would lead to the fall of his cabinet.

common sense, and their "social" authority and legitimacy are considered.

Political authorities are expected to use their discretion in applying the law, taking into consideration common understandings as an unwritten law. On the one hand, legally unauthorized bureaucratic intervention in the form of administrative guidance is demanded, and when the political authorities go against these expectations, they are criticized for being hard headed. On the other hand, compassionate justice that ignores the legal codes, the kind that was shown by Ōoka, a famous magistrate in the city of Edo during the Tokugawa period, is sought, and when this is not displayed by the authorities, they are criticized for being inhuman and devoid of blood and tears.

Special Types of Criticism

Common understandings do not represent the only basis for political criticism. Expert knowledge possessed by specialists also forms a basis for political criticism. For example, the question of whether the government agencies acted in accordance with the law can become an issue in political criticism, as well as among political parties. Because there are, among parliamentary politicians, a number who are lawyers and have had legal experience, political criticism and the power struggle among political parties often takes the form of legal arguments, and develops into a legal dispute. With respect to Article 9 of the Constitution, the maintenance of the Security Treaty with the United States, and strengthening of the defense forces, the LDP has taken the position that these measures are constitutional.

As a result, the controversy over the constitutionality of Japanese foreign and defense policies has divided the ruling and opposition parties within the National Diet. The essential points of these controversies have been reported and interpreted by the mass media. These controversies have also been injected into numerous Supreme Court decisions. However, debate over the Constitution also occurred before the war. For example, there were legal controversies over such matters as the control of the budget by the House of Representatives, the joint responsibility of the cabinet, the independence of the supreme command, the relationship between military command and administration, and

Minobe's theory of the Emperor as an organ of the state. These controversies were a form of political criticism as well as a manifestation of power struggles over political issues.

Technical Discussions

The functions performed by the various government agencies affect a wide range of matters pertaining to the lives of the people. In the performance of these functions, specialized knowledge, not only of legal science, but of economics, management, the humanities and sciences, engineering, agricultural science, medicine, and pharmacology are utilized. Thus, political criticism must in many instances be based on technical knowledge provided by these specialists. The response to such criticism takes the form of technical rebuttal. There are many examples where political criticism based on specialized knowledge has elicited a technical rebuttal in that specialty, and where a political problem was settled by a specialized decision that only specialists could understand. Examples are nuclear power generation, radiation, building materials, civil engineering works, foodstuffs, public health, carcinogenic materials, exhaust fumes, and atmospheric pollution. In establishing and revising standards relating to the foregoing, technical discussions were involved in many cases.

With the development of an industrial civilization, the mass media, in response to the public's curiosity, has endeavored to provide the most up-to-date knowledge about science and technology. The people, too, were happy to buy and use the products of modern technology as a blessing of civilization. However, in order to enjoy this blessing, all that was necessary was to flick a switch. Knowledge about science and technology was not necessary. Moreover, despite the efforts of the mass media, there is a wide gap between the specialized knowledge possessed by the experts in a particular field and the ordinary knowledge possessed by the general public. Accordingly, the general public has no alternative but to accept without question the authority of the specialists, and their scientific and technical views, and to give in to their technical decisions.

From the point of view of the public, this is the establishment of an enlightened despotism by specialists. What gives legitimacy to this despotism are the benefits derived from the blessings of civilization. When this enlightened despotism meets with technical failures and leads to political criticism, such criticism may be viewed as a complaint that the specialists had not devoted themselves fully to their jobs. From another point of view, it is a criticism of the failure to supply the blessings of civilization. In many instances, the specialists will say that at present there are limits to science and technology. The assertion that their abilities are limited and so are their responsibilities absolves them of any responsibility for the situation. The combination of limited ability and unlimited authority, needless to say, is a characteristic of the world of politics.

The Believers

Government by Truth

Seiron is based on the vision of order. It detects violation of the order and criticizes it. By contrast, there are doctrines that are based on the Truth, and reject systems and orders that go against them. They not only advocate a "correct" order that is consistent with the Truth, but also, as a part of what they advocate, they criticize violations of rules taking place in one's presence. In this book, we will use the term orthodoxy to designate the doctrine that relies upon the Truth. In the case of those who advocate a true order, presumably they became such advocates when they were possessed by the Truth. When the Truth is the traditional one, the advocates have no need to preach a new faith. All they must do is to appeal for a return to the traditional faith that has been shared in that society. An appeal to return to the past indicates that there has been a rejection of tradition. So, the appeal to return to it means that it has more or less a characteristic of fundamentalism.

By contrast, there are instances where a new religious authority or Truth enters from outside of the traditional faith. In that instance, news of an event occurring in a foreign country could become the occasion for revelation of a new Truth. Also, pamphlets and books and other forms of published material could produce the same effect. In that case, the advocates of a new order must preach both a new faith and a true order that is based on that faith.

A classic example of someone who advocates a revival of a true order are the prophets in the Old Testament. Jehovah, the creator God of the Jewish religion, gave the Ten Commandments to the people of Israel and asked them to obey these commandments loyally. When the king and the people of Israel abandoned the faith and disobeyed the laws, it was the prophet who received the command from Jehovah to tell them to return to the faith and laws. At that point, the laws themselves represented an order that was different from the on-going rules of the historical society at that time. It was in the context of this dualistic structure that the prophet directly received the words of criticism and orders from the God, Jehovah, and spoke to the king and the people. Elijah conveyed to King Ahab the Lord's denunciation of a murder (1 Kings 21:19), and Amos said, "But let judgment run down as waters, and righteousness as a mighty stream." (Amos 5:2)

The Politics of Truth

In the course of secularization, God, Jehovah, gave way to Truth. In the place of prophets, there emerged advocates of Truth, who are in touch with Truth, and convey its words to the people. And the people who hear these words of Truth also are in touch with Truth and become its followers. In this way, the advocates of Truth increase the size of their following, and also present the true order based on Truth, and ask its acceptance. They compare the existing system and order to the standards of Truth, and find the former to be wanting. They advocate social change that would institutionalize the true order. The prophets, now secularized, became advocates of Truth as well as advocates of social change. There are many examples where, with modernization and the spread of literacy and the art of printing, one pamphlet or book would convey the Truth, win over many people, and pave the way for social progress. Moreover, as people's lives become more complicated, there are numerous instances where they got the Truth in the form of scientific and technical knowledge. Since the people found such knowledge to be useful, the Truth often paved the way for change relating to various aspects of life.

Now, the advocates of Truth have a monopoly on judging the truthfulness of the order based on Truth. When the true order is achieved in practice, the advocates of Truth have some choices to make. That is, first of all, should they cooperate with the ruling authorities and maintain the system based on Truth, or second, should they remain apart from the ruling group and criticize them and stand in opposition? A third possibility would be for the advocates of Truth themselves to split into two factions: one that allies itself with the ruling group, and another that stands in opposition. Just as there are false prophets, there can be advocates of falsehoods, or demagogues. Indeed, many things rest on the distinction between these two. This is the lesson of human history.

Parliamentary Politics

Constitutional parliamentary government demilitarized the struggle for power by substituting elections. Parliamentary politics is characterized by two features. It is money politics that requires vast sums of money for election purposes, and it is word politics that uses verbal explanations to win the support of the voters. Arguments made orally or via printed materials, and public opinion that is influenced by verbal and written expression represent the tools and stages of politics. Depending on how one characterizes voters, the politics of words divides into two types. One is to assume that voters are endowed with a high level of intelligence, and that they are rational in their choice of goals. In this case, a kind of social-engineering approach is possible, using legislation as the technical instrument. In that event, as in the case of academic lectures, intellectual materials form the core of word politics.

The other alternative is to assume that voters are biased, given to defending their interests, and are easily moved by emotional appeals and agitation. In that event, rabble-rousing sentiments are expressed. This is the end product of what Max Weber called charisma of eloquence. And if the eloquent words of the advocates of Truth cum advocates of social change are indictments that reach the inner hearts of the listeners, it will shake them emotionally. Thus, depending on circumstances, Truth will organize not only the intellect but also the emotions and impulses. The followers of these advocates, whom Eric Hoffer called True Believers, will engage in the politics of passion, and give rise to the world of chaos of violence and destruction.

Japan's Orthodoxy

Seiron of the Repose of Souls

In Japan's tradition, there is no explicit statement of the true order, as there is in the case of the Ten Commandments. But, of course, that does not mean that there is no true order. One type of order is related to serving the divine spirits and numinous powers that move freely within this world. The spirits of human beings both dead and alive are also included in the divine spirits. It is taken as a matter of course in the religious beliefs that the enmity of the spirits of the living and the dead will bring a curse. Accordingly, in order to avoid enmity, one should not go against the feelings of the living and the dead. One must give priority to satisfying their feelings. When engaged in negotiations, one usually tells the other party, "I understand very well how you feel about this matter," and try to pacify the feelings of the other party. With regard to the dead, the repose of the soul of someone who has met a violent death away from his birthplace is terribly important.

The Yasukuni Shrine, where the Emperor worships, was established for the repose of the souls of the soldiers and sailors who had died in action. Moreover, with regard to the negotiations with America in 1941, one of the conditions put forward by the United States was the withdrawal of Japanese troops from the Chinese mainland. The Japanese army rejected this condition on the ground that "if we withdraw, we would be letting down the spirits of the dead soldiers." This was a *seiron* that no one could rebut. With respect to the living, the tragic harm that is the result of misgovernment, and the accumulation of the bitterness that is not assuaged, leads to the formation of groups of angry people who are victimized as well as other groups of people who join in the indictment. Both of these are to be regarded as a manifestation of the maltreated spirits of the living and the dead.

These groups become supreme judges of the situation in this world, and attack the government agencies and firms that are responsible for the harm that was done. As a result of journalistic reporting and campaigns, these attacks develop into political movements. Thus, there are various movements, such as those comprised of victims of the nuclear bombing of Hiroshima and Nagasaki, and victims of industrial pollution. Since the demands of the true order are for satisfactory consideration being given for one's feelings, and for the repose of the souls of the dead, it is natural that if the government agencies and firms do not understand the feelings of the victims, negotiations break down.

Truth from the West

Even though there were no prophets in traditional faith, with modernization there came Truth and advocates of Truth. In the course of modernization and Westernization following the Meiji Restoration, there appeared in 1871 a translation of Smiles's *Self Help*, and in 1872 the *Encouragement of Learning* by Fukuzawa Yukichi.[3] Through these books, many people came into touch with Truth, and the way was shown for the advancement of oneself, as well as for the country as a whole. Also during the freedom and people's rights movement, Ueki Emori's[4] *On Popular Rights and Freedom* was issued in 1879, and the translation of Rousseau's *Social Contract* followed. These works also let the people in on Truth. In Japan, where the literacy rate was already high, and where printing techniques became quite advanced, printed materials contributed greatly to the advance of civilization following the Meiji Restoration. In the process of Westernization, Western civilization itself was considered a true order. The reading of the original works imported from the West and the accumulation of Western knowledge represented the wellspring of authority. When standards in Japan did not reach those found in the West, there emerged the *seiron* of Western learning that criticized what prevailed. Finally, many people who came to depend on the Truth in Western civilization were able to improve various aspects of their daily lives.

Despite this importation of Western civilization, Christianity, which was the source of the traditional beliefs of the West, was pretty much excluded. In 1873, the ban against Christianity was lifted, and Catholic and Protestant missionaries became active. But its rejection by the people has remained strong, and even though a century has passed since then, the number of Christian converts is less than one percent of the population. However,

3. Fukuzawa Yukichi (1835–1901) was a well-known figure in introducing Western civilization into Japan. He was a journalist and the founder of Keio University.
4. A popular movement to try to force the Meiji government to establish parliamentary government. It started in the early 1870s and lasted to about 1884. Ueki Emori (1857–92) was a leading theorist of the movement.

Christianity has made many contributions. Education in the schools, particularly of women, the anti-prostitution and the women's liberation movements, hospitals and social work, social welfare programs, and social and labor movements have been strongly influenced by Christianity.

With the coming of the twentieth century, the intellectual level rose, and there was a move to delve into the inner world of human beings. During the World War I period, social and labor problems became important. The publication in 1916 of Kawakami Hajime's *Tale of Poverty* pointed up the problem.[5] The success of the Russian revolution in October of 1918 led to the influx of Maxism and made it one of the branches of the socialist movement in Japan. In the 1920s and 1930s, Marxism, to its believers, became the Truth that would provide an overall solution to the problems of one's inner life and social and labor problems. The number of young people and students who believed in this Truth and joined the revolutionary movement was not small. From the point of view of practical politics, the believers of Marxism, as members of the Japan Communist party and front organizations and as fellow travelers, were, as part of the plan to defend the Soviet Union in international politics, under the control of the Soviet Communist Party and the Comintern. Domestically, the believers of the Truth were hunted down by the Special Higher Police and the Japan Communist Party disappeared.

Politics of Divine Judgment

Missionary Work and Learning

There are two ways in which believers of the Truth can get into action. One is to increase the number of believers. The other is to attack those who deny the Truth and reject it. The way to increase the number of believers is through missionary work. Those who have not accepted the Truth will have some exposure to it if they attend lecture meetings and study groups organized by the believers. At these meetings, and on other occasions, they will be given newspapers, magazines, pamphlets, and books, and

5. Kawakami Hajime (1879–1946) was a professor at Kyoto Imperial University and an influential teacher and writer of Marxist theory.

will be encouraged to study them on their own. These materials have been to some extent systematically organized so that one will begin with elementary materials and proceed to the more difficult, arriving at the core of the Truth at the end. Even though one may be permitted to join the band of believers on the basis of having mastered the elementary materials, the study process will not come to an end. As believers of the Truth, they will be required to engage in a lifetime of study.

When the rankings on the basis of the mastery of the material, and the pecking order in the organization coincide, the leaders of the organization become, at the same time, the top interpreters of the Truth. Power struggles within the organization of believers or the political movement wing of the organization involve splitting into factions, which is paralleled by differing interpretations of the Truth. Another way of putting it is that fine distinctions in the interpretation of the Truth correspond to differences in policy line or in changes in leadership.

Words of Admonition
Those who do not know the Truth may be ignorant, but they are not the enemy. The enemy are those who attack the band of believers, openly scoff at the Truth, and reject the faith. They are nothing but mistaken, deceitful, and vicious clods. There is no middle ground between Truth and lies, and so the enemy must be annihilated. When they attack the enemy of Truth, the believers of Truth become one with Truth, and become manifestations on this earth of the eternal Truth itself. And the words used to harangue the enemy must be so sharp and extreme as to cause his face to turn white. In this case, the verbal attack is almost warlike. But if one accepts the interpretation that speeches represent another form of fighting with guns, then one can have the equivalent of military exploits in speeches.

As a result of the transfer of the conflict between the Meiji government and the movement for freedom and popular rights to the halls of parliament, speeches and questions in the National Diet are interpreted to be wars of words. Speeches in the parliament became occasions to confront and attack the government like on the battlefield. The so-called bomb questions in the National Diet are an extension of this. And the method of defense designed to confine the damage to the minimum are the perfunctory responses made by the government to the questions from the opposition.

The Charisma of the Mystagogue

It is not enough for a political movement that seeks to establish the true order based on the Truth to increase the number of its followers and publicly attack the enemy. Such a movement will make an appeal to the people by promising to establish an ideal society that, for instance, would get rid of poverty, unemployment, and recessions, or eliminate poor health and conflict. But, in order to get the many people who do not believe in the Truth to accept this promise and support the political movement, it is necessary to make use of the traditional authority that the people do understand. As we have already explained in the possessed individuals' code, there is a system of acquiring magical powers to control the spirits. This is done by mystagogues who abandon the routines of ordinary life and take up ascetic practices, whereby they experience a religious rebirth. And these mystagogues, in response to the demand of the secular world, say their prayers that summon these magical powers, and provide the material secular benefits that are sought. Thus, the daily performance of ascetic practices and the efficacy of magical powers go together.

The socialist movement of the 1920s and 1930 developed in the foregoing style of the mystagogues. That is, the socialists refused to take up the more usual pursuit of success characteristic of students and graduates; carried out their ascetic practices in the face of repression by the Special Higher Police; rejected luxuries and continued their studies and political activities in circumstances of poverty; and led the kind of private lives not hidden from view, but there for their fellow travelers and sympathizers to see. This kind of lifestyle and the realities of the socialist movement gave to individual socialists the kind of charisma and authority that the mystagogues traditionally enjoyed. It converted those who did not believe in the Truth to become followers of and believers in individual socialists. Because this tradition has been carried over into the postwar period that saw the liberation of the socialist movement, people have come to expect left-wing politicians to engage in clean politics, and lead austere personal lives. Accordingly, when politicians are implicated in scandals, exposed by the mass media, that involve money and/or women, the disappointment felt by the people and party supporters is greater when the guilty party belongs to the left wing than to the conservatives.

Yet, the ordinary people are both realistic and practical, and prefer to take a balanced view of this. Hence, such people do not fall for the promise to build an ideal society because that runs counter to common sense. They recognize the mystagogue charisma of the socialist members whom they know personally, respect them as fine people, and even vote for them. But their judgment is that these socialists, to the extent they are clean, are also unworldly, and not very effective in the real world of politics. They view the activities of the left wing as a political diversion. This is how the ordinary people see it.

Politics as Judgment

As mentioned earlier, political criticism begins with violations of rules and the harm it does. But ordinary people do not become involved in politics, even though they may criticize it. But a few people do volunteer their services. This is contrary to the dictates of common sense, and it means joining the world of political activities. So long as involvement in a political movement is done in one's leisure time and is not paid, one is a volunteer activist in the true sense. There are relatively few volunteers, and political activity that is started on one's own initiative requires much time and money. Eventually, volunteers are forced to make a choice between their work and political volunteer activities. When they choose between their work or politics as their profession their status as a volunteer ceases.

The world of politics is one where people make a living at it. Those who are in politics professionally, in order to preserve their position of leadership externally, and to increase their power internally, will work hard to organize volunteers and bring them under their influence. It is not easy for political activities carried on only by volunteers to produce results without the protection of the professionals. As a result of the tendency for building organizational structures, when volunteers choose politics as a profession, they are often recruited into existing political organizations, such as political parties or factions, or as staff members of support groups of individual politicians. Labor unions and student organizations are notable as recruiting grounds for professionals.

Activists as Energy Per Se

Sometimes when volunteers get into politics, they are pushed into it by their raw inner energies. They engage in a kind of formless, directionless action of violence. The prototype of this kind of behavior was the action of the young samurai on the eve of the Meiji Restoration. They left their feudal lords and joined the forces pushing to restore power to the Imperial Court. The next outburst of energy took the form of direct-action members of the movement for freedom and people's rights. They then reappeared as right-wing agitators, adventurers on the Asian mainland, and hangers-on in the political world. They became part of the direct action group in the conservative parliamentary parties. This direct-action group became one of the sources of parliamentary politicians at various levels. The style of the direct-action group was also seen in the junior army officers who attempted coups in the 1930s.

People in this category are activists who love intrigues and feel they are outside of the system. They tend to be given to the use of violence. Since they are young and full of energy, they like wine and women. They are known for lamenting over their wine glasses and for bombastic talk. They never become accustomed to ordinary lifestyles. They are not able to control their energies and are given to frenzy and reckless courage and are even given to lawlessness. Their political activities are dominated by unplanned violence rather than long-term planning, and the desire to start something as an avant-garde of society. Their political activities incline toward the use of violence. They might try to disrupt political rallies with violence and, when pushed, might engage in assassination attempts. It was natural that in the 1930s ordinary people felt the manifestation of chaos of destruction and death in the face of violent right-wing activities.

The Politics of Judgment

Another form of political participation on the part of volunteer activists is to be called by the Truth. From the point of view of someone who has become one with Truth, what is important for bringing to this world a true order that is prescribed by the Truth is not self-reflection and self-reform on their part but the reformation of others who do not accept the Truth. Aggressive extrapunitive behavior that is directed to others will presently lead to bloodshed and bring about rule by force. Politics guided by this kind of Truth often leads to the worst kind of brutal politics. Bands of believers in Truth are manifestations on this earth of eternal Truth by their own definition. Therefore, cruel violent actions perpetrated in the name of Truth represent the "judgment of god" and "punishment by Heaven."

From the point of view of ordinary people who do not share in this belief in the Truth, "punishment by Heaven" is another form of the chaos of death and destruction. Violent behavior that is legitimized by the Truth becomes the application of force that is devoid of judgment and self-control, and takes the form of sadistic behavior that uses excessive force. Such was the grilling and torture by the special high police. The assertion that human beings, who are finite, are manifestations of Truth cannot be supported from the point of view of outsiders. In order to avoid self-awareness and self-reflection, and to perpetuate the system of forceful rule, believers of Truth must, by means of strongly held beliefs, fortify their inner world, and freeze their sensibilities, imagination, curiosity, and even their spontaneity. This is what the people observed in the first half of the 1940s.

Chapter Seven

Ideological Politics

The Advance of the Believers

Words

Seiron is to criticize and seek remedy for violations of rules from the side or from below. Those who advocate *seiron* and work for it politically are the *seiron* group. Political activity is not only an isolated, intellectual endeavor. It is also a process to organize many people to cooperate, and in this sense, is an activity that seeks to mobilize even their emotions, impulses, and urges. In their daily activities, the political actions of the *seiron* group take on, to some extent, the characteristic of the politics of passion. When the features of the historical society are set, the *seiron* group also has a tendency to become doctrinaire. In this way, the *seiron* group, in their political activities, tends to become more like a band of believers of Truth.

The advocates of truth cum advocates of change will also reach the point in the course of their political actions where they cannot ignore questions of strategy. When the lone voice in the wilderness adopts a strategic approach, extreme charges are toned down, and attempts are made to persuade by mild discourse. Thus, in terms of political activity, the band of believers tends to become like the *seiron* group. In short, in terms of their concrete political methods, the band of believers and the *seiron* group become very similar. Hence, in what follows, I have, for the sake of convenience, taken up both groups under the rubric of *seiron* group and will explain their political activities.

Explanatory Literature

When the *seiron* group engages in political activity, whether it is to correct violations of rules or to establish a true order, they have a goal or a series of goals. To this extent, the *seiron* group has "policies," and they are different from the policies of those who want power for power's sake. Accordingly, *seiron* groups, as a means to explain their activities and to expand their influence, distribute literature describing their objectives. The tactics of the various groups are not uniform, but vary, depending on their strength, political background, and financial resources.

One form of activity is to hand literature to friends, and the material is explained orally or mailed to a limited number of people. Another is to hold mass meetings, have parades, hold press conferences, and by such means get their movement reported by the mass media. They may also prepare all kinds of literature and mail them out at great expense. From the point of view of the recipients, this literature tells them what the *seiron* group is all about. So they may keep it for a long time even after the issuer has forgotten about the "promissory note," and use it to judge whether the *seiron* group has kept its promises.

Persuasion

The *seiron* group expands its strength by converting outsiders into participants and supporters. One way of achieving this is to persuade by the spoken or printed word. In situations where the *seiron* group is strong, and the opposition is weak, persuasion begins with friendly or affectionate persuasion. In a reverse situation, there is a tendency to use angry accusations. Friendly and affectionate persuasion is a method that *seiron* groups use to preach penitence and submission. Not only *seiron* demands from above, but *seiron* demands from below are often made in face-to-face meetings of the two parties. Submission to the *seiron* group is achieved if the other party repents and says "we were at fault," "we made a mistake," in response to the *seiron* group's sincere and very considerate efforts to persuade the latter. And with this the pursuit comes to an end, and those who have changed their minds now join the *seiron* group or support it and start life anew.

If efforts at friendly and affectionate persuasion are rejected, and there is no response but silence for a long time, these efforts are repeated several times. If the rejection continues, the *seiron* group suffers a loss of self-confidence, their definition of their role and self-image threatened. So they move in the direction of angry accusations. Toward the other party that sulks and rejects its sincere overtures, the *seiron* group vents its anger and uses harsh words and, at times, might resort to violence.

There is another kind of angry accusation, that is, planned attack by the weak *seiron* group on the opponent which is much stronger. The *seiron* group, which would have been defeated if it had resorted to force, uses the authority of order and of the Truth as a shield, and attacks the enemy stronghold with shells in the form of words. This is a barrage that is carefully planned with its probable outcomes meticulously calculated. The enemy, suffering from psychological blows, might surrender, or it might disregard the attack. These are the likely outcomes of psychological and verbal warfare.

Seiron and Zokuron

What the *seiron* group advocates cannot be refuted unless one attacks their premises. This is because their position is based on the reasoning that has as its premise both the order and the Truth. If one denies the premises, it is possible that one will be expelled from society as one who does not believe in the order and the Truth. Accordingly, in arguing with the *seiron* group, one must preface his remarks by saying, "This is *zokuron*," [literally earthly, secular, or worldly argument] and enlarge the area under discussion by changing its contents and premises. Thus, the *zokuron* group is one that opposes the *seiron* group without giving into it and uses a different approach to the arguments. Ordinarily, the core of what the *zokuron* stands for, in terms of the power struggle, is "We don't like to submit to the *seiron* group." The *seiron* group's response to the attitude of the *zokuron* group is that the latter is selfish and self-willed, and that it is refusing to face the Truth. If the *zokuron* group answers that "we just don't like it," then that is the end of it.

But sometimes the *zokuron* group might shift the argument toward the utility of the *seiron* group's position, and refute it on the grounds that what they advocate is not practical. Such arguments as follows are used: "*Seiron* is inconsistent with the reality of human life"; "The arguments are false, they are not realistic";

or "*Seiron* leads to unbearable hardship." In rebuttal, the *seiron* group shifts the argument to the level of obedience to the Truth and says to them: "That just shows you don't want to give in"; "Unbearable hardship is already taken into account"; or "We realize that we all have to make sacrifices." In response, the *zokuron* group denies that their stand is just an excuse to refuse obedience, and elaborates in detail how great the hardship and sacrifice could be if the *seiron* group prevails. Finally, the *zokuron* group puts forward an ethical argument, that is, "human beings have to live," "for human beings, existence comes before order and Truth."

Thus, the conflict between the *seiron* and *zokuron* groups takes the form of both a political contest, between "Submit to us" and "We don't want to," and an ideological conflict between "living in the true way," and "living in order to exist." Since living in order to exist is what the ordinary individual wants, potentially, those who are on the side of the *zokuron* group are in the majority. This shows that the "domination" of the *seiron* group tends to depend to some extent on threats and force, and that its dependency on threats and force increases as time goes on, as demonstrated in the early 1940s.

Compulsion

Compulsion to Be Silent

Since what the *seiron* group advocates has order and Truth as its premises, it is superior to other arguments in terms of legitimating their right to rule. In order for those who are in positions of dominance in groups and organizations to overcome potential resistance or opposition and thus reaffirm the ruler-ruled relationship, they may temporarily act as if they are the *seiron* group and perform political rituals that serve to affirm that there is no resistance to its dominance.

The ritual, say a meeting, demonstrates group unity if there is no potential resistance or opposition. But, in this instance, potential opponents might be intimidated in advance ("It will be to your advantage to keep quiet") or at the meeting harassed by a lot of noise or threatened by the display of weapons. And with the announcement that "I presume no one opposes," the dominant group reaffirms for the time being the position of the *seiron* group and the submission of the others attending the meeting. Participants who were forced to submit feel that, even though they had to attend the meeting, they kept their silence and did not give their positive approval. With firm inward reservations, they feel that at some other time and place they might oppose even publicly: "What is unbearable is unbearable. We had better protect our daily lives by ourselves."

People divide their attitudes into two layers. The upper layer, the part that is made public, is *tatemae*, and the lower part that pertains to life situations satisfies the *honne*. We mentioned the case of feigned obedience. Those who participate in the political ritual also engage in this feigned obedience. Accordingly, the act of affirming the ruler-ruled position by means of political rituals of this kind loses its effectiveness as time goes on, and *tatemae*, also, comes to exist only in name.

Compulsory Responses

Compelling people to be silent means that potential opponents cannot be smoked out. An old method, used against Christians in the Tokugawa period, of exposing resisters and opponents was by forcing people to make a clear response by *fumie*, or treading bronze plaques decorated with Christian icons. In this case, people in a position of dominance set up two possible responses: the acceptance of the *tatemae* and the opposition of the *tatemae*, and individuals were compelled to make a choice. This is the *fumie* method.

Examples of choices between two alternatives are actions of a ritualistic nature, such as worshiping at Shintō shrines, saluting the flag, and participating in group rituals. Examples of choices in symbolic behavior are worshiping the portrait of the Emperor, as in the so-called Uchimura Kanzō incident,[1] and dealing with symbols that represent the Truth. Signing a petition that states the *seiron* position and giving money to *seiron* fund raising are examples of supportive behavior. Examples of choices in public-relations type of behavior are repeating orally the slogans of the *seiron* group and quoting *seiron* phrases in written material. In this way, in the eyes of the dominant group, individuals are divided

1. Uchimura Kanzō (1861–1930), a Christian and teacher at the First Higher School, refused to bow to the Emperor's portrait in a school ceremony in 1891 as was required. This caused an uproar, and he was fired from his job.

into two groups: those who agree with the *tatemae* and support it publicly and those who disagree and refuse to support it.

Even though the *seiron* group is not part of the ruling group, by using the *fumie* method, it can unilaterally force its opponents into two camps, the supporters and resisters. The latter, as the enemy, is made out to be subversive and could be the object of persecution, and on occasion might even be forced into "martyrdom." And, when this kind of persecution becomes more frequent, those who have openly accepted the *seiron* begin to include more potential resisters. This is because when freedom becomes more restricted and one is forced into action of a supportive nature, one begins to resort more to feigned obedience.

Moreover, when, in the midst of a threat of persecution, members of groups and organizations become convinced that verbal and written statements are being used as a *fumie* for judging one's loyalty, the unimpeded transmission of objective reports about the real state of affairs becomes difficult. As a result, members of groups and organizations, both in internal and external communications, will merely say what is expected of them. The flow of objective information will be cut off, thereby making action difficult and even threatening the very existence of groups and organizations.

Conquest

From the point of view of the *seiron* group, those who oppose them represent an evil power that refuses to admit that it is going against the order and the Truth. Such people could have been good individuals but are now rotten to the core. They have lost their human qualities and need no longer be treated as human beings. On the basis of this conclusion, the *seiron* group now takes the offensive and brandishes the sword of righteousness against its opponents. And, as indicated before, the "divine wrath" that pits the absolute good against absolute evil takes the form of unlimited violence. Violence, as a political technique, is also a method of making threats, so excessive terrorism is usually not necessary. Many people, under an atmosphere of threat and violence, in order to maintain their lives, keep quiet or accept things passively or even resort to flattery. The *seiron* group takes advantage of this silent acceptance to stay in control. In the case of a nation, the press reports that "the dark clouds have dissipated, the sun is shining, and the people's lives have changed for the better."

When the *seiron* group achieves victory, there are changes in the system. What the group advocates is transferred from the spiritual realm to the real secular world, becomes the law of the land, and is incorporated into the lives of the ordinary people. As one might expect, behavior that is contrary to this true order develops, and a new *seiron* group that is upset by that behavior comes into existence. Everyone on this earth, including the *seiron* group itself, is finite.

The Growth of Power

The Psychology of Participation

The methods, already discussed, that are used by the *seiron* group to control those who are opposed are found in the world of such small groups as family, coworkers, and neighbors, whose membership numbers in one or two digits. It is also found in large political movements, whose membership runs into the hundreds, thousands, and tens and hundreds of thousands. However, the number of people involved does affect the psychological basis of action. Moreover, that the psychology of the participants is more varied the larger their number is clearer to the outside observer. It goes without saying that the number of people in the *seiron* group who are sincere believers of the order and the Truth is not small. But even if those in the *seiron* group publicly state that "I believe in the order and the Truth; what I advocate comes from this belief," the question of the psychological basis of such belief is another matter.

Even if the individual thinks that he faithfully believes in the order and the Truth, there is no guarantee that there is no motive hidden deep within the consciousness of that person, which guides his behavior without his knowing about it. Since the advent of depth psychology, one cannot maintain so easily that the individual knows best what his psychological attitudes are.

Outside observers will often note that involvement in the activities of the *seiron* group itself provides a certain psychological satisfaction, other than the feeling of engagement and achievement, to the individual. There are not a few cases where, as the individual might confidentially testify, he joins the *seiron* group under a disguise to hide his true intentions. Keeping in mind that there are such things as unconscious motives, satisfaction attained, and other goals which the individual is aware of, I will take up several examples of psychological reasons for joining the *seiron* group.

The Nervous Type and Security

When the *seiron* group poses threats for a time, justifying them as "Heaven's punishment," there will be an increase in the number of people who think and/or are afraid that they will be punished. There will also be an increase in the number of those who will feel and/or be afraid that they will be isolated when friends and colleagues, one after another, begin to join and support the *seiron* group. In that event, the nervous types and those who are already isolated and impotent and who often very calmly conclude that they cannot resist the *seiron* group will join it following the principle of survival for survival's sake as a preventive measure, a kind of insurance, so to speak. The *seiron* group will welcome this addition as a method of expanding their influence.

In terms of keeping one's options open in the future, it would be a smart move, upon joining, to take a passive role and try not to be too conspicuous. Once one joins, one cannot get by without taking some role in the organization. It sometimes happens that when one assumes a minor role in order to please the leaders, depending on developments, one ends up being a flag bearer, and eventually is pushed into a position of leadership. Since nervous-type people are in fact rather proud of themselves inwardly, they sometimes appear to be transformed in personality when they acquire influence. Depending on circumstances, the feeling of security and the vanity of having power will lead to degeneration and corruption.

The Hysteroid Type and Excelling

What the *seiron* group advocates is based on the order and the Truth, so with the legitimacy that this bestows, it seeks the unconditional obedience of the opposition. Accordingly, the *seiron* group arouses and satisfies the psychological needs of those who, in their interpersonal relationships, like to be in a superior position, thereby satisfying their need to dominate. Hence, among those who join the *seiron* group are people who, by temperament, dislike losing to others, or whose goal in life is to satisfy the desire for power and to dominate. Such people use their activities in the *seiron* group as a means of being superior to others. They will aggressively try to sell not only the *seiron* group's program to outsiders but also their utterances and activities within the organization will excel those of the lukewarm old-time members.

When this new type of member gains a leadership position, the *seiron* group will, on the one hand, be more radical or fundamental in their manifestoes and, on the other hand, more violent in persecuting their opponents. For such people, it is important and essential that their drive for power be satisfied. As a result, if their political movement flounders, or if they cannot attain positions of leadership, they might start another *seiron* political movement or join another one.

The Paranoid Type and Joining the Bandwagon
Even if what the *seiron* group advocates is based on order and the Truth, the other party may also be based on its own order and Truth, in which case, there are two faiths or philosophies standing side by side or there is a situation of conflict. The other party takes what the *seiron* group stands for and treats it as just another doctrine. The paranoid types are stubborn, so they do not pay much attention to the *seiron* group's threats. If such individuals do not deal amicably with the *seiron* group and continue to pay no attention to their influence and keep resisting, they will incur the wrath of the *seiron* group and become the target of violence and even assassination.

However, there are many instances where paranoid-type individuals, or those who believe in a different order or Truth, live only by the *honne*, that is, a faith that sanctions the pursuit of worldly goods. From that point of view, the emergence of the *seiron* group is the appearance of a new social force, and a sign of change in the distribution of power in the society. Stated in another way, the appearance of the *seiron* group provides an opportunity of seeking power and promoting interests, a chance to join the bandwagon. Some will perceive that there are opportunities for them, join the *seiron* group, and take part in the political rituals. And each person will benefit from it.

In the foregoing pages, we have described three examples of those who join the *seiron* group. As the *seiron* group's political movement grows like a snowball, there are all kinds of psychological reasons for joining it.

Priority of Political Consideration

As the *seiron* group grows from a small group to a large political force, the make-up of its membership becomes more varied. Of course, the number of pure members who believe in the order and the Truth increases. But, there are also increases in the number of those who, in the eyes of third parties, appear to join for other motives or goals. From the point of view of motives and goals, the *seiron* group seems increasingly to be a mixed organization, consisting of both pure and impure members. Moreover, as one observes the behavior of the *seiron* group members, it becomes clear that there are not only otherworldly, ascetic, and frugal types, as expected by the model of mystagogues; those who are in pursuit of worldly goods also begin to stand out. In this way, the *seiron* group, as its influence increases, begins to resemble the general run of political organizations that seek power within the political system. At the same time, it is confronted with the problem that is common to all political organizations, namely, its survival.

Two Objectives

The *seiron* group declares that its goal is to correct violations of rules and to bring about the true order. This is how it justifies its existence. Also, it starts a political movement to achieve its aims and becomes a strong political force. But there are numerous opponents, and their political influence is strong, making it difficult for the *seiron* group to attain its goals. Accordingly, the preservation and expansion of the influence of the *seiron* group, as a means of attaining its long-range goals, is set and honestly legitimized as an immediate goal. When the long-term and immediate goals are thus separated, an important change comes over the group's activities. This is because in the course of their daily activities, their preservation as a political force becomes in practice their long-range and ultimate goal. At the same time that this is happening, internally differences over policy develop.

For example, in recruiting new members or accepting applications, there are two alternatives. One is to stress the quality of members in a long-term view of the future of the organization. This means raising the required standards of understanding the publications of the organization, being more strict with regard to consciousness and everyday behavior, and adopting a policy of creating an elite with a high level of political consciousness. The other is to adopt a policy of placing priority on the political need of rapidly expanding the organization's influence and adopting the "mass line," a wide-open policy that accepts all applicants.

Conflict over Policy

Particularly when the *seiron* group is confronted with a crisis situation in which its survival is at stake, the internal conflict over policy becomes more intense. One faction will say, "So long as the *seiron* group survives, it will be possible to expand our influence at a later date under more favorable circumstances. It is more important that we remain in business, even if we have to lower our voices, sheath our swords, and even go into hibernation." The opposition will criticize this as right-wing opportunism. The opposition will say, "The *seiron* group remains as such only when it resolutely fights the enemy no matter how unfavorable the situation may be. Can we not bequeath the *seiron* to future generations only by raising the *seiron* banner and dying with honor?" They will be criticized as left-wing infantilism.

Since the goal of the political movements is the pursuit of worldly power, when they are confronted by this kind of political choice, it is natural that they choose survival. So long as the *seiron* group also makes its expansion of power and its survival the goal, it chooses survival. And this choice is justified not only as a sacrifice and dedication to the order and the Truth but also as a realistic policy that considers the security and convenience of the daily life of its members.

Even if the *seiron* group does not face the kind of political crisis that threatens its existence, it is not rare for it to experience a halt to its growth and expansion of its influence. Accordingly, it is often forced to make a choice between two kinds of policies, rapid advance or gradual advance, high posture or low posture, even if it does not have to make critical choices, such as between dying with honor or living to fight another time. In that event, too, usually the *seiron* group must give serious consideration to surviving as a political force.

As a result, sometimes the *seiron* group's ultimate political goal is divided between the *tatemae*, the ultimate goal, and the *honne*, the immediate goal, namely, to survive. The order and the Truth, which form the basis of the *seiron* group's position, are distilled into a political symbol. The order and the Truth are, in this instance, reduced to a liturgy that gives its members a sense of identity and a feeling of unity. On the other hand, what really assures the political unity of the *seiron* group is the satisfaction of *honne*, namely, the proper distribution of jobs and benefits. Thus, the usual course of development is for the *seiron* group to mature into adulthood and become like other organizations. Of course, there are always those who join the group on the basis of faith in the order and the Truth. However, even the new members, over a period of time, are confronted with the division between the *tatemae*, the goal of the group, and the *honne*, that is, the survival of the organization, whereupon its new members either become adults and stay, or become disillusioned and leave. When the numbers of those joining and leaving are about equal, the *seiron* group survives in a state of political stagnation.

Restoration of the Non-Believers

"Wait-and-See" Phase

Even when the *seiron* group begins its activities and presently develops into a political movement, the general public, which is not directly involved, does not pay much attention. Ordinarily, most people are not concerned with matters outside their work and personal lives. But influential people and those in positions of authority, that is, people who could later become the *zokuron* group, and who are likely to become the targets of *seiron* group attacks, learn about the activities of the *seiron* group from reports because they are interested in it. For them, the central problem is that of political leadership in micropolitics or macropolitics.

So long as their leadership is not threatened, they are like by-standers. But if the *seiron* group begins to threaten their leadership position, they rise up to defend it as the *zokuron* group.

However, when the threat from the *seiron* group is not that acute, when the *seiron* group is still small and weak, and, again, when the potential *zokuron* group is the paranoid type and stubborn, there is a wide social and psychological gap between the two parties. In that event, there is a feeling of security, since the danger of their political leadership being usurped is remote. The potential *zokuron* group recognizes the *seiron* group as a new political force, and watches and evaluates it from a distance.

Approval of Activities

The *seiron* group asks those in positions of authority who have engaged in violations or rules to mend their ways and acknowledge responsiblity for their misdeeds. Or as advocates of the Truth and of change, they seek, if necessary, to establish a new true order, even if they have to dispose of the ruling authorities. Hence, what the *seiron* group wants is in direct conflict with what is acceptable to ordinary adults. The potential *zokuron* group looks upon all this with tolerance. "This is good; you have a lot of energy. When you are young, naturally you should be energetic like that," they will say in acknowledgment. They affirm this as a manifestation of the energy inherent in the universe. The leaders sometimes admit from their secure positions that "I myself behaved like that when I was young." They do not merely show high regard for the *seiron* group's unbridled undirected energy. Within limits, they admit that what the *seiron* group advocates is partially true.

Since the eternal being is immanent in everything in the universe as explained in the equality code, what the *seiron* group advocates also reflects this being. If one were to call this being Truth, what the *seiron* group advocates also incorporates a partial Truth. However, even if what the *seiron* group has is a partial Truth, it is not the Truth itself. If the *seiron* group is going to argue that what it has is the highest, absolute Truth, then it is a mistake; it takes what is limited in time and space, a partial Truth, to be the whole Truth. And criticism of what the *seiron* group advocates starts from this point.

Criticism of What Is Being Advocated

I have already explained that when the *zokuron* group talks to the *seiron* group, there is need to change the dimensions and basis of discourse, that is, to broaden it. When there is enough social and psychological distance from the *seiron*·group for the *zokuron* group to feel secure, then the crux of the criticism by the *zokuron* group remains the same as before. That is, they criticize what the *seiron* group stands for on the grounds that what is vital for human beings and society has been ignored, that the area of debate is too restricted, and that what the *seiron* group seeks is narrow, limited, and one sided.

The essential points would be as follows: The *seiron* group is made up of sincere and honest people. One can see why they impress youth and students, but they do not understand the realities of human beings and society. Human beings carry a heavy burden of having to live every day. The social reality is controlled by opportunism, which is based on the belief that for human beings sex and money are paramount. What the *seiron* group advocates ignores this human and social reality and so has no solid foundation. In this way they criticize the *seiron* group's position as against common sense and immature. Accordingly, they conclude that the *seiron* group is not fit to assume the responsibilities of leadership. And those in positions of leadership and authority tell the youth and students who join the *seiron* group that "people might have to come down with measles at some point in their lives, but, in time, they must recover and become adults."

Waiting for an Opportunity

Eventually, the safe period that one can enjoy as a kind of bystander comes to an end, and the *seiron* group seeks to impeach those in power. Even though the *seiron* group might be small in number, because it represents an aggressive threat, it is not pleasant for those in power to have to deal with them. When in a meeting, the size of the *seiron* group becomes unexpectedly large, or when what is being said becomes unpleasant, or when those in power become insecure, those in control sometimes make excuses to avoid meeting with the *seiron* group or simply ignore them. But, the problem cannot be solved if they run away from it, and in the end they have to contact them and talk, even if reluctantly.

At that point they sometimes may give in to the *seiron* group, which is on the attack, and sometimes they may not. Since the *seiron* group not only refuses to give in to rebuttals but also does not permit one to remain silent, if those in power maintain silence for a while, the *seiron* group may decide to resort to violence. When those in authority experience these kinds of problems with the *seiron* group, they begin to understand fully that the issue of who is going to rule is at stake. At that point, as the *zokuron* group, those in power will resolve to defend their position against the *seiron* group.

Buying Time

There are a number of important steps that the *zokuron* group, in its political struggle with the *seiron* group, can take to assure victory. The first is for the *zokuron* group itself to consolidate its power. Second is the weakening of the power of the *seiron* group. Third, in micropolitics it can secure the support of third parties, and in macropolitics the support of the general public. Fourth, it can buy time to prepare for the attack. A traditional example of the tactics used to buy time is transactions within the parliamentary chambers. In parliamentary politics under the Meiji Constitution, as noted earlier, speeches and interpellations represented a battlefield to inflict wounds on the government in power. Under this system, the government, in turn, used the traditional weapon of dissolution to attack the opposition, which used the *seiron* to put pressure on the ruling authorities.

Accordingly, in the government's response, the element of trying to buy time to prepare for the counterattack was important. The first tactic was to let the *seiron* group have its say, and then ignore it. Even if the *seiron* group's statements may be extreme, if one ignores the provocation and remains cool, the time available to the opposition speakers runs out and the attack fades away. But one does have to respond to the questions. This brings us to the second tactic, which is to adopt the so-called parliamentary response. That is, in responding, one dodges the question, is evasive, and avoids saying anything that would commit oneself to the *seiron* position adopted by the opposition and thereby compromise one's freedom of action in the future.

Outside of the parliamentary halls, one would often resort to the tactic of giving vague answers or of limiting the time allotted to talking with the *seiron* group. In this way, one would buy time and wait for changes in conditions and relative power positions.

Changes in Conditions

The expansion in the power of the *seiron* group is influenced by the situation or by the so-called objective conditions. When some incident occurs that attracts the attention of the public, those who had previously been unconcerned now become interested and might join or support the *seiron* group. Accordingly, when a different kind of problem comes up and the situation changes, that is, the public becomes concerned with matters that another *seiron* group had been pointing to, third parties will abandon the old *seiron* group and join the movement started by the new *seiron* group.

Especially when the mass media's attention shifts to the new *seiron* group, the old one becomes weaker and, on occasion, the movement it represents comes to an end. The mass media lives in a competitive world, so it makes it its business to dig up and popularize what the new *seiron* group is advocating and to support its political movement. Competition in the mass media business rests on the premise that the public's interest is short lived. There is not much point in supporting the old *seiron* group over a long period of time. It is sometimes necessary to discover a new one and sell it to the public. With the advent of new problems, the support of the mass media thus fades, the people's interest declines, and the long established *seiron* group may even disappear. In that event, the *zokuron* group that had been trying to buy time to wait for some change in the situation no longer needs to attack because its position as the power holder remains assured. Those who had been active in the *seiron* group, after their anger has been dissipated, return to their everyday routines. The memories of those who did harm may be short, while those of the victims are long.

Of course, not all change is of disadvantage to the *seiron* group. Incidents and events, especially incidents involving personnel, underscore the rightness of the *seiron* group's position. Moreover, "put at rest the souls of the deceased" is the most persuasive *seiron*. When there is a change of this kind in the situation, and people begin to say that "we should not permit the victims to have died in vain," what the *seiron* group has been advocating becomes ruling the consensus. In terms of macropolitics, laws are enacted, budgetary provisions are made, and government agencies make it part of their regular duties. When necessary, construction on long-delayed roads, bridges, and the like are rushed. In this way, what the *seiron* group wanted is attained, and its political movement successful. But, by its very success, its contribution is moved backstage, while the practical steps taken by the *zokuron* group occupy center stage. What had been previously advocated by the *seiron* group now becomes part of the politics of distribution. This also means that the power of the *zokuron* group that had bought time to wait for a change in the situation has been preserved.

"Strike-back" Phase

If while the *zokuron* group is trying to buy time the *seiron* group becomes weaker, or if it becomes isolated because it has lost the support of the third party or the general public, it becomes easier for the *zokuron* group to strike back. Now the weakening of the *seiron* group can come about through internal conflict. The *seiron* group's publicly stated goal is to correct violations of the rules, or to bring about a true order. But, as has been explained earlier, in expanding its political influence, it becomes a mixed organization composed of people with diverse motives and goals. Depending on circumstances, it becomes concerned with preserving its position within the political structure. The *seiron* group also might seek to maintain its unity by manipulating the allocation of jobs and benefits. In that event, there is conflict over organizational policies on the one hand, and over personnel policies on the other. These two kinds of conflicts could proceed along parallel paths, or perhaps become intertwined, and eventually lead to factional strife. This in turn could result in a group splitting off, or a splintering of the *seiron* group itself. It goes without saying that this internal conflict and splintering would weaken the organization.

This situation could result in mutual recriminations through the mass media to the general public. There are instances where the "purists" criticize the *seiron* group itself. There are also cases where those who are dissatisfied with personnel arrangements, either in response to prompting from the outside or to make public their dissatisfaction, leak information to outsiders to engage in mutual recriminations. The leaking of information, particularly of a confidential nature, is a blow to the *seiron* group, and, depending on its nature, may have the effect of destroying the support of the organization by the general public.

Disillusionment and Secession

When the *seiron* group, despite the fact that it proclaims itself to be an organization dedicated to the order and the Truth, is actually like any political group that is given to corruption, the result will be disillusionment of the pure members, who joined because of their belief in the order and the Truth. Such members eventually leave the organization. Accordingly, the *seiron* group sometimes attempts to purify itself in response to these purists in order to maintain or strengthen its political influence. Such efforts sometimes succeed. However, if it remains like other political groups, it is possible that its self-purification will be more ritualistic.

In order to prevent the defection of the purists, the leaders of the organization take steps to prevent information about the corruption from getting out. It tries to discourage the reading of material other than what is printed in the official newspapers and magazines of the organization. If outsiders report anything about the organization, such reports are dismissed as irrelevant noise, or as conspiracies by the enemy. Members are urged not to pay any attention to such reports, or not to believe them if they do read or hear about them. Strict controls are exercised to prevent information about the daily lives and consumption patterns of the corrupt leaders from being reported to the rank and file. Since people tend to see, hear, and read about what they believe in, control of information has little effect on those for whom it is intended.

Isolation of the Seiron Group

Sometimes the *seiron* group becomes isolated because it has lost the support of the third parties or the general public. If an organization composed of those who believe in the order and the Truth threatens others as a manifestation of the numinous force, and resorts to violence in the name of divine punishment, its opponents will experience fear and hate, and third parties will feel revulsion. Just as members of the *seiron* group have various motives and goals, so those on the outside also have various motives and goals, and respond in various ways. There is envy and jealousy. If one puts aside the goals of the *seiron* group and looks upon it as an ordinary political organization, there are in it individuals who are very much like oneself in terms of family background and career patterns, who hold positions in the organization and who enjoy its benefits. This makes one envious. On the one hand, this makes for psychological identification and provides the basis for political support, but on the other, it is also a source of jealousy. And jealousy turns to hatred.

Another response of outsiders is repulsion and enmity. When the influence of the *seiron* group is ascending, members sometime behave rudely and push other people away. Since the members of the *seiron* groups are devoted to the pursuit of organizational goals, they do not care how they are regarded and evaluated by those around them. Some people are willing to forgive the *seiron* group's behavior as youthful excesses, but others feel a sense of repulsion because of the group's arrogance. And repulsion becomes enmity. Thus, although what the *seiron* group stands for in terms of its legitimacy is worthy and respectable, depending on the way it pursues its political activities, it creates negative feelings among those on the outside, such as envy, jealousy, hatred, repulsion, enmity, and fear. In this instance, while the *zokuron* group is patiently waiting and buying time, the support of the third parties or the general public for the *seiron* group is steadily ebbing, even while the latter is not fully aware of it.

Counterattack

In order to regain leadership from the *seiron* group, the *zokuron* group waits for a good opportunity, and when the propitious time comes, it launches an attack. Attacking the *seiron* group and, if necessary, suppressing it by legal methods may look like warfare, but really is not. It is a case of ordinary politics. Accordingly, the attack on the *seiron* group, and the subsequent disposition of the matter, must be the kind that the third party or general public understands and supports. The time for a counter-attack is indicated by a change in the atmosphere. Sometimes, while the *zokuron* group is buying time, the *seiron* group does something that is too extreme, especially in terms of violence. When ordinary persons, who prefer to be well balanced, hear of such actions, they become upset and use the occasion to withdraw their tacit support.

At the same time, an atmosphere that will accept an attack by the *zokuron* group develops. Given this atmosphere, the *zokuron* group cuts off the *seiron* group from the base that gives it its legitimacy, namely the order and the Truth. For example, Marxism, which advocates "scientific socialism," was labeled as a form of dangerous thought that sought to change the national structure (*kokutai*) and that violated the authority of the Emperor, "whose lineage is unbroken for ages eternal." It was a false doctrine that went against the eternal Truth. Again, in suppressing the so-called new religions, the argument was used that they were false doctrines that violated the principle of Westernization and Western scientific truth. Finally, the disclosure that will be discussed next will cut off the *seiron* group from the principle of order that gives it its legitimacy and from the mystagogue model that gives it its authority.

The Disclosure of Corruption

When the *zokuron* group discloses the true situation with respect to the *seiron* group to the mass media, or through the media to the public, two aspects of the situation will be stressed. The first is the orgiastic worldly aspects of the *seiron* group, particularly the "sex and money" life that characterizes its leaders, rather than the mystagogue model with its frugal ascetic practices. Matters pertaining to sexual ethics, such as having mistresses, abusing women, immoral conduct, and blind passion are brought up. Next are disclosures about the *seiron* group's financial dealings: collecting large sums from members, securing large contributions from outside vendors, and the like. Other disclosures are that the *seiron* group's leaders are spending large sums on personal luxuries, amassing private fortunes, and spending lavishly to gain political support both internally and externally. In this way, it is revealed that the *seiron* group is acting quite contrary to the ascetic life that is expected of them, but rather it is behaving like any ordinary political group.

The other aspect that is revealed is that the *seiron* group is not even an ordinary political group, but is a collection of criminals. In other words, they are lawless and not to be trusted. With respect to sexual morals, instances of criminal behavior are cited. And in regard to internal discipline and external conflict, examples of violent behavior, use of torture, lynchings, assassinations, and terrorism are cited. In this way, the *seiron* group is separated from the principle of order, which provides it with legitimacy. The *seiron* group is no longer a political force, but is merely a band of criminals that should be under police surveillance.

The press plays an important role in projecting the image of the *seiron* group to the public. Accordingly, when the *zokuron* group discloses the corruption that characterizes the *seiron* group, it must impress upon the media the credibility of the evidence. As has been noted, the purists, the disgruntled group within the *seiron* group, and the spies that the *zokuron* group had planted within the *seiron* group all testify and present convincing evidence. Moreover, those who were victimized by the corruption or injured by violent acts serve as first-hand witnesses.

In response to these disclosures, the *seiron* group seeks to preserve its status as a political force by trying to refute the charges before the media. The *seiron* group argues that the charges are malicious and that the evidence and testimony are false. Following the charges and the denials, the image of the *seiron* group held by third parties and the public is sometimes tarnished as hoped by the *zokuron* group. At other times, the disclosures might be seen be to be malicious, and the anticipated decline in the image of the *seiron* group does not take place. Finally, sometimes within the *seiron* group the sense of unity might be strengthened in an effort to ride out the crisis, or many members who are shocked by the disclosures may decide to leave the organization. The results of disclosure are not uniform.

If the third parties or the public comes to the conclusion that the *seiron* group is a band of criminals, it will no longer be a political problem, but a criminal matter. Ordinarily, what is expected of the accused in criminal cases is an admission of guilt, an apology, and repentance. When these are forthcoming, the public will accept the accused, who by such actions, has been restored to the status of a true human being. The principle of order and Truth that once cut the life of *honne* to pieces has now been reabsorbed and melted into the life of *honne*. And the political leadership of the *zokuron* group also is reestablished. But to the purists, who had participated in the *seiron* group, its defeat will produce a sense of anomie and the loss of the meaning of life and the guidelines to behavior. In many cases, with the passage of time and in the course of ordinary daily life, psychological trauma is cured by itself, though old scars may sometimes reappear.

Chapter Eight

The Power Struggle

The War Model of Politics

Alternating Order and Disorder

When we try to explain changes in power holders, three approaches or models are possible. The first model is one where in a long established, unchanging political regime the order is maintained in a steady state, and changes in power holders take the form of periodical shifts in personnel in accordance with the legally established political system. Personnel changes in government and in business ordinarily take this form, as well as changes in the prime ministership and the other cabinet members under a parliamentary system.

The second model is one where in an unchanging political regime chaos is present and powerful, and has weakened or destroyed the order. But a new force has overcome chaos and restored order. This is a rebellion model or a rebellion and restoration-of-order model. As will be explained shortly, in the power struggle in Japan between political parties or political factions, those involved sometimes behave in accordance with this model.

The third model is one where there has been a conquest or a revolution. Along with the complete replacement of one group of power holders by another, the order and, more often than not, the political regime is replaced. The Meiji Restoration was in fact close to the third model, but in terms of its legitimacy, it is closer to the second model.

175

Rebellions and Wars

General elections in Japan do not result in a change in ruling parties, as we have already noted. Accordingly, they do not provide the function of releasing chaos that lies at the base of society and then bringing it under control again. However, so far as the professional politicians are concerned, the political struggles that go on among the parties and factions may be likened to rebellions where chaos prevails. This originates from the power struggles that went on in the popular rights movement and the interventions of the police in general elections in the Meiji era, and party politics in the 1920s and 1930s, when the prevailing psychology was to "annihilate the opposition."

It has been said that running for office in an election is somewhat like going off to a civil war, and large amounts of "provisions" and "ammunition" are consumed. In the political world there are "war councils" held in many "regiments" and "divisions" of troops. In political fighting, they "attack at night or at dawn." In the minds of the political professionals, parties and factions on their side have the mission to restore the order that chaos has destroyed. The opposition parties and factions represent the forces of evil, and the chaos that destroys the order. Accordingly, political struggles represent, for both sides, good against evil, and orthodoxy against heterodoxy. To refuse to take part in this struggle between good and evil and to remain neutral also represents evil. Political struggles may be looked upon as an all-out war of the good against evil, and are a form of punishment meted out by Heaven. It is at this point that the forces of chaos are released unbridledly and the politics of believers comes into play.

Compromise and Dying with Honor

If we divorce political struggles from such concepts as Truth, orthodoxy, and justice, and liken them to business transactions and to diplomatic negotiations that, in a practical way, make social coexistence possible, the result of negotiations and compromise is a creative solution to the achievement of mutual coexistence of the adversaries. Both sides derive some satisfaction from it and will consider the compromise a success and a victory. However, if the political struggles are likened to a contest between good and evil, mutual coexistence, negotiations, and compromise do not enjoy legitimacy. This is because the good must always win out.

But victory and defeat are based on hard realities. Often, perhaps almost always, the good is weak, and evil is strong. In the final analysis, from the point of view of evil, victory is what counts. But from the point of view of the good, which is weak, compromise that is needed to continue to live represents giving in to evil—prostituting one's self and behaving in a wicked way. Hence, according to the rebellion model, the minor party or faction, that is, the weak, which has justice on its side, must either compromise and submit to evil and live in shame under the shadow of the tyranny of the majority or attack and "die with honor," making a good show even in defeat, and, in that way, hope for a comeback at a later date. It must always be confronted with the choice of compromise or death with honor. And this choice is one of the factors that conditions the operation of the National Diet.

Treatment of the Defeated

The victors, that is, the majority party or faction, are a manifestation of the great life force in the universe, and the representative of justice that has destroyed the chaos and restored order. The victors attract to themselves many opportunists, who come to share in someone's good fortune. In the court of power, things are decided on the basis of actual strength. There is nothing in the traditional Japanese language that corresponds to lost cause. There is no self-restraint among those who represent the Truth and power. The losers, that is, the minor party and factions, are ignored, treated cruelly, pushed around, and forced to put up with all kinds of indignities. Of course, under the common understandings, the minority parties and factions are a part of the National Diet, and socially they are influential. But others that do not have this political background, the minorities, the weak, and the losers, are expected to exercise self-control and shrivel up. And sometimes they, on their own accord, choose to do so.

While there is the old tradition to agree with the strong, and help the strong and destroy the weak, there is also the conventional wisdom that it is better to avoid open conflict situations, where one's defeat will be made evident to everyone. If people, contrary to common sense or the will of the strong, create problems, and are exposed to the public via the mass media, they must bear the burden of defeat and shame. In that event, some members of the camp of the minority faction or the weak might say that "those who created the problem are at fault, since they could have anticipated what would happen," but few will seldom come to the support of the person who is in trouble. To take steps to avoid a collision, and to exercise self-control is to act wisely. Moreover, since it is obviously smart to lead a normal life and avoid anything that could become the subject of newspaper stories, leading an ordinary life entails exercising self-control and lying low.

Disorder in the National Diet

Diplomacy, defense, and the organization of the government were the prerogative of the Emperor under the Meiji Constitution. But, under the postwar Constitution, these matters were put under the jurisdiction of the National Diet. Moreover, Article 8 of the postwar Constitution established local autonomy. But, under the situation where there is supposedly only 20 or 30 percent local autonomy, the solution of many local problems came to rest on the decisions of the central government. In this way, the present system of party politics shifts the burden of solving many problems in a variety of areas to the National Diet, or to the central government.

In addition, given the system of universal suffrage, the number of voters has steadily increased over the last 40 years, and presently stands at about 80 million. As a result, even though the various political parties have not evolved into organizations with many millions of members, since the political parties enjoy the support of the mass media, the election outcomes increasingly depend on the party label, on the party leader, and on the publicly stated party platforms. Under the circumstances, the need of parties to carry out party promises becomes greater. Another way of putting it is that the freedom of action that parties enjoy to disregard policy promises in order to negotiate and come to an agreement within the halls of parliament has diminished. Parliamentary debates, too, have to some extent become more of a formality without real substance.

Under these circumstances, the monopoly of power enjoyed by the LDP has continued, and the opposition parties, beginning with the Socialist party, have remained perpetually in opposition. With regard to policy positions, the ruling and opposition parties have continued to disagree by maintaining their basic stands with regard to the Security Treaty, with the United States, and other diplomatic, defense, and internal security questions. Accordingly, those who are perpetually in the opposition have not been able to achieve the campaign promises they made to those who voted for them. They must tell their own politicians and the voters who support them why their policy of refusing to compromise with the LDP is realistic and legitimate.

Thus, making a good show of the conflicts between the ruling and opposition parties in the National Diet, the dying-with-honor tactics of the opposition that end in their defeat, and showing all this on national television has become common practice. In the eyes of the opposition politicians who are engaged in these struggles and in those of the supporters who vote for them, the justice of their cause as well as the evil nature of the LDP is revealed. Also, this continuous struggle in the Diet is highlighted, and the legitimacy of the opposition parties is reaffirmed.

The Structure of Disorders

The drama of struggles between the ruling and opposition parties and the dying-with-honor tactics of the opposition are important political rituals that show the conflict between the two sides, and the defeat of the opposition. With regard to the conflict between the two camps, this political ritual has a vital function. It shows that even with a long-term LDP monopoly of power, we do not have dictatorial politics, and that parliamentary politics with its ruling party-opposition party conflicts are here to stay. Accordingly, it is very difficult for political professionals to get rid of the drama of parliamentary conflicts and replace it with parliamentary proceedings that are more like an academic debate.

The political professionals are aware that disorderly proceedings are not a part of the normal Western-style parliamentary government, and so they would like to avoid it as much as possible. They are also aware that, even though the National Diet is the center of power struggles, disorderly behavior appears to the electorate as unworthy. Moreover, there are both physical and psychological limits to organizing the members to engage in disorderly behavior in the halls of the Diet. Even the effectiveness of violent behavior has its limits: there ought not be more than several in one session. Thus, in using violence, the choice of locale, preparations, and concentration are important. In this way, the stage is set for an outbreak of violence in the Diet when the opposition states that it will resolutely prevent the passage of a treaty or a bill, and mobilizes its members for a parliamentary demonstration, and the press supports them by stating that the outcome deserves attention.

A Close-up View of Violence

Some disturbances are triggered by relatively minor incidents, such as a policy mistake, an offending remark by a cabinet minister, or a "bomb" question. The latter is a question, the gist of which had not been revealed in advance, that is asked by the opposition in the interpellation period. This type of disorder is called an unexpected encounter. When this happens, the proceedings will come to a standstill, and later the opposition may decide to boycott the sessions. Today, the mass media demands that the sessions be resumed and be normalized. This also becomes necessary when there is a need to pass the budget or to save important laws that contain an expiration date in one of its articles. But conflict within the ruling party, and among the opposition partners does not always make it easy to settle the matter and resume the sessions. Eventually some equivocal statement that is meant to be apologetic and that all parties can agree upon is read by a minister or a chairman of some Diet committee, or a minister might resign, and the matter will be settled. Thereupon the parliamentary proceedings will be resumed.

Another case of disturbances involve previously planned interparty confrontations to highlight disagreements about the ratification of treaties and pending legislation in either the committee meetings or the plenary sessions. At this point, the voting procedures take center stage. The ruling and opposition parties come to an understanding about having a rather peaceful confrontation while Diet members vote. It will start with the introduction of a large number of procedural moves by the opposition that have to precede the consideration of the bill itself. Since all members present have to vote individually on all of these moves in accordance with official rules, voting can last for several days and nights. Members of the House can stay in the chamber, bringing in sleeping bags. If snail's-pace tactics (known as "cow walking"), in which members of opposition parties walk as slowly as possible to the rostrum to cast their votes are adopted, in spite of the Speaker's warning that the ballot box will presently be closed, even more time will be required.[1]

The third case is a more direct form of confrontation. If the LDP as the ruling party decides to ratify a treaty or pass a controversial bill, and the opposition does not accept defeat peacefully by participating in the voting, there will be an impasse. In that event, the ruling party resorts to extraordinary tactics and tries to ram the legislation through, resulting in some dramatic scenes. There may be informal prior consultations with the opposition, but the LDP, without a formal agreement of the House Management Committee or the councils of the committees, cuts off debate on the bill and schedules a series of votes. When this happens, the committee meetings or the plenary session are the scene of much confusion, and sometimes violence breaks out. There was a time when in an effort to prevent a vote in the plenary session the opposition resorted to sit-ins, or tried to block access to the chamber or the rostrum, and the police were called in to remove those members obstructing the proceedings. All this had a good deal in common with military uprisings in terms of preliminary intelligence work, detailed planning, placement of personnel, and skills involved in its execution. In these confrontations, the Diet members and their secretaries gave vent to their feelings and emotions and had the satisfaction of participating in a common enterprise.

Settlement of the Confrontations

Proceedings in the Diet chambers ordinarily follow a script, in

1. According to the rules, after a member's name is called, he proceeds to the rostrum with a wooden ballot, which indicates approval or opposition by its color, and puts it into the box. The ballots are counted and the Speaker is notified of the results, which he announces. Since there are 511 members, voting can take up more than one hour. So in order to speed up the voting process, there is an established procedure whereby the Speaker announces that the voting will take place and that all those members who approve of the bill should rise. Accordingly, the LDP legislators stand up while the opposition remains seated. The Speaker (or chairman, if it is a committee meeting) states that the majority is in favor and that the bill has passed. Thus, when there are interparty conflicts, the opposition insists on voting by casting ballots in order to delay the parliamentary proceedings.

which the various political parties have come to an agreement in the House Management Committee, and in the councils of the various committees. Accordingly, the ramming through of legislation by the ruling party is not considered legitimate. The opposition parties will boycott the proceedings professing their anger, and everything comes to a standstill.

Thereupon, the mass media criticizes the ruling party for having used steamroller tactics, and the opposition parties for always opposing everything. It asks that the two sides get together, restore order through talk, and resume their legislative work. Presently, the representatives of the Diet strategy committees of the various parties enter into negotiations and make some agreement. In some instances, the basis of the agreement is an apologetic statement that is read, rulings to be followed, or the Speaker's resignation. As a result, the parliamentary session is resumed. There was a period when important legislation was rammed through with some frequency, resulting in changes in the Speakership so often that it gave rise to a saying, "one bill, one Speaker," but in recent years, things have quieted down.

The Model of Unity and Harmony

So far as professional politicians are concerned, the power struggles among political parties and factions have been likened to warfare. But, as has been noted, during the last thirty years or so, general elections have not resulted in the replacement of one party by another. Even in the case of the monopoly of power enjoyed by the LDP, electoral victory for the party has not amounted to much more than a series of individual victories of politicians in their own districts. From the point of view of voters, the change of cabinets has represented nothing more than a periodic change of personnel. For the voters, elections were not occasions to discharge their emotional feelings, nor were they substitutes for an internal war in which the submerged chaos rises to the surface.

Accordingly, in terms of governing the people, the LDP regime had to depend more or less on the traditional order that rests on unity and harmony. For example, even if a leader has emerged victorious in the interfactional struggles within the LDP, and has a great deal of power, he will enjoy more popularity if, in running the party, he lets bygones be bygones, and seeks reconciliation, and shows the public that he seeks party unity and harmonious collaboration on the part of everyone concerned. Moreover, in ruling the country, he is expected to treat everyone, irrespective of the party they support, on equal terms and work to improve the welfare of each and everyone.

The Rejection of Partisanship

In the traditional conception of the order, those who have the responsibility of maintaining in-group order are expected to treat everyone fairly. The demand for fairness and impartiality has some implications for party politics. What is expected is that in party politics, political and party strife should be avoided, and that, even if it would be formally contradictory, party politics should not favor one party over another. On the basis of this idea, the Japanese army, in the 1930s, took over political power, on the grounds that they should get rid of the existing parties because they were financially corrupt and engaged in partisan politics.

During the last 30 years, the press has persistently demanded that the LDP, which is in effect a federation of factions, do away with factions. Both the ruling party, which rests on its laurels with its "tyranny of the majority," and the opposition, which "opposes everything," have been the subject of negative comment by the mass media for their open partisan character. Professional politicians are people who are involved in party and factional matters, and are engaged in party strife and warfare. At present not only Diet members but even local assembly members are forced to build their own personal support groups in their electoral districts. Under these circumstances, warfare and party strife spreads throughout the country and becomes rather commonplace.

If we accept fairness and impartiality as the standard, the spread of party politics would have to be considered an unfortunate development. From the point of view of ordinary individuals who denounce anything that goes to extremes and approve well-balanced approaches, too much partisanship is undesirable. Some political critics who wish to see open partisanship reduced have advocated such measures as the growth of middle-of-the-road parties, making the House of Councillors non-partisan, and the revival of the Green Breeze Society in the House of Councillors.[2] In reality, with the development of the politics of distribution, one can say that a pseudobureaucratic system, where the party politician holds office as a representative of local interests, has come into being. This represents a certain dilution of partisanship.

Human Finiteness

If one rejects partisanship in party politics, one's expectations are turned to arenas other than the world of professional politicians who engage in political struggles. That is, what would be desired is a world of technocrats, who are above partisan struggles, who are under strict discipline, who are fair and impartial, and who do not favor any one party or faction. Or, perhaps an autocratic form of rule by bureaucrats would be desired. It cannot be denied that in response to this, during the last 40 years, the higher-level bureaucrats have maintained a strong sense of mission to promote the national interest and have pursued a policy of enlightenment through more Westernization. However, bureaucratic autocracy by enlightened civil servants does mean that they participate in political struggles and are partisan to the extent that they seek to perpetuate and extend their political power.

But human beings are finite creatures. Given their limitations, human beings have no alternative but to make choices and decide here and now. As is said in Western textbooks, party politicians seek the votes of the electorate by making a choice and assuming responsibility for such choice. The voter casts his vote by making a choice and assuming responsibility for such choice. Accordingly, the partisanship of both the politician and the voter represent the carrying out of individual choices and the assumption of individual risks, that is, consciously living in a finite condition. Thus, the approval or disapproval of partisanship is closely related to what life means to every individual.

Harmony in the Legislative Halls

The system of arriving at collective decisions on the basis of voting,

2. Ryokufūkai (Green Breeze Society), the House of Councillors' second conservative party from 1950 to 1959, had more ex-bureaucrats than the other groups.

along with the principle of majority rule, is Western in origin. It also has legitimacy originating from democracy. In the decision process, a clear-cut division into a majority and a minority, and the defeat of the minority are made visible to the participants. In the case of the National Diet, the number of seats in both chambers that are held by the majority and the minority are fixed until the next election. In the Diet, decisions are by majority vote. It is also a place where confrontations are put on display in the struggle for power, and so the participants are not especially bothered by defeat.

In the case of meetings where small groups of people who know each other well are involved, it often troubles people to see the group divide into a majority and a minority and to witness the defeat of the minority before one's own eyes. Because of this, in many cases there will be a good deal of premeeting discussions and informal negotiations so that unanimity can be obtained. In this way, the embarrassing difficulty of having a victorious majority and a defeated minority can be avoided.

The Avoidance of Majority Rule

I have already explained *nemawashi*. The participants, or their representatives, meet a number of times beforehand and prepare an agenda and a draft proposal, which they agree on unanimously. Then the meeting is held. There are statements of "no objections" by a member who is assigned to speak up, and the chairman of the meeting, having ascertained that there are no objections, determines that the decision has been made unanimously, thereby bringing the meeting to an end.

For example, even in political party conventions, when factional strife takes the form of the election of officers, there can be confrontations. But, in conventions that have no factional confrontations, decisions are made by acclamation. In local assemblies, such as city, town, and village councils, where there is less partisanship, and where the number of council members involved is still quite small, other methods, in addition to *nemawashi*, are used. If during the proceedings, there are differences of opinion or controversies, there is a recess, and the council members reconvene as an informal discussion group. In this informal setting, they spend a lot of time to come to an agreement. Then an agenda and a proposal that can obtain unanimous approval are prepared, and the formal session is reconvened.

Political Skills

The National Diet has to produce enough legislation that is required to run the country so that it can be called a legislation factory. But it does not meet all that many days each year. The ruling LDP must pass the needed bills in a limited period of time. Accordingly, carrying out committee meetings and the plenary sessions without untoward incidents, and getting bills enacted expeditiously are yardsticks that party leaders and colleagues use to judge the political skills of those who manage the Diet. It goes without saying that when no delaying tactics are used by the opposition, and everything goes according to script, the productivity level of the legislative factory is high. By contrast, when the proceedings come to a standstill because the opposition refuses to cooperate, the ability of those who manage the Diet is not likely to be regarded highly.

Collections of Anticipated Questions

Diet proceedings can often come to a standstill when, during the interpellation period, the opposition asks a bomb question and the government is unable to come up with a satisfactory response. Accordingly, in order to prevent this sort of thing from happening, usually the junior officials of government agencies go to the opposition party members who registered to ask questions the next day and try to find out exactly what questions will be asked. With this information in hand, the senior officials of the various government agencies prepare a handbook of anticipated questions and suitable answers. On the appointed day, usually the following day, the cabinet minister or a government official committee member is able to respond to the question that has been asked on the basis of material that had been prepared beforehand. If the response is an appropriate one, it cannot become an excuse to stall the proceedings. Any cabinet minister who has the ability to give satisfactory answers, and is able to reassure the party leaders and those who manage the Diet proceedings is called a "safe" minister.

Those in the government feel that it is important in running the country that they maximize the options that are open to them, given the fact that it is hard to predict what will happen in the future. Therefore, the government's responses to questions are often minimal in their scope and are more often vague than clear. Moreover, when the opposition asks questions that tend to be "divine judgment" of what the government is doing, the latter often tries to dodge the question. Thus, when the proceedings are televised, the viewers are presented with a spectacle of the opposition making imperious accusations, and the govenment responding in a pro forma way.

The Power to Choose Bills

Another cause of a stall in parliamentary proceedings is the handling of "confrontation" bills. In foreign relations, defense, and internal security matters, there are sharp differences between the ruling and opposition parties. When it comes to legislation relating to these matters, the opposition parties, within the framework of established procedures, try to filibuster in order to delay passage. But the opposition parties will also try to speed up passage of bills that pertain to certain matters in order to distribute benefits to their own supporters. Some examples are budget, salaries of government workers and those working on semigovernment corporations, social welfare, and benefits for local communities. Thus, both the ruling and opposition parties enter into "diplomatic" negotiations to agree on a timetable for the passage of bills. These negotiations take place in the meetings of the councils of the various Diet committees, of the management committees of the two houses, and of the Diet strategy committees. Informal negotiations that take place, inside and outside of the two houses, in various sites and at various times, proceed almost as if they were diplomatic contacts. In the course of these negotiations and compromises, the opposition parties, in the case of certain bills, demand that statements be added, or that the wording be changed, or that the debate be continued to the next session, or that the bill be tabled. If the government, as part of the negotiations and compromise, accepts some of these demands, the effect is that the passage of the bill appears to depend on what the opposition demands. This means that the opposition has, under some circumstances, the power to choose bills.

Political journalism has always criticized confrontations between the ruling and opposition parties in the Diet, and has strongly urged that every party should work together in harmony so that the legislative task can proceed in an orderly manner. After the large-scale political upheavals in 1960, which erupted in opposition to the revision of the Japan-U.S. Security Treaty, in response to the press's demands, the Diet strategy committees of all of the parties began to hold informal talks for the smooth operation of the National Diet. As members of opposition parties began to participate in the operation of the parliament, in time, some members of both the ruling and opposition parties came to establish close personal ties, from which there developed a feeling that they were all involved in a common enterprise. In this way, the principle of harmony and unity in the operation of the National Diet became such a commonplace matter that nowadays the media reports that some opposition parties are accompanists if not accomplices of the LDP.

Change of Prime Ministers

The Prime Minister and the Cabinet

"Capacity" and "Gilding"

When the factional alliances in the LDP shift and a new factional coalition, which is a majority in the party, comes into being, a new party president and prime minister appears, resulting in a political change. The new party president and prime minister is not only the leader of his own faction, but will become the symbol of the LDP and of the Japanese government. He is expected to play the lead in the drama of politics. The power inherent in him as leader of his party and the legal authority vested in him by law serve as his stage props, letting his dignity and stature come through. Accordingly, the question whether he has the capacity and the character to be party president and prime minister is asked within the party and in political journalism. At least during his term of office, he will be evaluated in those terms. Moreover, professional politicians ask themselves whether they have these two qualities.

But the political influence that a politician has within his own party, faction, or among his close associates is quite different in character from the authority he has with the public, from whom he is separated and with whom he has little direct contact. This is because authority contains another element, namely, the respect that people have for him. For that reason, there was a time when so-called *haku* (gilding), which is an element in respect, was much talked about in political circles. During the Occupation, knowledge of the West and foreign countries or diplomatic credentials, which stood for foreign knowledge, were valued as *haku*, as well as for their practical utility. Also, as a carry-over from the Meiji Constitution, the same held true for the credentials of a higher civil servant and the schooling that provided a basis for such status. However, due to the spread of the idea of equality that destroys the notion of status, the loss of authority and respect for politics, and because of constituency service that exchanges benefits for votes, *haku* is no longer important for the prime minister or for politicians in general.

Suggesting Oneself or Having Others Recommend You

There is a saying concerning elections that it is better to vote for someone you would like to see running for office than for someone who came forward because he wanted the job. This shows the deeply rooted traditional view that recommendation by others is better than self-promotion. There are two aspects of passivity involved in recommendation by others. When a person, in assuming office, prefaces his remarks by saying, "I unexpectedly was chosen . . . ," he is trying to show the passive nature of his actions, that is, that he is there, not by virtue of his initiative, but because others asked him to serve. When a representative of a politician's support organization prefaces his remarks in a speech at a banquet celebrating the politician's electoral victory by saying, "On the basis of public support given to you . . . ," he is telling the victorious candidate that he was carried into office by the assent of those who are being ruled. The former suggests that one is prepared to be carried around like a portable shrine by his supporters. The latter is a premonition that after the public loses confidence in him, the shrine will be put down and forgotten.

In parliamentary politics, one is not only free to run for office, but is free to nominate himself. Thus, even though it is difficult for politicians to gain the confidence and support of their fellow politicians, given the spread of the idea of equality, those who are self-assertive and can get financial backing come forward. This gives rise to fierce competition to control the intraparty majority for nominations of party president and prime minister. This leads to rumors about money politics in the press.

Protecting the Prime Minister's Power

Becoming the president of the LDP and the prime minister represents one process. Protecting that power and maintaining it is another process. Now among those conditions that make it difficult for the prime minister and his faction to remain in power is, first, the biological nature of human beings. The health and life of the prime minister lie in the biological realm. Even though he will receive the best of health care, given his position, in the final analysis, the matter of his health and life lie beyond the reach of his political power. The second condition is the limited nature of power. Even the most powerful figure cannot anticipate beforehand and prepare for incidents and problems that may occur in the world or within Japan, nor the solutions which will become the responsibility of the prime minister or the cabinet. An analysis of the changes in LDP prime ministers shows, depending on the criteria one uses, that four were for reasons of health, two for having to take political responsibility for something that happened, three because of the struggle for power, and one retirement. The single case where the prime minister was able to retire on his own volition was that of Satō Eisaku, whose regime lasted seven years and eight months.

Incomplete Information

The first problem the party president has in maintaining power in the intraparty struggle within the LDP is the conditions that happen to prevail in the political arena. Among these conditions are the ambitions and reputations of the faction leaders, whether there are in the party powerful factions that could challenge the faction in power, and whether these powerful factions are prepared to form an antimainstream faction to mount a challenge. The second problem is the various defense stratagems. Those who belong to the party president's faction are quite aware of the need for defense. But as has been noted, individuals and groups that sit at the pinnacle of power do not get enough accurate information because their followers want to flatter them. As a result, unpleasant news about what is going on in the party and what other factions are doing tends to be withheld from them. The leaders may be unaware that the basis of their power is being eroded.

Disaffection Within the Party

When a new coalition of factions achieves dominance in the party, and a new government is formed, those prominent in the winning coalition are rewarded with positions in the National Diet, cabinet, and the party. This results in two groups of people: those who are given positions and achieve power and are happy, and those who are left out and harbor feelings of resentment. The system of shuffling cabinet, Diet, and party positions every year is designed to alleviate these hard feelings over a period of many years. But every time there is a cabinet shuffle, for every person that feels elated, there are many who are dissatisfied. Hence, with every cabinet change, dissatisfaction tends to accumulate, thereby weakening the foundations of the government in power.

In order to remain in power, it is not only necessary to appoint a suitable politician to the office of the Chief of the Cabinet Secretariat in order to run the government and cabinet effectively, but also to pay a great deal of attention to managing the party and to delegate responsibility over party affairs to someone in whom the leader has a good deal of confidence. For these people, the distribution of Diet, cabinet, and party positions, as well as money is important in reducing dissatisfaction and strengthening the foundations of power. And those who are directly responsible for giving out positions and funds may end up gaining personal power and influence in the process. There are instances where the basis of a faction leader's power has been eroded step by step and eventually crumbled due to the machinations of a trusted follower to whom he had delegated the "dirty work" and who had the hidden intention of succeeding to the leadership.

The New Government

What Goes on in the Political World

The power struggle in Japan takes the form of factional strife within the LDP. Those who participate in this struggle, in a formal sense, are the **LDP** Diet members, who number between 400 and 500. Among these, only about one in ten possess leadership qualities. Thus, power struggles are a "tempest in a teapot," as Yoshida Shigeru once said. There are differences in fitness and make-up among those party politicians who have been reelected any number of times. Not all are talented in the way of political machinations, and the prowess of those who have accumulated a great deal of experience and training is revealed.

The process of attaining a dominant position in the LDP begins with setting up plans for building a winning coalition. This involves strategists and general staffs. It is a struggle that takes place in a limited arena, and as political journalism says, "There are no great strategists in the political world." Both from the point of view of the need to maintain secrecy, and the wish to maximize one's options, faction leaders often keep their strategic plans to themselves. Thus, the process of building a winning coalition often proceeds on the basis of conjecture or wrong inferences of plans that the faction leader had in mind.

Next, there is the matter of information gathering. Politicians, their secretaries, and political journalists accumulate news in their everyday contacts, and exchange and evaluate information about the goals and plans of other politicians and factions and changes in interpersonal relationships among members in each faction.

Finally, there is the mechanics of coalition building. It does not differ much from diplomatic practice. There are telephone calls, and face-to-face meetings that take place between people who know each other well, or have been arranged by intermediaries. In this process, who met whom, when, and under what circumstances, who were the intermediaries, who is going to meet with whom, all are pregnant with meaning. Among meetings, there are those that are informal and secret, and those that are formal and public that announce the formation of alliances.

Some will try to guess the probability of an alliance being formed. There will be factions that will benefit from an alliance being formed as predicted, and some that will be disadvantaged. In this coalition-building process, information can be very important. They may send signals or send up trial balloons by holding press conferences in the office of the faction, or in a train while traveling from one place to another. They may send out false information in an effort to increase suspicion among factions and individuals and thus separate them.

One difference between this process and diplomacy is that agreements among factions are not spelled out in formal documents. There have been so-called abdication agreements between faction leaders. In a formal but secret document, a contestant for party president agrees to hand over power to another contestant at the completion of the former's term. However, if a winning coalition which has the power to force compliance with the abdication agreement can be put together, that coalition can take power, whether or not there was such an abdication agreement. Moreover, it is a foregone conclusion that if one faction joins a winning coalition, there are more rewards in the form of Diet, cabinet, and party positions, so a written agreement to confirm the traditional practice is not necessary. Thus, in many cases, factional alliances are based on informal and tacit understandings. For this reason, when it comes to the details of these agreements, there is a good deal of room for interpretation, a fact that encourages political maneuvering later on. In this way, sometime after a new government comes into existence, there is movement in the political world, and the process of new coalitions forming and old ones dissolving begins again.

The New Government

The first job of the new prime minister is to distribute Diet, cabinet, and party positions, and finalize the line-up. These positions are the spoils of victory and can be divided into those that are politically important, those that produce benefits for their holders, and others that are of lesser importance. The new government in practice distinguishes between the mainstream and antimainstream factions, and gives something to all factions. Since the LDP is the ruling party, it must be able to unify and mobilize all of its members when they have confrontations with the opposition parties in the National Diet. It cannot afford to discriminate against the anti-mainstream members for fear that they might go over to the opposition, leading to a split in the party.

In allocating cabinet posts, whether the prime minister does so according to a list that ranks eligible candidates proposed by each faction (usually on the basis of the number of times a legislator has been elected) or whether he chooses those he wants from each faction, makes a difference in terms of political consequences, even if the number of ministers in each faction remains the same. In the former case, factional and party make-up is not likely to be affected, and dissatisfied factions do not join the antimainstream coalition because the nomination is based on seniority in that faction, that is, the number of times one has been reelected. In the latter case, the new prime minister's power in the party is demonstrated, but also the number of people whose expectations are not met increases in that faction as well as the number of those who sympathize with them. Thus, the atmosphere in the faction is not always favorable to the mainstream. Furthermore, the elderly members do not retire so easily, and, as these senior politicians keep getting named to cabinet posts, the waiting list of those eligible for cabinet positions becomes longer. The middle-aged and younger faction members often complain and want the older generation to make room for them. But, of course, that is not so easily done.

Influencing Public Opinion

The establishment of a new government with a new prime minister and cabinet, cabinet reorganization, and shifts in Diet and party positions, all are important events in the political world whose staple food is political strife. Political journalism will report and interpret to its readers almost everything that goes on in the process leading to the final announcement of a new government. In this way, it prepares the public for the event. It will cover the political process, from the early to the final stages. This kind of political news represents, on the one hand, political journalism's participation in the political process, and, on the other, reporting about political maneuvering on the part of various factions. Political journalism is, to some extent, a house organ of the political world. Accordingly, it has other functions in addition to enlightening the public. It prints news items that are "about, from, and for the benefit of" the political world or the various factions. It is an instrument for providing the political world with complicated and subtle intelligence activities.

Now, after a new government has been established, the new prime minister, in order to consolidate his power, wishes to call for an early election. So long as the LDP is always able to win more than one-half of the seats in general elections, the authority of the new prime minister, who has dissolved the House of Representatives, depends on whether the election results in an increase or decrease in the number of LDP seats.

The timing of the election thus becomes important. Two indicators that help determine the timing are public opinion polls carried out by the mass media on the percentage of those who support the present cabinet and data on party support. A government that is contemplating dissolution tries to manipulate public opinion by announcing a new policy, for example, tax reduction. Also, a new prime minister and leaders of major factions might run new candidates from their own factions, in an effort to expand their power base. Thus, after the passage of a few months or years following the creation of a new government, there rises the problem of restraining the prime minister from using his power to dissolve the House of Representatives. Moreover, political journalism that had restrained itself during the few weeks that followed the ascension of a new prime minister begins to criticize the government. The new government has now become the present government and is confronted with the problem of defending itself. The days of political strife have returned.

Chapter Nine

The Politics of Policy Making

The Mass Media, Especially the Press

Structure

In the case of Japanese newspapers, aspiring reporters must first be hired by newspaper companies. The latter give them in-house training, and they are then launched in journalistic careers. In these careers, journalists stay with one firm, and those in the management track are promoted from reporters to division chiefs and chief editors, while others become editorial writers and are promoted to chief editorial writers. To the extent that the firm provides a setting for competition for promotions, it is inevitable that there are office politics, cliques, and factional strife. In this regard, newspapers are no different from any other business.

There is a system whereby reporters, depending on their specialties, are attached to departments. Departments are vertically segmented units that are in charge of a page or pages of the newspaper. As a result, the material in the various sections of the newspaper may not necessarily be consistent. It is often noted that, in particular, there are differences between the editorials and commentaries and the news sections. The fact that the pages are not carefully controlled to conform to a single editorial policy is a convenience for careful readers who do not overlook small items that may contain important news.

The Conditions of Competition

Many families read only one newspaper, and their preference

for one paper, which is often inherited, is quite stable. This situation assures the survival of the home-delivery system, and, in turn, the system helps to maintain the stability of readership. Most families do not have the interest, opportunity, time, or money to subscribe to many newspapers in order to read and compare them. If we exclude the situation where readers change from one newspaper to another because of differences in the price of subscriptions, the character of the reporting and the make-up of the sections does not have much influence on the number of copies sold. But this pertains to readers.

From the point of view of those in the business, their jobs and meaning in their lives are riding on the reporting and make-up of the sections. This results in cutthroat competition for news and scoops. If a reporter succeeds in getting a scoop, and subsequently wins an award, the higher-ups and colleagues can not only put the competition to shame, but the reporter, too, will be in a position to move up the ladder within the firm. In contrast, if another newspaper gets a scoop, and one's own does not, then that will hinder one's promotion. Because of this internal struggle for promotions, parallel with the competition to get news, there are ways to avoid being caught without news. Newspaper companies publish both morning and evening editions. In order to avoid being caught without news, the early morning editions that are sent to suburban cities by train used to be exchanged at the station platforms by reporters. By scanning the papers of other companies, they could determine whether their own paper did not carry the news.

Also, various newspapers tend to all contain the same news. Both the attempt to avoid being caught without news and the need for the government agencies to manipulate the news combine to give rise to a system "reporters' clubs," whereby a group of reporters of some companies benefits from news supplied exclusively to them by the government agencies. Reporters belonging to this special group, in addition to digging out news in a government agency, share equally with others in the club all official reports and announcements, and attend all news conferences. This way, the reporters are assured that they will not be deprived of news, and the agencies benefit from the public relations without cost through the distribution of information.

Moreover, it is well known that in Japan, as well as in the

United States, competition for news has resulted in a tendency toward sensationalism. In this regard, Japanese newspapers, too, have, in the last 120 years, taken to printing pictures, adopted new types of headlines, and used airplanes to speed up the reporting of news. In reporting accidents and incidents, the press, by saying, "the outcome deserves attention," tends to stir things up. This leads to the creation of a positive feedback loop between what happens and the reporting of it. When this common style of reporting is used in politics, for instance, the press making such comments as "the response of the opposition to this should be watched" or "a rejection from the opposition can be anticipated," it tends to have the effect of arousing or stimulating the opposition parties.

Newpaper Enterprises

Newspapers employ a large number of college graduates. They must also maintain and work their own printing plants almost around the clock to print numerous editions, including local editions. As a result, wages represent a large share of the costs. Hence, in the printing process, there has been considerable mechanization and the use of computers, which have led to reduced costs. At the same time, subsidiary enterprises have increased in number in order to absorb surplus management staff. There are a large number of such enterprises: publishing, television, pro baseball teams, computer institutes, cultural centers, travel agencies, and real estate. In response to the financial burdens these newspaper enterprises must bear, the government, as well as Japan's ruling groups, provide support in the form of selling them government-owned land.

The newspapers, of course, carry advertising. Since the advertising rates depend on the circulation, as certified by the Audit Bureau of Circulation, the number of copies sold is important from the management's point of view. Accordingly, there has been intense competition to increase circulation. There have even been attempts to deliver extra, unsold copies to their sales outlets and include these in the circulation figures.

In the case of television programs, the number of viewers is equivalent to the number of newspaper subscribers. When a program attracts few viewers, it is quickly dropped because its sponsors feel that their commercials are not very effective.

The activities of the mass media are covered by Article 21 of the Constitution, which protects the freedom of speech and publication. Its freedom from government censorship is protected as a basic human right. Of course, newspapers are limited by the number of pages, and radio and television by number of hours in a day. When it comes to reporting the news, interpreting and commenting on it, the various newspapers must make choices every day on what they consider to be "fit to print." The various newspapers exercise their discretion daily following their own policies on what to report or not report, and from what angle. But Japanese law does not guarantee the mass media, as a private enterprise, complete independence and autonomy. In criminal and civil courts, doctors, dentists, midwives, lawyers, patent agents, notaries public, and priests are guaranteed the right to refuse to divulge what was told to them in confidence. Those in the mass media are not included in this group of occupations. If reporters refuse to divulge the name of the person who gave the information or refuse to surrender television films, they may be fined by the court, or they may be brought to trial and fined or jailed.

Operations

Public Opinion

The mass media is not part of the government, and journalism, including political journalism, is not a direct government operation. If the public follows the political guidance provided by journalism, and this leads to a shifting of votes and of the number of seats won by parties, political journalism itself becomes "public opinion," a third political force along with parties and the bureaucracy. Against this traditional background, the newspapers, which represent political journalism, contend that they are public opinion. But in parliamentary politics, in which voters constitute the primary force, the political leadership of elected politicians is threatened if public opinion is monopolized by the press. Thereupon, politicians give expression to public opinion that has as its basis the living voice of the electorate, which they hear in their districts. Such views, which are diverse and varied, differ from that expressed by the newspapers.

The third form of public opinion is represented by public

opinion polls in which the nation's voters are statistically sampled and recorded in the form of responses to questions. When public opinion is expressed in numbers derived from a statistical analysis of the responses, we have something approaching a substitute for a national vote. It is well known that the three kinds of public opinion do not always coincide. Political forces represented by parties, bureaucracy, and political journalism do not necessarily reflect, in a passive fashion, the attitudes of the electorate. Such forces are sometimes ahead of the voters and lead them. Accordingly, even if the editorials, editorial opinions, and commentaries printed in a newspaper should differ from the results of the public opinion polls conducted by the very same paper, that should not be considered strange.

Political journalism purveys reports, information, and opinions about domestic and foreign affairs to the voters, and thereby gives direction to their views and forms public opinion. Among the information that is conveyed, there is not a little public relations material on policy planning that comes from the government agencies via the reporters' clubs. If this is all that they printed, newspapers would be nothing more than government handouts.

But there is a long tradition, dating back to the Meiji era, for the press to be critical of the government in power, that is, to be a kind of political opposition. As has been explained before, under the postwar Constitution, and also under the long-term monopoly of power held by the LDP since the amalgamation of the conservative parties in 1955, the press has been involved in depicting a political drama of the confrontation between the conservatives and the leftist groups. As a result, political journalism has protected the activities of the opposition parties. In the confrontation between the United States and the Soviet Union, and the resulting division between the hawks and doves, political journalism has been on the side of the doves.

Neutrality Toward Issues and Parties

The dovish stance of political journalism is not necessarily only the result of its partisan position. It also reflects the underlying isolationism of the Japanese people, who do not wish to get involved in international disputes. It also has the effect of reinforcing isolationist sentiment. Moreover, in a situation where there are multiple opposition parties, the press has endeavored to maintain a neutral stance toward all parties, and not favor any particular political party. For instance, it has tried to give equal space to all of them with regard to electoral activities.

Historically, by the beginning of the twentieth century, the educational level had risen and almost everyone had become literate. During the 1910s and 1920s, with the rise in the standard of living, a national press aimed at the mass level came into existence. Today, the various national newspapers manage to sell millions of copies each day. In order to stabilize their management, that is, income from advertising, newspapers find it necessary to maintain their circulation.

Accordingly, they must produce the kind of newspaper that will appeal to millions of families. They have to take into consideration demographic factors, such as sex, age, occupation, social class, income, standard of living, party support, religion, cultural level, and interests. They have to produce a product that will satisfy every group of subscribers to some extent and not antagonize any group. They have to be particularly quick to placate those groups that will use the threat of cancelling subscriptions. As a result, newspapers tend to get thicker, and their contents will include, in addition to politics and economics, material on all aspects of life, from food and clothing to housing and recreation. Moreover, they must adopt a neutral position in their writing. There has been a marked tendency for the press to separate their news reporting and commentaries from editorials and advocacy, and to stress objective and accurate reporting.

Public Forum

When newspapers begin to stress news reporting, they will all begin to have similar headlines and news stories. Given the need of the various newspapers to maintain the morale of their reporters and staffs, each one tries to become somewhat distinctive. Also, so long as they contend that "newspapers are public opinion," they must also deal with political guidance. Thus, newspapers, like general-interest magazines, now carry signed articles and essays written by novelists, commentators, artists, various specialists, and academics. These pieces are over and above the editorials and commentaries that newspapers ordinarily print and do not necessarily reflect the views of the newapaper, but may tend to support their editorial position.

Both general-interest magazines and newspapers provide a public forum of political journalism for social, political, and literary criticism, and the editors and writers preside over activities that go on in this forum. In conjunction with this, writers, commentators, and publicists have become more organized and divided into groups. This means, in turn, that the very choice of contributors becomes a reflection of the editorial policy of that particular newspaper. As a result, given the competitive situation that exists among editors and writers, both the stress on the use of established contributors and the search for new faces goes on simultaneously. Moreover, the competitive situation decrees that sticking to established editorial policy is not enough; change and the coming and going of fashions cannot be ignored. Hence, editorial policy wavers between the safety of doing the same thing over and over again, and the adventure of trying something new. Thus, political journalism presents a varied spectacle. However, with the emergence of a mass consumption society, the days when politics and the confrontation between the conservatives and the leftists were the main concerns of the people, especially of the young, have come to an end. And as the sharp decline in the sales of general-interest magazines indicates, public interest in political journalism has also declined.

World Situation as a Political Construct

Getting Chaos Under Control

Force, or the threat of its use, are common tools in politics and power. Also, the chaos of destruction and death always goes with politics and power. Deprivation, violence, and murder accompany war and conquest, revolution and civil war. Since ancient times, many people have sought to increase the predictability of life and human behavior, and to increase the security and stability of society and culture by suppressing the outburst of chaos in the form of the wanton use of force in wars and rebellions. And efforts have been made for a long time to bring about peace and order through the institutionalization of politics and power. Both the creation of a constitutional regime and parliamentary politics represent the fruits of this kind of effort.

Because the potential of chaos and the ability to do evil exist naturally in every individual, the effort to institutionalize politics and power means in effect to institutionalize human behavior. This is the reason that the political system institutionalizes the elaborate system of palace etiquette, and the political philosophy of propriety (*li*) as found in Confucianism. But institutionalizing politics and power and suppressing the appearance of chaos does not mean its elimination from nature and human beings, and from politics and power.

The Undercurrent of Chaos

Ordinarily, the world of politics rests on the legal system and operates smoothly. In contrast to the order that is on the surface and is more visible, in human life the potentiality of chaos lies deep beneath the surface. Sometimes it flows quietly deep down, and sometimes it bubbles up. For example, in the government, aside from some elected officials, most are appointed. Appointments represent discretionary choices made by superiors with the authority to hire personnel. Accordingly, one can think of two extremes. One is where the power of discretion lies solely in the hands of a dictator, and the other is one where there is a seniority system, which permits no discretion. In cases which are somewhere in between these two extremes, in other words in ordinary situations where both participation in and control of appointments are possible, there is the possibility of chaos beginning to act. Palace intrigues involving conflict among cliques has been commonplace phenomena since time immemorial, not only in China and Japan, but almost everywhere.

By contrast, under a constitutional government, elections represent an institutionalized, demilitarized kind of internal war. In the large-scale, festival-like political meetings with their displays of power and energy used to mobilize many voters, and in the lavish use of money, chaos makes its appearance. Occasionally, it is almost like an orgy, and people's emotions are aroused. When the voting is finished, control is restored. In these elections, the political parties are armies bent on conquest or campaigns to restore order, and the party leaders are the generals. In the case of the American presidential elections, to the victor go the spoils, from several thousand to more than ten thousand jobs. In this way, in the ordinary course of operations, the legal political system sees both the outburst of chaos and the restoration of control over it. Herein lies another function of the political system.

The Politics of Mass Society

The development of an industrial, technological society has led to the growth of cities and urbanization. In these cities, there are skid-row districts where chaos is present in the form of prostitution, gambling, drugs, and violence. These are the districts of darkness. In the classical prosperity of the Victorian era, modes of life in the cities were classified as dark and sunny. And both of these modes existed side by side. With industrial and technological development, the governance and control of life in the sunny parts of the cities became more effective, leading to the emergence of a managed society.

With the growth of a mass consumption society, taboos against sex, drugs, and violence were weakened, and society became more tolerant of chaos. For this reason, the sunny and dark societies merged to some extent. In terms of politics, this tendency took the form of the display of naked force and the use of propaganda. This was the beginning of modern politics that makes wide use of violence and the display of power. For instance, the Nazis had private armies. Under these circumstances, the function of elections, which serve first to release and then to regain control over chaos with the counting of the vote, is important. It is often said that changes in ruling parties that the United States, Great Britain, France, and other countries have experienced since the end of World War II were not necessarily beneficial for continued economic growth. This was because they brought about important changes in basic policies, and rampant waste and disorder in both the economy and society. However, it cannot be denied that changes in ruling parties produced by voters participating in elections also had the important effect of regaining control over chaos and reuniting the people under the conditions of mass consumption society and international politics.

Leftist Local Governments

By contrast, the situation in Japan is different. Every year, newspapers print news about expected appointments of bureau chiefs and vice ministers. They also report gossip about conflicts between the high-level bureaucrats, who seek autonomy in such appointment matters, and the ministers, who have the power of appointment. Even though the annual shuffling of personnel may be for the authorities involved an opportunity to work behind the scenes to release and recontrol chaos, it is not an opportunity for the people to participate. Moreover, elections have not produced a change in the ruling party. The LDP remains the majority party. General elections do not have the effect of releasing and regaining control over chaos and reintegrating the people. The political maneuvering that occurs over the realignment of LDP factions does serve, for elected politicians, as a reopening of the field of battle and provides an opportunity to reassert control over chaos. But it does not provide the people a chance to participate in this process.

What has provided the people with an opportunity to participate and has served as a substitute for bringing about a change in the ruling party has been local elections. Elections to choose the chief executives of prefectures and cities, that is, governors and mayors, provided a good opportunity for the conservatives and leftist groups to fight it out on an one-for-one basis. In addition, problems produced by the mass consumption society were particularly acute in the big cities. In the latter half of the 1960s and into the 1970s, many leftist chief executives and leftist administrations were voted in by the electorate in the large cities. The large financial deficits and administrative inefficiencies that resulted may be considered the price that had to be paid for regaining control over chaos that lies beneath the surface of mass consumption society.

The oil crisis of 1973 led the people to think that the period of high economic growth was over, forcing them to tighten their belts. Voters who were fed up with deficits and administrative inefficiencies began deserting leftist chief executives. Those employed in the local governments were generally happy with the status quo, but there were not enough of them to assure reelection of leftist chief executives, with the result that they were defeated one by one.

The Role of Competition
Parties and elections do not sufficiently perform the function of permitting the people to participate, give expression to their emotions, and allow chaos, which lies at the bottom of society,

206 THE POLITICS OF POLICY MAKING

to burst forth and then be brought under control. Something else performs this function. One is the work group, and the other is their country. As has been already explained, there is the outer world as the battlefield where competition takes place. So conditions in the outer world are taken as reality, and the group assumes the role of the battle unit organized to fight a battle for life or death. The competitor is designated as the enemy, and what is to be won is looked upon as the goal or prize, and strategy and tactics to achieve the goal are dictated.

The leader of the group is expected to be concerned with these factors. The members of the group are expected to participate in the competition, and do their best so that their highly disciplined group can achieve victory, while the members show initiative and give expression to their emotions. The success of the effort to release and control chaos can be observed everywhere in the competition among firms to increase their share of the market and to raise their position in the ranking among business firms. Also, we have witnessed the frenzied national effort to catch up with and overtake the West during the last thirty years—particularly during the decade in which income doubled.

World Developments

With respect to the country as a collectivity, since the arrival of Commodore Perry's Black Ships, Japan has occupied a marginal position in relation to the Great Powers, and in international politics, which were first led by Great Britain and later by the United States. Accordingly, the world situation was that Japan, being unable to resist the Great Powers, had to adopt a passive stance. And Japan had to come up with policies that represented a passive response to world developments. The formula of "world-developments response" and "reality-responsive policy" was first adopted in the middle of the nineteenth century. In the beginning, the reality was defined as the coming of the Black Ships, and the proposed response was limited to the policy of "expel the barbarians." Later, reality was construed as the world-wide spread of Western civilization, and the responsive policy was defined as a combination of Westernization, industrialization, and building modern armed forces by the Meiji government, which launched a program of modernization.

The Politics of Pragmatisim

Since then, a new political tradition has been established. When something new takes place in international politics, a new definition of world trends becomes necessary. The new reality thus constructed demands a new policy in response. The need for new policies justifies and provides rationale for the emergence of a new political leadership. This pattern has been repeated over and over again since the Meiji Restoration and has become a new tradition.

Thus, new developments in international politics can lead to domestic power struggles, and also become a burning issue. Hence, reporting by political journalism of international news, such as the intentions of the Great Powers, the basic trend of world history, the course of historical necessity, and trends in international public opinion, and the recognition, evaluation, and definition of the international environment and foreign pressure have come to carry great weight in the domestic power struggles. The pragmatic evaluation of whether a combination of new political leadership and new policies in response to new international trends would be appropriate or inappropriate has become an important factor in domestic politics. Accordingly, when it is construed that there is little change in the stable world situation, power struggles and political change take place within the framework of a stabilized institutional system. And without the dramatic appeal of new policies, the people have the impression that nothing new is taking place.

By contrast, the bureaucratic system prefers the fossilization of the world situation and of reality. Bureaucrats will not easily accept a new definition of reality. In the bureaucratic structure, its functions, authority, personnel, and budget are set up on the basis of some policies in response to the world situation, which was constructed in relation to the business of the particular agency. As a result, usually the bureaucracy resorts to policies that were thought to be appropriate responses to global trends which were defined and institutionalized in the past. So their operation tends toward orthogenesis. It is difficult for the bureaucracy to come up with newly revised conceptions of reality or of the world situation, which is the very basis of their existence, organization, and operation. The task of revision belongs more to the politically oriented groups, namely, elected politicians, the upper levels of the bureaucracy, and political journalism.

Political Definition of "Reality"

Demands for Revision

When the definition of reality and policy are expected to correspond, we can conceive of two kinds of revision. One is the case beginning with a demand for a policy change, which leads to a revision of the definition of reality. The other is starting with the revision of the definition of reality, which leads to a change in policy. In the first case, difficulties and confusion stemming from existing policy result in social instability. This eventually leads to a demand for a change in policy or the establishment of a new policy. In this instance, when, in the course of a power struggle, it is argued that in order to deal with social instability, it becomes necessary to adopt long-term "radical" policies and that as short-term policies are not sufficient, the revision of the definition of reality eventually becomes necessary.

In the second case, there are demands for a new policy based on the recognition and evaluation of new situations, such as a change in the international power system and changes within the country in polity, economy, society, and culture. In this instance, the power struggle is over recognition of the new reality, which leads to a choice of one policy over another.

The Release of Chaos

The on-going definition of reality forms part of the order. Reality is constructed and defined as the world situation. The definition is authorized, established, and widely shared among the population. The political structure, policies, and the order, which correspond to the definition, rest on this shared knowledge. Accordingly, from the point of view of demanding a change in policy or the adoption of a new policy, and, again, of demanding a change in the perception of reality, it will be necessary to release the chaos from the lower layer of human society, let it come to the surface, and then challenge the order, which provides a cover over the surface of society, forcing it to be more fluid. Thus, whatever is troubling people, whether it is demand for new policy or is nothing more than mere dissatisfaction with the status quo, is expressed publicly under the aegis of the freedom of expression guaranteed by the Constitution. This expression takes various forms, such as meetings or street parades, which, being reported in the mass media, may elicit a wide response. Since this is the public appearance of chaos, there may be unusual displays, such as bizarre forms of dress, and placards, floats, and music, which are out of the ordinary.

In the present mass consumption society, the older, more formal styles have been replaced by those that are more relaxed and informal. For this reason, sometimes unusual behavior that expresses dissatisfaction is no longer noticeable in the confusion that marks the mass consumption society. One of the elements connected with the display of dissatisfaction that shocks the order is the matter of quantity. That is, the very fact that large numbers of people are mobilized for mass meetings and marches draws the attention of both the people and the mass media. Accordingly, the sheer number of people participating have a political effect. However, when a large number of people are involved, whatever actions they take tends to be organized, and, therefore, institutionally commonplace.

By contrast, another element that strongly shocks the order is quality. Resort to violence and organized terrorism represents direct action by a small number of people, so it has a strong impact on the political world and on the people's mind, even though it may not lead immediately to any political change.

The Role of the Mass Media
In all this, the mass media, which sounds a warning bell in its effort to change the perception and definition of reality, is very important. It seeks to maintain an objective, neutral position in reporting the news, as we have described. So, when chaos surfaces from the depths and seeks to make force felt, the mass media recognizes this, and reports it, either by printing it in the newspapers or putting it on the television screen. Often these activities are undertaken so that they may be reported by the mass media. The mass media also provides a forum for those who participate in this activity, and reports their stated purposes and goals.

By taking notice of these activities, the mass media accords them social recognition, which in turn gives legitimacy to the political movement. All this has the effect of revising the definition of reality, and a new policy responding to this new version of reality is sought by the mass media, either explicitly or implicitly. If, in response to the warning bell, a new policy is put into practice, the mass media legitimizes both the new policy and the definition of reality that goes with it. Moreover, the mass media endows this combination of policy and definition of reality with names, labels, and slogans, which become accepted by everyone and become a part of shared knowledge.

As has been noted, the mass media is characterized by competition among the firms who are in the business. Hence, this newly articulated definition of reality can be likened to a new piece of merchandise that has become fashionable. Accordingly, competition to investigate new developments in the world situation goes on, and, at the same time, the new definition of reality becomes popular and fashionable, only to be relegated to oblivion with the passage of time. In this way, the structure of reality is divided into two layers. There is the reality that is closer to the surface and changes frequently after months or years, and a deeper layer that corresponds to the stability of the political system. The problems that emerge from the day-to-day political struggles, in many cases, refer to the definition of reality that is near the surface.

Political Effects of the New Definition of Reality

What brings about change in the image of reality or becomes an essential feature of a new image of reality are new facts and changes that were not noticed previously. Thus, the first step in the revision of the image is to send an expedition to discover what is new. Given the century-old tradition of catching up and overtaking the West, the search is directed to the outside, especially the Western world. Field trips abroad, foreign study, correspondents abroad, dispatching study groups composed of politicians and/or bureaucrats to foreign countries, and the like result in the inflow of new information and factual reports on the world situation. The search could include library research involving foreign books and articles. As a result of dissatisfaction with the status quo and political demands, there are also efforts to study the domestic scene. Field work, surveys, dispatching reporters, and groups of politicians and/or bureaucrats provide material for a new definition of reality. Those individuals and businesses involved adopt a new definition of reality and devise new policies to meet it.

New Policies

When as a result of these searches and studies, a new situation is perceived to exist in the international arena, which leads to a new image of reality, those in power come under criticism. They are accused of having carried out policies based on the old definition of reality, and of having failed to adapt to the new version. There are demands that the policies be changed, and that the cabinet resign to make room for a new government.

By contrast, if it is established as a result of search and study that the world situation has not changed in a fundamental way, it is judged that the policies of the government in power are proper, and, thereby, its right to continue in office is recognized. In this instance, the political struggle is not over policy, but over personnel matters: a younger generation replacing the old or bringing in new faces. Power struggles are part and parcel of politics, and the new definition of reality does not bring an end to them. However, for those in power, whether or not they have the legitimacy to continue to rule makes a great deal of difference in terms of the power struggle. Accordingly, whether or not there was a change in the world situation, and whether this change was big or small, the recognition and definition of reality becomes central to the political debate. And the various newspaper companies that take part in and lead the debate often disagree about the definition of reality.

The Art of Constructing Reality

The construction of an image of reality and the struggle for power are closely related, and the image of reality has the function of serving as a political symbol. So the artistic construction of reality needs a nice combination of perception, evaluation, and orientation in order to mobilize people emotionally. For this, the skills of a copywriter become useful. Some clever phrases to define a new version of reality are invented by gifted people. When these phrases are passed from one person to another, or are used in the mass media and become fashionable and gain the capability of mobilizing the public, social and political forces that can be organized around such expressions are found in specialized groups, or even in the country at large.

As public opinion, these forces are used by the parties and factions and play an important role in determining the outcome of political struggles. Some examples of such expressions that look backward to the past are: "This is no longer the postwar period"; "High economic growth has come to an end"; and "The 1970s have come to an end." Others that look ahead to the future are: "It is a new era in Japanese-Chinese relations"; "It is a new era in Japanese-American relations"; "This is the 200-mile period"; and "We are now in the 1980s." Other famous examples that succeeded in the 1930s because they appealed to the traditional feeling of order are: "Don't miss the bus" and "Don't become an orphan of the world."

The Officially Sanctioned Definition of Reality

The definition of reality that has been recognized heretofore forms a part of the system and of the order. The new image of reality that is portrayed by the appropriate expressions is accepted by everyone and becomes common knowledge. Thereupon, the new image of reality is adopted and sanctioned by official documents and government pronouncements in such forms as statements, speeches, and orders. In this way it receives official sanction.

At that point, not only the expressions but also the authoritative interpretations of such expressions are officially established as a system. Since the new definition of reality demands a new policy orientation, and must be incorporated into the system of positive laws and the daily operations of the various government agencies, the interpretations of the expressions also must be given unique and unequivocal interpretation. The new definition of reality that is officially sanctioned is explained to the people by political journalism and the mass media. And a set of new policies that goes with this new definition of reality leads to laws defining jurisdiction and increases in the number of government personnel and budget items, it becomes part of the official daily duties of the government agencies. In this way, it is carried out automatically until the next revision of the definition occurs. The official sanction of the image of reality in some cases gives legitimacy to the new regime in the event that there is a change in the cabinet or government (more of this later). And, again, official sanction might be given without a change in government. Just as the political system enjoys stability, so the definition of reality in a fundamental sense as it relates to the political system does not change every few months or even over a period of years. Most of the time, even if the definition of reality may contain elements that suggest revolutionary change, it is nothing more than a surface phenomenon.

Bureaucracy

Organization

After the Meiji Restoration, a new regime came to power by virtue of victory in the civil war. In staffing the government agencies, initially the new regime adopted a policy of giving preference to those who came from the same home towns and the same feudal fiefs as those who belonged to the winning coalition. However, with the introduction of a Western-style educational system, there was gradually established a system of recruiting officials on the basis of academic records and examinations that were open to the public. In this way, the bureaucracy became accessible to all.

On the basis of the new educational system that was set up all over the country, graduates of special academies that were created by the government for training specialists, such as army and navy officers, and graduates of colleges under the control of the Ministry of Education who passed the higher and lower civil service examinations were hired for work in the government agencies. This system based on merit paved the way for bureaucratic dominance.

On the one hand, the national bureaucracy became a channel for achieving success in life and getting close to the center of power. With the fading away of the political leadership that had led the Restoration movement, the higher bureaucracy became the recruiting ground for those political groups that were destined to rule the country. On the other hand, both the middle and lower levels of the bureaucracy provided stable and secure employment in an era when there was slow economic growth, and jobs were hard to get because of the excessive supply of workers. It was in those days that the traditions that characterize the Japanese bureaucracy were established and remain to the present time.

Personnel Management

The bureaucracy is organized much like the military, that is, it has a three-tiered arrangement consisting of officers, noncommissioned officers, and privates. The top layer consists of the officers. In the case of the prewar army and navy, the officers were graduated from the academies and started as junior officers and eventually some of them became generals and admirals. In the case of the civil service, aspirants must pass the higher civil service examination. They are classified as "career qualified," and can become bureau chiefs and vice ministers.

The second tier are the noncommissioned officers. In the prewar army and navy, after they were graduated from the middle-level service schools, they became noncommissioned officers and could advance to the middle ranks of the officer corps. In the case of civil service, individuals must pass the middle or lower level examinations. They can eventually become division chiefs of the ministries, or bureau chiefs of branch offices. The third layer are the enlisted men. In the prewar army and navy, they were conscripted, and some were volunteers. In the government, individuals other than those who have passed the higher, middle, and lower examinations fill non-specialized jobs.

The first chracteristic of this type of organization is that it is based completely on the educational level that the civil servant has completed. The number of various positions in the government agencies is set by law. Depending on the school one has graduated from, or on the type of examination one has passed, the entry position, the kind of promotion, and the rate of advancement are set at the time one is hired. There is also a selective system that provided for faster promotion on the basis of internal examinations and in-house training.

The second characteristic is that in many instances graduates of certain schools are given de facto preferential hiring. By contrast, graduates of schools with lesser reputations are disadvantaged. Some conspicuous examples are preferential nomination of graduates of national universities for civil service positions, the discriminatory advancement of officers promoted from among the noncommissioned officers and from reserve officers in the army and navy before 1945, and the personnel conflicts involving groups of teachers who are working in the same prefecture but happen to be graduates of different normal schools.

The third characteristic is that in many instances, individuals who passed the examination for law positions have been chosen for the top jobs, such as vice ministers and bureau chiefs. This has been criticized as the "LL.B. monopoly."

Regulation of Personal Lives

Members of the bureaucracy do not lose their jobs when a change in the ruling party occurs. In exchange for this guarantee, they are required to be neutral toward political parties and groups. According to the regulations of the General Personnel Administration, they cannot engage in political activities. Moreover, they are required to devote themselves to their official duties and maintain confidentiality. They are not to become involved in labor disputes or to engage in actions that would result in the loss of trust.

But civil servants also enjoy a variety of benefits. They can buy food and clothing cheaper through special stores and coops, and have access to subsidized, inexpensive housing. They are provided with medical insurance and a pension, as well as hospitalization, and access to halls and resort hotels maintained by governmental organizations. In practice, there is a system of mutual aid for expenses incurred in weddings and funerals for bureaucrats and their families, and aid for the dependents of deceased civil servants.

There is informal help for those who retire, either at the normal age or earlier, in the form of employment in the private sector. The system of retired, high-ranking bureaucrats taking jobs as top executives in government corporations and in private business has been widely reported in the mass media, and so it has become well known. But postretirement employment through the informal help given by those still in the government is not limited to those in the upper ranks of the civil service.

Providing a Meaning for Life

In Japan today, one finds mostly small families in which two or three generations live together under one roof. The bureaucracy looks after their personnel, the heads of such households, both publicly and privately from the time they are hired until they retire, and sometimes literally until they are in their graves. It also provides group affiliation and a sense of identity. The stipulated and professed goals of the various ministries and agencies give their members a sense of mission. Because of their contribution to the national interest, a sense of mission and patriotism give legitimacy to their work and also guide their policy making.

And, for groups, their survival and growth are self-evident goals and are what gives them meaning. The expansion of functions, competence, personnel and budgets of the various ministries, bureaus, departments, and sections are the meaning of life so far as bureaucrats are concerned. Planning and advocating new policies and getting the required personnel and funds give those involved meaning as well as a sense of participation and satisfaction. Moreover, since the size of the national budget is by definition limited, departments and agencies compete with each other. The sense of unity and esprit de corps felt by members of departments and agencies through their hard work carried on day after day is reinforced by conflict with outsiders. In this way, vertically segmented administration and interagency conflicts are perpetuated, making administrative reform extremely difficult.

Operations

The Ringi System

The well-known way in which the Japanese bureaucracy performs its job is the so-called seal administration. In this system, relevant documents circulate within it, and the appropriate officials indicate approval by stamping them with their seals, thus providing a record of their actions. The names given to such documents vary, depending on the agency, but here for the sake of convenience, we will call them *ringisho*. The system of using *ringisho* is known as the *ringisei*, or the *ringi* system.

There are two types of *ringi*. One is related to routine administrative actions, such as the disbursement of money for office supplies. In this case, the documents proceed virtually automatically. The other is related to policy making. A *ringi* document in the second category is a kind of "diplomatic document" that confirms the agreement of relevant departments for the policy that is being proposed. In terms of jurisdiction, the division in a ministry is the basic unit. The particular division involved studies and discusses the matter over which it has exclusive control and comes to a consensus on the policy that is to be proposed.

The division chief and other members informally take this matter up with the other divisions. It then goes up to the bureau level and the ministry level, and eventually to other ministries that are involved to obtain their informal approval. The entire process starts from informal contacts and discussions, and, for purposes of confirmation, ends in a formal conference or conferences. The whole process may proceed smoothly, or it may run into snags. This depends on what is being proposed, on the interests of the other departments involved and on the political skills, assets, and capital of all those concerned.

After an informal approval is obtained, the particular division has one of its junior members prepare a *ringi* document. This is then circulated, according to stipulated rules, to all of the divisions and bureaus from whom the informal approval was previously obtained, and all division and bureau chiefs stamp it with their seals. This is an example of the *ringi* process. A good deal of time is required for preparation and negotiations before the document begins to circulate. On the other hand, the system assures integration of related divisions, which tend to want to go their own way. It also assures that the relevant divisions and bureaus will come to an agreement on how they should operate.

In the *ringi* system, those divisions and bureaus involved have the power of veto. So the approval must be obtained politically from those individuals who happen to be chiefs of divisions and bureaus at that time. Accordingly, if a reshuffling of personnel has occurred prior to the stamping of the document with the seal, it becomes necessary to obtain the approval of the chiefs who have been newly appointed. For this reason, sometimes it is necessary to make changes in the details of the policy that is being proposed.

"Inferiors Usurping the Powers of Superiors"

Since the divisions are the basic units in a ministry, in terms of matters that are under their jurisdiction, they are the government of Japan. The actual formulation of policy is in the hands of the various section chiefs within the divisions. The power to manage the divisions and start the process of obtaining policy approval lies with the division chiefs. They also have the power to take policy proposals originating in other divisions and push them along by giving their approval, or to block them by opposing them. In the government, the locus of formal competence and the locus of actual decision-making power do not coincide. The actual power to make decisions has been unofficially transferred from the cabinet meeting to the vice-ministerial conference, from that body to various ministerial conferences, and from the ministerial conferences to informal discussions among division chiefs. In other words, what is required of ministers, vice-ministers, and bureau chiefs is the art of governing that rests on mutual adjustment among the division chiefs. It is something like the portable shrines that are carried around during festivals. This is the well-known system in the Japanese bureaucracy in which the inferiors usurp the powers of their superiors (*gekokujō*). There was also criticism of a similar system in the prewar army, where the colonels ran the show.

This system of inferiors usurping the powers of their superiors may also be viewed as one of adjusting meritocratic principles to the rule that promotions should be based on seniority. Unlike the traditional society, at present we see constant technological progress. As a result, the actual ability to initiate policy has shifted from the older generation to the younger. Accordingly, given the ossification of the bureaucracy, where the system of promotion by seniority prevails, and where the selective promotion based on merit is impossible, if effectiveness in the bureacracy is to be assured, there is no other way but to kick the older people upstairs, and let those with ability do the work. In the period from the 1890s to the 1920s, it was important for the bureaucracy to constantly obtain new information from abroad through field trips, study abroad, and observations made by officials stationed overseas, and in that way upgrade their abilities.

Maintenance of Monopoly

Since the divisions have a monopoly over matters under their jurisdictions, only those policy proposals that originate endogenously within it are viewed as "authentic" or "legitimate." But the allocation of responsibility for governing different aspects of human life to various government agencies is determined by law on the basis of convenience. So it is quite possible that some matter will fall under the jurisdiction of more than one agency. As a result, policy proposals that are quite similar might originate from divisions other than the one that thinks it has legitimate jurisdiction. When that happens, those originating from other agencies, sections, etc., or those proposed by the public receive cool reception and are ignored by the agency claiming jurisdiction. But, if there are two policy proposals that cannot by ignored for political or social reasons, they may end up cancelling each other. If, however, the interagency conflict is criticized in the mass media, or the coordination of these two policies is pushed through by the LDP, an "add up and divide by two" type of compromise proposal may be adopted. Or, alternatively, they may decide to hold back rather than to adopt a compromise arrangement that was forced upon them on the ground that they need to examine the matter carefully. The result is that nothing is done until some incidents or accidents occur. In that case, the civil servants take great care to avoid legal responsibility by arguing that there is no law that empowers the agency to take up the matter. When some accident, incident, or problem makes it imperative that a policy be adopted, the affected agencies all propose new policies and try to have their own adopted and block all other policies being proposed. That results in the recurrence of interagency rivalry.

Planning New Policies

The Role of the Bureaucracy

Within the context of the LDP as a ruling party, when a change takes place in the coalition of factions, and a new alliance comes to dominate the party, a new prime minister and a new cabinet come into being. This represents a change in personnel resulting from the struggle for power, and is not a change in the ruling party. This means that the contending leaders of major factions are restrained from promoting policy changes, as might be the case when a general election takes place and parties try to propose new policies.

Even though the change may be nothing more than a reshuffle of LDP personnel, in parliamentary politics, the people and public opinion require that the change have some justification. For that reason, some new policy proposals must be made in response to the new definition of reality. There is the case where after the political struggle that took place in the latter half of 1972, a new policy toward mainland China was adopted. Usually, after a new prime minister comes in, a series of new policies is announced in connection with the preparation of a new budget.

When new policies are announced after the new cabinet has started to function, the sum total of all of the policy proposals that had been prepared heretofore by the government agencies defines the policy objectives of the new cabinet. Sometimes such objectives are epitomized in slogans. Then all of the policies of the agencies are tailored to conform to the slogans. If the new government does not show interest in new policies or slogans and thus fails to provide copy for the mass media, it is categorized as a "routine cabinet."

Planning New Policies
The secretaries of the Diet members are most involved in constituency service and do not have much ability in policy planning. Among the staffs of the political parties and factions, there are some people who do research on policy problems, but they are not equipped to deal with the broad range of domestic and foreign policy issues. The bureaucracy is the only one that is able to engage in policy planning in an organized and systematic way. In the budgetary system, funds are appropriated for each fiscal year, and continuing appropriations are assured for set budgetary items. Funds needed for new projects are added on to the set budgets in the form of incremental appropriations in a certain fiscal year, and become part of the set budget in the following year.

Accordingly, when government agencies, in response to the new definition of reality, come up with new policies that require new projects, new or supplementary laws, authority and competence, personnel, and budget are needed in order to carry them out. Another way of putting it would be that, if the agencies, for their survival and prosperity, seek to expand their operations, authority and competence, personnel, and budget, they must come up every year with new policy proposals. In this way, agencies

have to maintain, all the time, their ability to engage in policy
planning.

Training in Policy Planning
Bureaucracies also have the problem of organizational management. Within the bureaucratic system, there are standards for
bureaucratic behavior. That is, internally, precedent must be
followed, and regulation and discipline maintained. To outsiders,
they explain that they do not have legal responsibility. When in
positions of responsibility, bureaucrats avoid making serious
mistakes and pass the time without getting into trouble, while
waiting for a transfer to another position.

It is possible to follow another, more achievement-oriented
line of action. If one wants to do something that will be re-
membered, one can encourage research on new policies, and
when the opportunity presents itself launch a new project, after
having obtained backing for it by informal discussions and negotiations. There are considerable differences among individuals in
terms of temperament, character, ability, interest, knowledge, and
sociability. Thus, it is inevitable that there are some who are
oriented toward bureaucratic control, while others are achievement oriented.

In addition, there is a system for educating the younger group
destined to become the top bureaucrats. They are removed from
day-to-day administration and given research projects, told to
study specialized materials, and, in particular, they are made to
read and study foreign newspapers, magazines, and monographs.
In this way, they have been given an opportunity to judge what
goes on in their agency from a broad perspective. It has been a
way of developing staff capabilities that are useful in policy planning. But in recent years it has become more difficult to provide
such training because of cuts in personnel.

Seminars
In the final analysis, intellectual development depends on one's
own motivation and initiative. Topics for study suggested by
one's superior are now carried over into the informal seminars.
As has been noted, a new definition of reality and new policies
in response to it have often originated in the Western world.
Hence, the planning and development orientation of the high-

level officials augments the desire of individual civil servants to become better informed. Traveling, studying, and living in foreign countries provide opportunities to do research, import new ideas, and transmit foreign material into Japan. Seminars serve as a forum for exchanging and absorbing this new information. In this way, seminars offer opportunities to listen to reports of foreign experiences and to hear lectures by experts in various fields. One can also listen to book reviews and reports on research findings in these seminars.

There are small gatherings that convene in one's division after five o'clock. These may be considered study groups built around colleagues and work associates whom one knows well. The circle of participants may later be broadened to include individuals from other divisions, and bureaus within the ministry. It may also come to include those from other ministries and even from private companies. Some study groups continue in that form, while others may grow into loosely organized informal groups that cut across various ministeries and business organizations. As has been noted, the *ringi* system often requires informal discussions and negotiations that cut across various ministries, so these informal gatherings have the capability of facilitating this process. In this sense, these study groups may be viewed as political groups incognito. Moreover, contacts between high-level bureaucrats and LDP politicians for explanations of pending bills, and for expediting their consideration can lead to social interaction between leaders of LDP factions and members of study groups. In that event, faction leaders are in a good position to obtain first-hand information about policy matters from the members of the informal group, who are versed in policy planning and who have many new policies up their sleeves.

Brain Trusts

Federation of Ministries
The various activities of the people and the world of business that sustain such activities are regulated by one or more ministries of the government. In a functional sense, all aspects of the lives of the people are divided and governed by ministries that are more or less independent. Another way of putting it would be that a functionally organized federation of ministries regulates the

people's lives. Just as the states are sovereign in federal systems, in federations of ministries, each ministry is more or less sovereign and tries to guard its own turf and go its own way. Except for those newer, weaker ministries, whose top jobs are held by bureaucrats on loan from other stronger ministries, the reshuffling of personnel is limited to positions within the same ministries, and the movement of personnel from one ministry to another is extremely rare.

Moreover, only those policies that are developed endogenously within the ministry are likely to be implemented. Interministry cooperation on policy matters is extremely difficult to achieve. The most famous example of this is the interservice rivalry between the army and navy that existed until August 1945. On the other hand, there are many examples where similar, overlapping policies are proposed by a number of ministries when a season for new policies approaches, as when a new prime minister is nominated or the time for the preparation of the new budget approaches.

Demand for Centralization

In response to fragmentation and conflict, and overlapping of functions and competition among ministries, political journalism has long demanded that there be more centralization in government. The demand is not only for centralization in diplomacy to counter pressure from foreign countries but also for centralization in the implementation of policies in domestic affairs. The White House under the American presidential system has often been cited as a model for a system that puts the implementation of diverse departmental policies under the unified control of the president.

In this connection, two topics have been discussed over a long period. The first is, how would the prime minister's policies be developed, and, second, how would a brain trust that is independent of the ministries be created. Another topic under discussion has been how to get public opinion reflected in the prime minister's policies, since people generally feel that the bureaucracy does not reflect their wishes and desires. However, it is a fact that centralization has never been achieved. This is because the ministries jealously guard their independence, and the bureaucrats fiercely resist any attempts to bring them under central control.

Commissions and Discussion Groups

The federation of ministries governs the people, but what individual citizens may be thinking is outside of its purview. Accordingly, the ministries have public relations staffs and reporters' clubs, and try to manipulate the mass media and public opinion. Each ministry has something like a brain trust. They also use commissions and discussion groups to obtain expert opinion and to try to get public opinion reflected in their policies.

The make-up of these organizations varies. Some are established by law, others are set up on an ad hoc basis. Among participants are retired high-level civil servants, influential people in business and the mass media, academics, and other distinguished individuals. The ministries suggest topics for study, provide data and staff people, and pay for the costs of meetings. The participants meet a number of times over a period of several months to several years, and eventually come up with recommendations that are, in essence, often prepared by the ministries. There are reports, commentaries, and reviews in the mass media when the roster of participants is announced. Depending on the subject, there might be progress reports, and, when the final recommendations are made, they, too, are reported in the press. All this does affect public opinion and serves to educate the voters.

Individuals and Personal Connections

In addition to commissions and discussion groups, there are more informal groups as well as individuals, who anonymously or otherwise, serve as brain trusters to professional politicians, faction leaders, cabinet ministers, and prime ministers. The best-known case of an individual is the relationship between Shimomura Osamu and Prime Minister Ikeda. In the case of groups, there are instances where an informal study group composed of high-level bureaucrats, businessmen, academics, and journalists has developed into an informal, loosely organized group, and then has come to maintain an informal network of people in the course of interacting with faction leaders. Such a group is not a pressure group established by representatives of the business establishment, but an informal brain trust incognito. When they are mobilized in anticipation of a change in government, they will informally and behind the scenes take part in preparing new policies and influencing public opinion. Moreover, when well-known personalities are involved, they are often used, not so much for their knowledge as for their halo effect in influencing public opinion and election outcomes. Examples are celebrities and show business people running in the national constituency in the House of Councillor elections.

Epilogue

One way to approach the Japanese political system is to view it as a hybrid variety. It is a hybrid because it draws on two different political, social, and cultural traditions. As has been described in earlier chapters, the institutional structure, that is, the National Diet, political parties, elections, and the civil service as well as the underlying constitutional order and legal system, was in essence imported from the West. But the political leaders and the voters who function within this structure are products of a different tradition. To be sure, the Japanese have, in the last one hundred and twenty-odd years, become increasingly Westernized. Yet, it is also true that social institutions, cultural values, and religious beliefs and practices continue to display a remarkable degree of continuity with the historical past.

Now, one of the consequences of the hybrid character of the political system is that one finds certain anomalies. For example, the imported legal system is based on the idea of constitutionalism that goes back to the medieval period in the West. Constitutionalism states the principle that not only commoners, but kings and power holders are under the law. This stands in contrast to the tradition in Japan and in other East Asian countries that emperors, kings, warlords, and power holders can issue decrees that stand above the laws of the land and that, moreover, such rulers are not bound by existing laws.

According to the 1947 Constitution, all citizens are equal before the law (Article 14), and all citizens are to be treated equally in elections (Article 44). Because of rapid industrialization and urbanization that has occurred since 1955, the allocation of seats among electoral districts has become badly distorted, leading to cases of severe underrepresentation and overrepresentation. Under existing law, the Diet is responsible for correcting the situation. But, as has been noted, since the reallocation of seats would work to the disadvantage of the ruling party, which is strong in the overrepresented areas, no attempt has been made to date to bring about fundamental change.

Quite clearly, the present system violates the constitutional doctrine of equality before the law, but this has not moved politicians to action, nor led to press criticism or public outcry. When the Supreme Court, under Article 81 of the Constitution, held in a case brought before it that the imbalance in representation was unconstitutional, a prime minister commented that the Supreme Court was on the verge of exceeding its competence. It would appear that the long-established cultural tradition that power holders are above the law is still alive.

Corruption

Another example of an anomaly concerns election campaigns. Because such campaigns are expensive, politicians need to raise money. The borderline that separates contributions from bribes can be very thin, so politicians are sometimes likened to performers walking a tightrope. Sometimes they fall and are prosecuted for bribery. But no code of professional ethics has been developed in the political world that would force such individuals to be automatically expelled from the political arena. Several defendants in bribery cases have run for reelection repeatedly and have won. In terms of professionalism and morality, the world of politicians appears to be characterized more by tolerance of wrong doing than by strict self-discipline.

Another consequence of the hybrid character has to do with constituency service. The prime goal of all politicians in a parliamentary system is to be elected and reelected over and over again. In the present multimember electoral system, which was first used in 1928, LDP politicians have to compete with one another in the same electoral district. Hence, they must organize a stable group of supporters whose votes can be counted on. Since the 1960s, LDP politicians all over the country have formed their own support organizations for this purpose. These organizations are sustained by constituency service, such as providing public works projects, securing government subsidies, and the like. Presumably what makes these activities legitimate is the dependency mentality of the Japanese people. It is something analogous to caring parents giving sweets to their children.

Regional Development

Twelve decades of modernization, industrialization, and urbanization have produced regional diversification if not bipolarization. That is, the central, southern, and western areas of the country that face the Pacific Ocean are warmer and have developed more rapidly and achieved a higher standard of living. By contrast, the northern and eastern sections that face the Japan Sea are colder and have lagged behind in terms of economic development. But the constituency service of parliamentary politicians has had the effect of redressing the balance to a considerable extent. Thanks to government aid, living conditions in the north and east have greatly improved; but it has not been without some cost. Scattering small-scale public works projects and subsidies piecemeal throughout the country has often meant a waste of tax money. Since distribution was based on the principle that every claimant should receive equal treatment, tax money was often spent on similar public works projects and subsidies irrespective of long-term planning at the local and national levels. Today, there are many reminders of the inefficient expenditure of public funds in the form of deserted public buildings, abandoned rights-of-way of lines of the Japan National Railways that were never completed, and so on. Parliamentary democracy has not always been successful in optimizing the public good.

The Common Welfare

All this suggests that if the common welfare of the nation is to be promoted, the making of public policy must be done with foresight, that is, leaders must give some consideration to problems that could develop in the future. In Japan, policy making is carried out mainly, but not exclusively, by bureaucrats in many ministries of the central government. Ministries, bureaus, and divisions are typically concerned with competence, budgetary allocations, staff personnel, and administrative activities. For members of the bureaucracy, the growth and expansion of these four elements are of vital interest, materially, psychologically, and ideologically. They always seek organizational expansion, even though to "scrap and build" may sometimes be called for. Thus, bureaucrats do not want to give up any part of these elements, even when changes in the outside world might suggest otherwise. This naturally leads to bureaucratic fossilization.

When they do try to develop new projects, they build on what has gone on before. Usually they are reluctant to engage in a radical reexamination of the basic sociopolitical assumptions and policy orientations of their ministries, bureaus, and divisions. They are thus motivated to "carry on." Trained, efficient bureaucracies with a mental outlook that values the status quo, doing what they have always done, tend to lack foresight. Such bureaucracies are incapable of adapting quickly to a changing environment.

One might note, with the advantage of hindsight, that the outbreak of trade friction and economic conflict between Japan and the United States and the countries of Western Europe could have been anticipated as early as the 1960s and 1970s. As least the policy makers should have been able to see that the problem would develop, although they may not have been able to anticipate the severity of it. Another case of the failure to engage in anticipatory policy making is the plight of the Japanese fishing industry in the northern Pacific Ocean.

What we have been saying about the bureaucracy may also be applied to individuals in relation to their work. Many individuals look upon their jobs and work, either in terms of skills or of their niche in the world, as one road to self-improvement, which will ultimately lead to unity with the eternal being, such as the *tao* or Way. Such people toil diligently all the time and make hard work an end in itself. The division of labor through which the skills and motivation of individuals are brought together in firms and other organizations is not questioned. The basic assumptions concerning the methods and goals of these firms and organizations are taken for granted.

When Japanese work hard in a group situation, their mental attitude tends to be very conservative, that is, they are dedicated to keeping the status quo and "carrying on." It is rather difficult for anyone who has the foresight to suggest new policies in anticipation of changes that may be in the offing to win the support of his fellow workers. Instead, people insist on working together in the pursuit of established organizational goals. This works for a certain period, which may be long or short. But suddenly the situation may change, and the people are told that they are on a collision course. At that point, they feel perplexed and at a loss about what to do. The Japanese people have often suffered from the lack of foresight on the part of management.

Political Leadership

When people are perplexed, they tend to look for political leadership. But political leadership in Japan is not without its problems. The strategy of the opposition parties is to secure at least one-third of the seats in the House of Representatives in every election in order to prevent the revision of the Constitution. But they have never been able to form a government, resulting in the continued dominance of the LDP.

As the LDP sees it, national security is provided by the Japan-U.S. Security Treaty and the U.S. armed forces. Their domestic policy of economic growth has been supported by a national consensus, and carried out with skill by the economists and technocrats in the ministries of the government. All of this has made it possible for the LDP politicians to spend their time and energy on the game of power struggle.

Because of the electoral system and other considerations, LDP politicians, except for a few independents, are organized into factions. Factions are involved in coalition politics, which has never been very stable. As a result, many politicians have been nominated for the position of prime mininster or cabinet minister. In the period of high economic growth, there was not much demand for capable national leadership, either in the world of politics or the nation at large.

But after the oil crisis of the early 1970s, and later the onset of serious economic conflict, people yearn for effective political leadership. Whether Japan will be fortunate enough to find leaders who are capable of meeting the challenge remains unclear at the present time. Only future generations will know the answer.

Suggestions for Further Reading

This list is intended for readers who are not specialists on Japan, but would like to learn more about some of the topics and themes developed in this book. It is not meant to be exhaustive. The titles are grouped in broad categories, and, within each category, are placed with the more general works preceding the more specialized ones.

Historical Background

Hall, John W. *Japan: From Prehistory to Modern Times*. New York: Dell Publishing Co., 1970. A readable and authoritative account of Japanese history.

Sansom, G. B. *The Western World and Japan*. New York: Knopf, 1950. On the early Westernization of Japan by a distinguished British diplomat and scholar.

Maruyama, Masao. *Thought and Behavior in Modern Japanese Politics*, edited by Ivan Morris. New York: Columbia University Press, 1969. Contains important essays on militarism in Japan by a leading authority.

Kosaka, Masataka. *100 Million Japanese: The Postwar Experience*. Tokyo: Kodansha International, 1972. A good account of Japan's history through the 1950s and 1960s by one of the younger generation of Japanese scholars.

Titus, David Anson. *Palace and Politics in Prewar Japan*. New York: Columbia University Press, 1974. Japanese politics of the 1930s as seen from the vantage point of the Imperial Palace.

231

Social Organization

Nakane, Chie. *Japanese Society*. Berkeley: University of California Press, 1972. A somewhat controversial account that provides insights into Japanese society.

Fukutake, Tadashi. *The Japanese Social Structure: Its Evolution in the Modern Century*, tr. by Ronald Dore. Tokyo: University of Tokyo Press, 1982.

Vogel, Ezra F. *Japan's New Middle Class*. Berkeley: University of California Press, 1963. A study of white-collar workers. It would be good to have a more up-to-date account.

Cole, Robert E. *Japanese Blue Collar: The Changing Tradition*. Berkeley: University of California Press, 1971. The author collected his material by actually working in a Japanese die-cast plant.

Rohlen, Thomas P. *For Harmony and Strength: Japanese White-Collar Organization in Anthropological Perspective*. Berkeley: University of California Press, 1974. A participant-observer study of a Japanese bank.

Religion

Space, Joseph J. *Shinto Man*. Tokyo: Oriens Institute for Religious Research, 1972. Although the author is a Catholic priest, he gives an objective account of Shintō most of the time.

Dore, R. P. *City Life in Japan: A Study of a Tokyo Ward*. Berkeley: University of California Press, 1958, especially Chapters 18 to 23. A semi-classic work by a British sociologist.

Politics

Richardson, Bradley and Scott C. Flanagan. *Politics in Japan*. Boston: Little, Brown, 1984. The most recent general treatment of Japanese politics.

Thayer, Nathaniel B. *How the Conservatives Rule Japan*. Princeton: Princeton University Press, 1969. Somewhat outdated, but many of the points the author makes are still valid.

Pempel, T. S. *Policy and Politics in Japan*. Philadelphia: Temple University Press, 1983. One of the few works that is explicitly oriented toward policy making.

Baerwald, Hans H. *Japan's Parliament: An Introduction*. London: Cambridge University Press, 1974. Offers additional information about factions, confrontations, and related matters in the Diet.

Kurt Steiner, Ellis S. Krauss, and Scott C. Flanagan, eds. *Political Opposition and Local Politics in Japan*. Princeton: Princeton University Press, 1980. A detailed account of the rise of leftist local administrations, but the work was finished just before many of them were voted out of office.

Fukui, Haruhiko. *Party in Power: The Japanese Liberal-Democrats and Policy-Making*. Berkeley: University of California Press, 1970. The most detailed account that is available of the ruling party.

Bureaucracy

Campbell, John Creighton. *Contemporary Japanese Budget Politics*. Berkeley: University of California Press, 1977. A study of the powerful Ministry of Finance. After the author completed his research, Japan entered a period of slower economic growth, which must have affected the nature of budget politics.

Johnson, Chalmers. *MITI and the Japanese Miracle*. Stanford: Stanford University Press, 1982. An insightful historical account of the Ministry of International Trade and Industry that tries to guide the country's economic development.

Index

235

sovereignty, 3, 5, 6, 8, 9
spirits, of dead, 46
State Shintō, 7, 8
submission, 67, 75, 154, 157
submission and resistance paradigm,
  59-62
subsidies, 96-97, 109
suffrage, Meiji, 9
support organizations, 12, 113, 114,
  227
supreme command, independence of,
  7, 9
Supreme Commander for the Allied
  Powers (SCAP), 5, 17, 101
Supreme Court, 140; on voter imbalance, 10, 227

tamamushi-iro, 70
tao, 50, 51
tatemae, 59, 60, 61, 135, 157, 158,
  164
taxes, 129-30
television, 29
terrorism, 158, 209
tertiary industries, 30, 31
Tōjō Hideki, 3, 52
tolerance, 55
trade: conflict, 28, 32-34, 131; restrictions, 32, 33
traditional values, and democracy,
  126
traditionalism, 66
transportation, 100
Treaty of Mutual Cooperation and
  Security, 14, 21, 179; movement
  against, 19, 20, 23, 188

Uchimura Kanzō, 157

Ueki Emori, 146
Umesao Tadao, 67
unions, 12, 30, 97, 126
United Nations, 4, 14
United States: decline of, 34-35; and
  Japan's defense, 14, 16, 17-18, 21,
  131; influence of on life style, 29,
  30, 36
unity and harmony, 42-43, 182-88

verbal warfare, 155
Versailles Treaty, 17
violations, 133-34, 135-36
violence, 158, 180, 209
violence paradigm, 72-76
violent behavior, 152
volunteers, political, 150
voter imbalance, 10-11, 23, 128-29,
  227
voter population, 12

wages, 30-31, 97
Weber, Max, 144
Westernization, 66, 67, 68, 98, 146
workers, 30, 126
World War II, 3, 4, 16-17

Yanagita Kunio, 67
Yasukuni Shrine, 145
Yoshida Shigeru, 14-15, 101, 139n,
  192

zaibatsu, 76
zoku, 117
zokuron group: arguments of, 155-56,
  166; formation of, 164-65; on
  offensive, 169-74